THE PROLETARIAT RELOADED

The Proletariat Reloaded
Badiou beyond Marxism and Anarchism

Jon Mazzalini

CounterPress
Oxford

First published 2021
Counterpress, Oxford
http://counterpress.org.uk

© 2021 Jon Mazzalini

Rights to publish and sell this book in print, electronic, and all other forms and media are exclusively licensed to Counterpress Limited. An electronic version of this book is available under a Creative Commons Attribution-NonCommercial (CC-BY-NC 4.0) International license via the Counterpress website:

https://counterpress.org.uk

ISBN: 978-1-910761-13-7 (paperback)
ISBN: 978-1-910761-14-4 (ePDF)

Typeset in 10.5 on 12.5 pt Sabon.

Global print and distribution by Ingram

Contents

INTRODUCTION 1

0.1 Methodology. 5
0.2 Chapter Outline 8
0.3 Terminology 9

1 MARX'S NON-PHILOSOPHY, 'IMPOSSIBLE COMMUNISM'
  AND A NON-ESSENTIALIST PROLETARIAT. 11

1.1 Introducing a Selective Reading of Marx
    and its Relation to Anarchism 12
1.2 The Poststructuralist and Postanarchist Critique of Class 15
1.2.1 *The Problem—The Invention of an Essentialist Proletariat* . . 15
1.2.2 *From Althusser to Poststructuralism* 20
1.2.3 *The Poststructuralist and Postanarchist Critiques of Marx*. . 24
1.3 Marx, the Performative Proletariat and Communism 29
1.3.1 *Class as an Analytical Concept* 29
1.3.2 *The Becoming of the Proletariat* 31
1.3.3 Performative Communism, Non-Philosophy and Non-Class in Marx . 33

2 POSTANARCHISM AND BADIOU'S EARLY DIALECTICAL MATERIALISM:
  FROM SARTREAN TO POST-ALTHUSSERIANISM
  TO ONTOLOGICAL ANARCHISM. 41

2.1 Philosophical Anarchism 42
2.2 Badiou Beyond Marx 44
2.3 Badiou, the Performative, and the Operational. 47
2.4 Badiou's Tussle with Postmodernism 48
2.5 Badiou's Journey Towards Post-Althusserianism 51
2.6 The Early Development of Badiou's Dialectic—
    Hegel Beyond Hegel 56
2.7 The Subject and the State in Badiou's Early Dialectic 61

3 BEING AND EVENT AND POSTANARCHIST ONTOLOGY:
  INEVITABLE INTERVENTION AGAINST INEVITABLE STATES 65

3.1 *Being and Event* and Badiou's Dialectic 66
3.2 The Regime of Presentation 67
3.3 Undecidability and Intervention 71
3.4 The Subject and the Approximate Truth 72
3.5 Badiou's Operational Theory and Postanarchism 74

4	No More Heroes: Badiou, the Proletariat, Communism and Permanent Revolution. 81

4.1 Anarchism and Marxism—
　　The Narrow Divide that Badiou Crosses. 83
4.1.1 *The Anarchist Charge against Marx and the Proletariat* 83
4.1.2 *In Defence of Marx and the Proletariat
　　against 'Ontological Essentialism'* 85
4.1.3 *An Anarchist Proletariat*. 86
4.2 Badiou's Communism 90
4.2.1 *The Unheroic Proletariat and the State* 90
4.2.2 *Antagonism and the Bourgeoisie*. 94
4.2.3 *Beyond Particularism—Subjects Doing It for Themselves* 96
4.2.4 *Badiou, Totalization and the Clinamen* 100

5	Ideology and Insurrection: 'Saint Badiou,' Postanarchism, and Servitude. 109

5.1 In Defence of the Concept of Ideology 110
5.2 Badiou, Postanarchism and Capitalism. 111
5.2.1 *Beyond Althusserian Interpellation* 111
5.2.2 *Badiou and the Problem of Capitalist Presentation* 115
5.2.3 *Postanarchist Ideology and Ontology* 119
5.3 Voluntary Servitude 122
5.3.1 *Liberal Democracy and Postanarchism* 122
5.3.2 *Voluntary Servitude in La Boëtie, Landauer and Abensour* 124
5.3.3 *Badiou, Liberal Democracy and Voluntary Servitude* 126
5.4 Overcoming Ideology 130

6	Post-Evental Politics: The Self-Pricing of the Proletariat 133

6.1 Why speculative materialism? 134
6.2 Correlationism. 135
6.3 Badiou, Metaphysics, and the Critique of Value 137
6.4 Value, the Event and Class 139
6.5 The Marxian Theory of Value 140
6.5.1 *The Problem*. 140
6.5.2 *The Mystery of Value* 142
6.6 Speculative Materialism 147
6.6.1 *'Factility'*. 147
6.6.2 *Speculative Materialism in the Derivatives Market*. 149
6.6.3 *The Post-Evental Pricing Process:
　　A Democracy of 'Self-Pricing'* 153
6.7 Countering Accelerationism 157
6.8 Violence 160

7	Conclusion	164
7.1	Badiou and Postanarchism—Unwitting Partners	164
7.2	Class—The Unheroic Proletariat and Theories of Action	166
7.3	Ideology and Post-Event Demands—The Self-Pricing of Labour	168
7.4	Limitations	169

Appendix: Terminology 172

Postanarchism 172
Communism 173
Badiou's ontology 173
The One 174
Multiple and Situation 174
Void 174
Belonging and Inclusion 175
The Event 175
The Subject and Approximate Truth 175
The Singular and the Universal 176
The Non-Essentialist and Performative Proletariat 176
Dialectical Materialism 176

Bibliography 178

Notes 193

Introduction

This book considers the interaction between Alain Badiou's theory of the event, and Marxian and anarchist thought. Its impetus, however, is a concern with what comes after great political events, and especially events against the exploitation of labour. Capitalism abhors a vacuum and will gladly fill a void with its own values, whether they are ideological values or exchange values. This is especially the case if the subjects of an event such as the Occupy movement that followed the Great Recession of 2008 waste crucial time while pondering what an event means, often broadening its meaning and diluting its consequences. One of the most important lessons Badiou gives us, I believe, is that those loyal to the consequences of an event need to embrace the singularity and universality of an event, whether it is a financial crash that brings into sharp focus the economic inequality in a society, or the death of black people at the hands of the authorities which brings into sharp focus the racism in society which targets one group in particular. Such a singular event—and the opportunity to change society—is rare, but it is of universal relevance to a society without other causes being attached to it and diluting the often horrific truth that an event exposes. Loyalty to the consequences of a singular and universal event is Badiou's lesson to us, and I want to establish what this means in practice, amongst the competing Marxian and anarchist theories that have been popular (and sensationalised) in recent decades, for events against capitalist exploitation. The aim, however, will be to hypostasize the politics of the event rather than merely cloak it in anarchist or communist theory.

We saw a wasted opportunity in the decade following the recession of 2008. The circumstances surrounding this recession were, of course, dubious for the way in which a recession of this scale was somehow unforeseen, but the consequences, and especially the response of ordinary workers and students, revealed how direct action remains part of the political landscape. Of course, it was not so much that the recession was unforeseen, but that it was not in the interests of the state and industry to admit as much, and they paid respected academics to perpetuate a myth that there was no financial crash on the horizon.[1]

This illustrates how Badiou sees ideology working in practice, with the dominant ideas quite visibly presenting the interests of the bourgeoisie.

The Occupy movement affirmed that there is still an awareness of class, and that class-based politics is alive and well. Despite years of being told that there is no longer such a thing as left or right wing politics, that the 'third way' in politics is the only way, and that the working class should be seen even by the centre-left as 'human capital' whose risk-taking should be incentivized (as Anthony Giddens would have it)[2], the proponents of the *status quo* were reminded, and will continue to be, that there is such a thing as a working class politics. It has, in fact, been a constant in liberal democracies that the ruling class needs to be reminded that labour is not merely capital, a point Mario Tronti made in the 1960s in a context where 'Capital *poses* labour—as it is forced to do—as the creator of value, but then *sees* value—as it is forced to do—as the valorization of itself ... it sees labour-power *only* as capital.'[3]

However, the parliamentary left in most Western liberal democracies struggled in the 2010s, with a few exceptions including Portugal,[4] and inroads made by Labour under Jeremy Corbyn in the UK until defeat in 2019. Indeed, the latter's performance in the June 2017 General Election was an example of contingency in politics defying mainstream journalists' interpretation of the opinion polls, which Badiou dismisses as being blind to evental politics.[5] (Badiou does not usually see the ballot box as an event-site,[6] although I would say elections can be indicative of a wider evental politics). While I refer to some of the problems with complex probability models in financial markets and beyond in the final chapter, and the implications for the wage struggle, election results in the 2010s demonstrate the redundancy of predicting elections based on previous polling and elections.[7] Furthermore, some predictions that gain traction in the mainstream media have little complexity or even a published method behind them, with probabilities for imminent elections or referendums being rounded to the nearest 5 per cent, something that is usually a tell-tale sign that they rely only on the author's informed opinion while pretending to be based on a mathematical methodology.[8] While such predictions might serve their authors' careers and entertain the mainstream media, they have little other practical purpose, and as I argue in the final chapter, contingency is the only absolute, and probability, as a way of describing our incomplete knowledge of a situation, is often futile in politics.

The fact remains, however, that the left has failed to deliver results for the most part, with the 'one per cent,' against whom the '99 per cent' of the Occupy movement pitted itself, entrenching its position in the past decade. The general trend for the decreasing value of labour as opposed to capital has been accelerated,[9] although even if this is disputed,[10] it is a moot analytical point for the subject if it is proven their labour is worth the same or more than in some idealized past if they are nevertheless feeling the effects of inequality. Furthermore, the notion of 'truth' (a variety of which Badiou has been an ardent defender of over the last four decades, as we will see) took a severe hit with the advent of 'alternative facts' and 'fake news' circulating on social media, and incredible and unsophisticated charges made by those in power against established news outlets that they are indeed fake news.[11]

If there is hope it lies in the proletariat, which has either been dismissed by those on the right, or rendered obsolete by those on the left. There will be many reasons why the proletariat has not been a successful political force in parliamentary politics—indeed, it is difficult to counter Giddens' view of workers as human capital when increasing numbers of workers are engaged in cognitive labour and do not oppose their labour to enterprise but, as Franco Berardi argues, see their labour *as* enterprise.[12]

My concern, however, is not with the electoral reasons behind the failure of the left, nor the psychological reasons behind the dismissal of the proletariat, but with the tactical and strategic dismissal of class as the unifying force within Occupy and wider protest movements on the left. This need not be the case, and a certain reading of anarchist and Marxian thought, with Badiou bridging the gap between the two, demonstrates that there is a place for universality and the proletariat in contemporary protests.

Indeed, what Marxian and *postanarchist* theory in particular have in common is that they both advocate direct action, while there has been a recent trend towards strategic approaches that focus on a certain intellectual wing of the working class. Negri sees cognitive labour as his designated political subject rather than reviving the working class as an agent,[13] while Aaron Bastani advocates engagement in electoral politics without being constrained by it, building a workers' party against work.[14] While I do not seek to designate a subject as such, I see the proletariat as broad and performative in that its subjects come to see themselves as exploited for their labour in the event. I set out the *tactical* approach that a Badiouan and postanarchist proletariat might take post-event, rather than set out a *strategic* approach for the future. My approach could easily form part of a wider strategic approach, but ontological thought can provide a strong philosophical basis for challenging the state and capitalism *now*.

I will therefore set out how Badiou's dialectical materialist approach, and that of other contemporary materialists, can provide the basis for immediate tactical action rather than dwelling on the flight of the owl of Minerva. This can include a challenge to capitalist values and the price of labour as a commodity expressed as wages, complementing the Marxian approach. The tactical approach toward challenging value I set out in the final chapter is not a departure from the labour theory of value that forms the basis for Marx's analysis of social relations, but is in fact built on an acknowledgement that while the labour theory of value may be at the centre of Marx's thought (that is, crudely, that the labour time socially necessary to produce a commodity determines its (surplus) value), there are for Marx complicating factors such as commodity fetishism, as well as scarcities, tastes, and so on that determine the value *form*. Ben Fine and Alfredo Saad-Filho argue that these factors are irrelevant for uncovering the social relations of production specific to capitalism, but they are factors nonetheless that help determine value form. Despite the definite social relations that result from the way in which capitalism organizes the production of goods and services, labour can still be reduced to a common price as another product of real world capitalism, without undermining the analysis of definite social relations that the labour theory of value provides.[15]

It should not be a controversial view that the price of labour is, or can be, determined by forces other than the spurious 'invisible hand' of the market, which Thomas Piketty, in his non-Marxian analysis, argues does not exist. Given that the market is embodied in specific institutions, including corporate hierarchies, 'hands in the till' might be a better metaphor as wage hierarchies are very difficult to explain solely in terms of supply and demand for various skills.[16] From a non-Marxian legal perspective, Katharina Pistor observes how the 'invisible hand' of the legal code of capital also relies not just on contracts and property rights, but asset-shielding devices to lock in past gains.[17] The invisible hand therefore needs to be countered constantly even for a capitalist economy to function effectively. I set out to do this from a philosophical basis, however, rather than an economic one, or by adding to the various alternatives to market pricing that have been developed, notably by W. Paul Cockshott and Allin Cottrell using rational economic calculation to determine wages,[18] or more recently by Viktor Mayer-Schönberger and Thomas Ramge,[19] whose work has been the subject of particular criticism.[20]

I argue that rather than rely on strategic approaches, it will remain essential, whatever the potential of technological advances, for the collective tactical insertion of workers into contemporary politics. This is another of Badiou's lessons to us, as I trace his development from Sartrean thought, to a student of Althusser, to what has been called post-Althusserian within postanarchist thought, and finally to his influence on his own student, Quentin Meillassoux, and the potential of speculative materialism for a post-evental politics. Against the trend of late capitalism, we then see a return of truth and collective action focused on the singular event of universal relevance, standing against the cult of the individual that must, to Badiou's chagrin, express itself[21] in the mistaken belief that its existing non-evental identity is unique, but is instead the handmaiden of a capitalism for which there is no such thing as society, but only a collection of individuals.

0.1 Methodology

The approach taken in this book, then, is an analysis of the key points of contention and convergence between the approaches of Marxian and poststructuralist anarchist political thought.[22] I still stress the continuing relevance of the proletariat as a potential political subject, but without relying on vanguard political parties or the strategy of taking control of a state. I will make this comparison by drawing on the works of Badiou to arbitrate between what may appear to be conflicting sets of views, but which I argue actually share significant common ground. This is important for two reasons:

First, there is the view that anarchist and poststructuralist thought is better equipped than Marxian thought to engage with the contemporary political challenge of economic inequality. This view has been expressed by a number of poststructuralist anarchist or postanarchist thinkers, perhaps most prominently, Todd May.[23] Moreover, continental thinkers like Badiou have also distanced themselves from the political legacy of Marxism, and Badiou has sought to salvage the term 'communism' from what he views as the oxymoronic 'Communist Party' or 'Communist State.'[24] While this position might, on the surface, suggest some initial common ground with anarchism—which is also a philosophy that rejects statism—Badiou has at the same time been dismissive of anarchism, and has avoided engaging with postanarchism. Even while coming to favour a politics 'without a party,' Badiou also warns against 'lapsing in the figure of anarchism, which has never been anything else than the vain critique, or the double, or the shadow, of the communist parties, just as the black flag is only the double or the shadow of the red flag.'[25] I will argue that this is an oversight on Badiou's part. It is also unhelpful. As Chiara Bottici has written, Marxism and anarchism have the potential to provide each other with the antidote to their own degeneration, maintaining their relevance. Anarchism can find in Marxism an antidote to 'a possible individualist twist in its absolutization of freedom,' while Marxism can gain from anarchism an antidote to the 'statist degeneration' of Marxism, with Bottici emphasizing, as I will, that Marx did not prescribe a clear path to freedom in his works.[26] I argue that Badiou and certain postanarchist thinkers, taken together, have largely arrived at this conclusion, both being concerned with the new rather than, for the most part, an old and needless obsession with black and red flags.

Second, while the questionable rift between postanarchism—which critiques the legitimacy of the state as well as forms of essentialism in traditional anarchist and other thought—and Marxism has had an impact on the ability to effectively contest economic inequality, the importance of class has also not been taken seriously enough by postanarchists. While postanarchism rejects essentialism and therefore a politics of identity, the problem has been that, in recent times, identity politics can be seen as displacing the idea of class and class struggle. We will see, for example, how Jodi Dean witnessed the dismissal of class in the Occupy movement, with the focus being on the multiplicity of the 99 per cent's 'incompatible groups and tendencies, and democracy as a process of integrating them,' rather than on class struggle and action against the factors that gave rise to Occupy in the first place. Indeed, Dean has noted that anarchist Andrew Koch's focus on pluralism assumes that such pluralism is just an ontological fact, without considering the role capitalism has in stimulating pluralism for its own gain.[27]

I focus on class because Badiou does, but I would argue that loyalty to the consequences of an event, without diluting its singularity whatever that may be, is vital for *any* effective post-eventpolitics. This is not to dismiss intersectionality, for example, but to focus on the singularity of an event. We will see how the event is too radical for the state to acknowledge its existence and belonging to a particular situation, with the state being unable or unwilling to acknowledge a void on the edge of a situation, or that which its ideology has excluded. This is true for all events, including Black Lives Matter,[28] where state violence against black Americans has long been ignored by the state. However, the sad prevalence of footage of state violence has led to *singular* events with *universal* relevance for those included in the state. Badiou describes an excess of inclusion over belonging in any state, meaning that of all the elements included in a state, there will be some which do not belong, and are not presented as such by the state.[29] As we will see, this is why subjects to the event make a wager and an intervention to determine that an event belongs to a situation.

From a non-evental perspective, however, the 'identity school,' as Jeffery R. Webber calls it, has neglected factors such as political economy, class, capitalism and history in favour of 'new' identities such as gender over the 'old' identity (if you can call it that) of class. Not only is it absurd that class is the older of these distinctions, it is characteristic of social movements to 'forget the crisis tendencies of capitalism, its stagnations and financial panics, or the system's necessarily uneven reproduction of inequalities at national, regional and international scales, and how these structural conditions influence the dynamics of any struggle under its sun.'[30] The point of evental politics, however, is to work with the approximate truth of an event, and not to determine in a detached manner what the most pressing matters for society are.

This brings me to the third reason for writing this book, which is almost to dispense with the overtly theoretical approach taken towards political events in practice. It will seem ironic that so much theory needs to be discussed to get to this point, but that is the approach that has had to be taken by so many action-oriented theories in order to dispute the claims of other theories or the legitimacy of the state and its laws. It is particularly relevant, as a general point, when considering the works of Badiou and of postanarchism, and Saul Newman in particular, as both sets of theories are aimed at making the case for the primacy of contingency. In the final chapter, a more specific point about contingency is made, utilising the work of Badiou's former student Meillassoux, which shows how contingency is the only absolute.[31] Speculative realism, a term coined for the purpose of a 2007 conference at Goldsmiths, has been one of the most interesting developments in philosophy in recent years, and Meillassoux's speculative materialism is particularly instructive for the politics of the event.[32] Embracing contingency provides the ontological ground for the proletariat to refute the legitimacy of the law, 'philosophy' or values of the state and capitalism, and affirms the right of the subject to challenge the legitimacy of all forms of power.

While Badiou's view of post-evental politics is to defend the consequences of an event—which, again, I would say means a focus on the original cause attached to the event, be it race politics, feminism, or the class struggle that Badiou is more interested in, so as not to dilute its consequences—the new philosophical tools available to us lend extra legitimacy to post-eventual demands, against any attempts by the state to impose its own values.

0.2 Chapter Outline

In the first chapter I explore post-Marxist and poststructuralist anarchist critiques of Marx in order to preserve aspects of Marxian thought that remain relevant to contemporary politics. This includes 'alternative' interpretations of Marx's thought to bring to the fore a non-essentialist understanding of the proletariat, a counter argument to claims of economic reductionism, and a performative 'non-philosophy' best suited to understanding events in their contingency. We will see how the proletariat continues to exist in an analytical sense (regardless of whether those who fall in this category see themselves as such), but more importantly in a performative sense as well (that moment when workers, or even those calling themselves 'middle class,' come to see themselves as political subjects similar to the proletariat, albeit often under a different name, such as the '99 per cent').

The second chapter considers the momentary state and ontological anarchy. It also considers the development of Badiou's dialectical materialism, from Sartrean, to Althusserian, to post-Althusserian perspectives, and, in the process, Badiou's relation to Hegel. Not only does Badiou, as a post-Althusserian, have something to offer postanarchist thought,[33] we see points of convergence throughout his thought, despite his frequent criticism of poststructuralist thinkers.

The third chapter takes a closer look at *Being and Event* and compares this to the postanarchist approach, including the question of whether Badiou is as opposed to Gilles Deleuze's approach (which is influential for Newman) as he claims, especially in light of Badiou calling his dialectic an *affirmative* one. In what is Badiou's most famous work, he has more in common with postanarchist thought than it appears at first, taking an ontological approach to understanding the subject (including the collective class-based subject) and its role in politics, with his notion of the wager to grasp what is only ever an approximate truth, leaving decision making in the hands of the individual.

In the fourth chapter, I take a closer look at Badiou and his relation to Marx. Badiou has not explored his relationship with Marxism systematically since the early 1980s, and there are a number of other Marxian aspects missing from his work, such as any significant discussion on political economy, with Badiou simply asserting that many of Marx's intuitions have proved correct.[34] Badiou is certainly not a conventional Marxist, and that is what makes him a good intermediary between Marxism and anarchism. Indeed, while Badiou has used Marx as a constant reference throughout his career, he refuses to associate the proletariat with a simple 'nothingness,' as he argues Marx does (apparently because they count for nothing in society), but instead identifies the proletariat as a genericity based on a complexity of differences, albeit with the potential demand for equality cutting across this identity.[35]

In the fifth chapter, other aspects of Badiou's thought that relate to Marxism are considered, specifically his approach towards ideology, alongside the postanarchist critique of ideology and insurrection. Badiou sees his own understanding of ideology (that is, ideology as the way things appear, reflecting the values of the bourgeoisie) as closer to Marx than Althusser.[36] The notion of ideology as presentation and appearance can be seen, albeit not always explicitly, in *Being and Event* and *Logics of Worlds*, and in avoiding reference to the unconscious and taking a mostly ontological rather than phenomenological approach, common ground is found with postanarchism. Both Badiou and Newman take a negative or subtractive approach to ideology, critiquing the unstable foundations on which it is built and pointing to a 'lack' in all ideology, rather than prescribing alternatives; moreover, they place the subject at the centre of any challenge to capitalism.

This leads us to the final chapter, in which I consider what a post-evental politics might look like, and especially how Badiou, as an unconventional Marxist, may add to Marx's legacy. While the consequences of an event may be many, I have focused on forms of economic inequality that cut across identity—that is, the exploitation of labour—and there have been attempts by some working in the field of Marxian theory to understand what kind of wage struggle Marx's thought may lead to. In this chapter I take as a starting point Kojin Karatani's[37] use of Kant to consider Marx and alternatives to capitalist values, and then use Meillassoux's critique of Kant (and Heidegger), and Elie Ayache's[38] application of this to the derivatives market, to move beyond this and develop a case for workers to *name their price*—a self-pricing of labour. This, I argue, is where Badiou's theory of the subject takes us after the event.

0.3 Terminology

Badiou's work can be a challenge to follow, and I clarify terms used in his works as and when I refer to them. In doing so, my aim is to elucidate Badiou to the reader without simplifying his theory in a way that risks losing its complex meaning. However, to aid the reader, I have also included a glossary in the Appendix, where I briefly explain a number of key technical terms in Badiou's works, including 'One,' 'multiple,' 'situation,' 'void,' 'belonging,' 'inclusion,' 'event,' 'subject,' 'truth,' 'approximate truth,' 'singular' and 'universal.' I also, very briefly, explain Badiou's dialectical materialism, as well as the terms 'postanarchism' and 'communism' used throughout.

1

Marx's Non-Philosophy, 'Impossible Communism' and a Non-Essentialist Proletariat

Marxism has failed and has been edging ever closer toward the perspective embraced by anarchism over the years, according to post-structuralist anarchist Todd May writing in the 1990s.[1] In this chapter I argue that aspects of both anarchism *and* Marxism remain relevant today, and should complement rather than oppose one another. Class in particular, and perhaps more than ever, continues to be relevant on an *analytical* level when considering antagonisms within society, cutting across identities and nationalities. However, class is often overlooked at the *practical* or *political* level in favour of identity politics, as if both approaches are mutually exclusive, as Jodi Dean noted with some frustration during the Occupy movement (in her case, on Wall Street).[2]

I agree here with Dean, who argues against anarchists' (such as Andrew Koch's) focus on defending the 'infinite pluralism of individuated meaning' as if 'such multiplicity were primarily ontological, rather than also stimulated by capitalism for its benefit and preservation,' hindering effective political action. I disagree, however, that the anarchist viewpoint, or Badiou's preference for a politics without a party, must lead to such a political impasse.[3] Both Badiou's theory and Newman's postanarchism force us to recognize singular and universal events, even if they contradict our pre-eventual worldview. That is to say, events do not simply confirm our analysis of class or identity, but reveal new ways in which people view themselves, with the '99 per cent' movement for example (even if the term was coined by academics and activists) gaining traction with a broad section of society.[4]

I consider the philosophical impasse that presents itself after Badiou's event (that is, whether subjects to a truth should defend the purity of an event, or alternatively develop ideological constructs to defend an event's consequences) in the fifth chapter. However, I am not interested here in discussing the (post-event) role of the political party as such, as Dean is, but rather with the singular and universal (including class based) political event *itself*, and ultimately its philosophical legitimacy, supported by both Marxian and anarchist political theory. Furthermore, not only does Badiou provide a philosophical basis on which to defend such events, so important to democracy and yet constantly undermined, but he also brings class to the fore.

1.1 Introducing a Selective Reading of Marx and its Relation to Anarchism

While this chapter will focus on Marxian theory, it should be said that the comparison I will make later with postanarchism, as well as with Badiou's theory, will help identify theoretical concepts associated with Marx (such as the proletariat, commodity fetishism and revolt) in a way that is not tied to the state, or to a statist interpretation of the dictatorship of the proletariat. This is something which I argue Badiou's use of Marx shares with postanarchism.

The move away from 'reductive' analyses of social struggle (that is, away from the proletariat as the key agent of change) that can be seen in Laclau and Mouffe's post-Marxism accorded with May's identification of a 'general trend' in twentieth century Marxism.[5] These theoretical developments notwithstanding, I defend a certain understanding of the proletariat and maintain its relevance. Indeed, to dismiss the future role of the proletariat as a subject almost amounts to a historicism which poststructuralists would (or should) be reluctant to follow. In this chapter I want to set out the critiques of the Marxian concept of the proletariat, which feature prominently in post-Marxist and postanarchist theory, and, in response, defend the concept of the proletariat as a 'non-class.' In agreement with the post-Marxist and postanarchist approach (notwithstanding their differences), this should not be a concept of the proletariat led by a vanguard, whose role is historically determined, but rather a contingent subject—a proletariat realized as subject only when it presents itself as such. This is in keeping with Badiou's references to the proletariat (as we will see in chapter 4) and avoids a pre-emptive dismissal of subjects. This concept also attempts to avoid prescribing political strategies based only on established identities or historical trends (or what could amount to dubious theories of probability, as we will see in the final chapter).

In addition to critically analysing the overhasty dismissal of the proletariat, this chapter will introduce the relation between Althusser's dialectical materialism, and post-Marxism and poststructuralism, which will be important when comparing Badiou's materialist dialectic to poststructuralist and postanarchist thought in the next chapter. In doing so, it will seek to defend Marx's philosophy as one which includes a performative concept of the proletariat. This is not a performativity in the sense critical theory usually means—that is, what Levi R Bryant calls the 'realist' approach which sees meaning as socially constructed through discourse, and focuses on the critique of such discourse because that is supposedly the closest we can get to understanding the real world.[6] This is not to dismiss entirely the discursive approach and the critique of performative power developed by Judith Butler, among others.[7] It is, rather, a way of understanding the proletariat as a subject which forces itself upon us through an event.

Perhaps the general side-lining of the proletariat is in part due to the numbing effect of capitalism on class consciousness. But, whatever explains the marginalization of the idea of the proletariat as collective subject *in practice*, it is the discarding of the proletariat as one of the most potentially viable subjects for affecting change through increasingly sophisticated *theory* that this chapter contests (without discarding contingency, or claiming that the proletariat is the only viable subject). Post-Marxism may be more than three decades old, but its legacy, which includes overlooking the proletariat as a viable political collective, lives on in theory and in practice. It could be argued that a certain understanding of poststructuralist theory contributes to the difficulty in practice that recent protests have faced when deciding on what and how to put forward demands for change. Again, this chapter will focus on Marxian *theory* rather than, say, lessons that can be learnt in terms of practical political organization in light of the recent 'Occupy' movement that claimed loosely to represent the less well-off '99 per cent' and seemed wary of any sort of vanguardism.[8] Dean, who as we know was involved with Occupy, has noted how the marginalization of class by others involved in the Occupy movement made effective political organization difficult, overlooking the one form of oppression out of many that those in the movement had in common.[9]

The criticism of Marx's view of the proletariat as collective subject by traditional anarchists such as Bakunin lives on, to a degree, in the works of May, Lewis Call and Newman.[10] Here I wish to defend aspects of Marx and Marxian theory in a way that need not be incompatible with postanarchism: in other words, a non-essentialist proletariat; a (non-historicist) dialectical materialism (which we will see has been developed further by Badiou, in chapter 2); and philosophy as having a performative component, working with events rather than creating them. Key postanarchist works have commenced with a discussion of Marx and Marxism. The survey of Marxian thought presented here leads us to another interpretation, and will lead us to Badiou's theory in later chapters. While Badiou has been dismissive of both poststructuralist and postmodern thought,[11] Newman takes care to distinguish poststructuralism from postmodernism, although he notes the latter is something we cannot ignore. Instead, the challenge is to ask how a notion of the universal can survive after postmodernism.[12] Badiou's theory of the One and the multiple, the universal and the event, and his relation to poststructuralism and postanarchism in this regard, will be considered in the next chapter, before his relation to Marx and the dialectic is examined.

In this chapter I will return briefly to the works of Marx, but not in a vain attempt to discover a 'true' Marx. Instead, I want to look at the room for interpretation that Marx left us. Marx, and Marxists, have often been associated with a clear teleological view of what the future holds for us and how it will be delivered (through an essentialist notion of the proletariat), although we can equally claim that Marx is concerned with a new, yet uncertain, future. Anarchist and postanarchist thought has long associated Marxism, and sometimes Marx, with the former view. Marx is concerned with the creation of political subjects against not just the state, but against power as it is dispersed throughout the economy under capitalism. Poststructuralists see power as dispersed, as does Badiou in his own way (there are many Ones, albeit temporary, as we shall see in the next chapter). But to view the proletariat as the emergence of a new political subject and the most effective challenge to capitalism does not make one an essentialist, even though some Marxian theorists (and Marx himself at times) decided to designate the proletariat as essentially the only agent capable of (and teleologically charged with) challenging capitalism.

This chapter will introduce the non-historicist branch of Marxian theory we see in Althusser's dialectical materialism, and which Bruno Bosteels wishes to revive along the lines of his reading of Badiou's materialist dialectic. This, I will argue in later chapters, offers a more convincing way out of the Althusserian impasse (which Bosteels sees in Althusser's unwillingness to see any political truth in the May 1968 events in Paris) that enables us to think about class without being entirely at odds with poststructuralism.[13] Dialectics is seen by Newman as a closure of politics, replacing 'practical politics' with dialectical guarantees, something that is seen as inimical to the contingency central to postanarchism.[14] However, in the next chapter we will see how

Badiou's materialist dialectic is not incompatible with postanarchism, and we will make the case for the continuing relevance of a universal political subject—albeit one which makes itself known through an event—such as the proletariat, without a loss of radical contingency. We will also see that poststructuralists are not necessarily opposed to Marx, and conversely, the case has also been made by Jon Roffe that the famously anti-Hegelian Deleuze, widely regarded as poststructuralist, is not the anti-dialectician that many, including Badiou, make him out to be.[15] This chapter will revisit Marx's notions of the proletariat and communism, ideology and what Étienne Balibar calls Marx's 'non-philosophy.' We will see that Marxian theory is compatible with more recent philosophy, capable of being a performative philosophy that engages with events. These points will be addressed following consideration of the critiques of Marxian theory found in post-Marxism and postanarchism.

1.2 The Poststructuralist and Postanarchist Critique of Class

1.2.1 The Problem—The Invention of an Essentialist Proletariat

Before looking at Marx as developing a performative philosophy that includes a non-essentialist proletariat and a non-historicist materialist dialectic, we must first consider the claim that it is essentialist to view the proletariat as the only political subject to challenge capitalism. This is a view that persists to this day, sometimes understandably, in postanarchist thought. However, viewing the proletariat as the most *viable* political subject to challenge capitalism at a particular conjuncture need not be essentialist. Furthermore, the poststructuralist thinkers that recent anarchist thought has drawn on are not steadfastly opposed to Marx, and often draw on Marx selectively. Drawing on any thinker selectively is how theory advances, just as postanarchism draws on anarchist theory selectively. As Simon Choat has argued, poststructuralists defended the concept of class, even if they were suspicious of its use in theory. According to Choat, poststructuralists read Marx selectively and critically, but they also set him to work instead of seeking the 'true' Marx, developing a materialist philosophy of intervention to bring about an unknown, undetermined, future.[16] Whether one agrees with Marx or not, any simplistic notion of an 'orthodox' doctrinaire Marx or Marxism should be avoided.

In a polemical but nonetheless historically relevant critique of post-Marxism published in 1986, Ellen Meiksins Wood referred to the then latest trend in political theory for class to retreat into the background as a 'New "True" Socialism' (NTS). Wood saw Laclau, Paul Hirst and *Marxism Today*, among others, as part of the NTS, comparing them to the original 'true socialists' that Marx described as those wishing to return to ideology, of the power of philosophical concepts to change the world in the interests of 'human nature' and not of the proletariat at a particular time.[17] The NTS moved away from a particular class, and towards other social collectives formed around identity and discourse. In doing so, the NTS moved away from grounding change in material conditions, and towards discourse itself. The true socialists, Wood argued, are the 'right-minded' intellectuals whose views on discourse are listened to. As the working class have shown themselves to be less likely than other social groups to form a socialist politics, the NTS have focused their efforts elsewhere. It is almost as if the NTS are more absolutist in their idea of what constitutes revolution than others on the left, having become frustrated with the various attempts of workers as agents, and their failure to deliver a new social totality. 'It is,' writes Wood, 'as if the only struggle that counts is the last one.'[18]

Wood's view places the poststructuralists of the NTS at quite some distance from the performative philosophy that I argue Marx espouses, being interested in how discourse is performative in bringing about a changed set of circumstances, rather than philosophy looking to events outside the realms of discourse, and working with these truths instead. The approach of Laclau and Mouffe, for example, where the social is comprised of various discourses, is one where no social agent can claim to be the foundation of society;[19] historical change is not conducted or determined by an 'essence' or historical inevitability, but is rather performed. We will soon see how a convincing performativity is already present in Marx's works, with subjects coming first, and philosophy second.

A move towards a focus on groups was already present in Marxian thought before Laclau and Mouffe's works. Fredric Jameson has written that Laclau and Mouffe's *Hegemony and Socialist Strategy* and Sartre's *Critique of Dialectical Reason* are the only two theories, after Fourier, to give the problem of groups and their constitution a central role, the former focusing on the 'culture' around which groups crystallize, the latter on concrete social relations.[20] However, in contrast to Sartre's variant of Marxism, which maintains a central role for matter and labour, there is little of Marx left in Laclau and Mouffe's works. Laclau and Mouffe maintain that 'Marxism is one of the traditions through which it becomes possible to formulate this new conception of politics.' This new conception of politics, what they call 'post-Marxist,' is also '*post*-Marxist,' the authors claiming it is 'no longer possible to maintain the conception of subjectivity and classes elaborated by Marxism.'[21]

In *Hegemony and Socialist Strategy*, their neo-Gramscian approach puts the stress on anti-essentialism, arguing that essentialism is still present even in Gramsci's work insofar as political struggle is still concerned with classes because, for Gramsci, 'a failure in the hegemony of the working class can only be followed by a reconstitution of bourgeois hegemony.'[22] This reveals an 'inner essentialist core' to Gramsci's notion of hegemony, pitting these classes against each other. Laclau and Mouffe take a poststructuralist approach in renouncing any discourse that claims universality through the discovery of 'truth.'[23] This does not mean, for them, that a radical idealist (or solipsistic) position is to be adopted, or that everything is what one wants it to be since there is nothing external to thought. For Laclau and Mouffe, every object exists within a discourse.

This has nothing to do with the old realism/idealism debate, but whether, as an example, the falling of a brick is discursively explained as 'natural phenomena' or as the 'wrath of God.' No object, they assert, can establish itself outside of any discourse. However, for Laclau and Mouffe, at the same time, no discourse can itself be totalizing; society consists of 'floating signifiers' and elements (ideas, beliefs, etc.) which once articulated discursively become moments. These discursive moments cannot be fixed eternally in a hegemonic practice; fixed moments would exist only in a closed system that excludes floating signifiers (that is, other ideas). The repetition of fixed moments, unchallenged by other ideas, would not exist in the poststructuralist, neo-Gramscian hegemony that Laclau and Mouffe advocate. While moments are not fixed and the impossibility of any discursive practice to over-determine and suture all elements is recognized, there has to be some level of fixity in a quasi-transcendental hegemony that recognizes equivalences. As Laclau and Mouffe write: 'If the meaning of each struggle is not given from the start, this means that it is fixed—partially—only to the extent that the struggle moves outside itself and, through chains of equivalence, links itself structurally to other struggles.' Antagonism is thereby recognized and converted into *agonism*, where each antagonistic moment recognizes its equivalence with other moments as they form a hegemonic nodal point through which floating signifiers are (temporarily) stabilized. For Laclau and Mouffe, the autonomy of the various discourses and the multiplication of antagonisms that results from their view of post-Marxist hegemony, enables an extension of the democratic revolution, which includes the abolition of capitalist relations of production.[24] However, Mouffe has indicated that Paul Hirst's theory of associative democracy (developing earlier forms of associationalism that can be found in Hegel and GDH Cole) could provide the practical dimension to Laclau and Mouffe's radical democratic theory.[25]

In response to Laclau and Mouffe, Žižek has famously taken issue with their lack of genuinely radical challenge to capitalism as 'the only game in town.' Links between social agents and their 'task' are contingent, with no attempt to map out possible agents that might affect revolutionary political events. For Žižek, 'the postmodern emergence of new multiple political subjectivities certainly does not reach... [the] radical level of the political act proper.' The overdetermination of the social totality through the class/commodity structure found in Georg Lukács's brand of 'Western Marxism,' for example, provides a global dimension that has been suspended in 'multiculturalist progressive politics,' whose 'anti-capitalism' is reduced to the level of how today's capitalism breeds sexist/racist oppression, and so on.'[26] Laclau and Mouffe demonstrate that it is possible for various elements in society, while different, to recognize equivalences (e.g. a common grievance with capitalism) and to manifest these discursively with the aim of developing an alternative hegemonic project, but there is no overdetermining cause such as the economy which bestows meaning or a particular destiny upon this struggle. As we will see in the next chapter, the same could be said of Badiou, who places less significance on political economy and the determining role of the capitalist mode of production, and more on the proletariat as a potential and contingent political subject.

Post-Marxism, as we have seen, proposes an anti-essentialism that comes at the cost of abandoning the proletariat as collective subject. Laclau and Mouffe draw on concepts from Marxian theorists, such as Althusser's notion of 'overdetermination' through which effects are determined by multiple, contingent causes. Yet, for them, even Althusser's theory has an essentialist core: contingent events and social relations are still determined, 'in the last instance,' by the capitalist economy. If the economy is a determinant in the last instance of every type of society, Laclau and Mouffe argue that this must be because the economy is defined without reference to social relations, or as a fixed entity rather than something constituted among social relations and just as open to overdetermination as anything else that is constituted.[27]

However one interprets Althusser's determination by the economy in the last instance, it would be wrong to dismiss the economy as not being an important determinant across different kinds of society, including capitalist ones. The difficulties the working class has faced in 'constituting itself as a historical subject,' as Laclau and Mouffe put it, does not mean that we must necessarily look elsewhere for agents or groups to challenge capitalism. Just because overdetermination, for Laclau and Mouffe, is seen at work through temporary expressions within discourse such as 'collective will' or 'masses,' it does not mean that the working class is a failed subject. For Laclau and Mouffe, the working class is not a historical subject, and the challenge now is therefore to weave those issues that matter to workers into discourse. The problem is that for Laclau and Mouffe there is no object beyond discourse. They sidestep this problem by arguing that what is at issue is the fact that objects as they appear for us are always embodied in discourse.[28]

Badiou's theory is much better at forcing us to acknowledge that some things are virtually inexistent for a situation, world, or a state, or appear minimally, as we will see. On the other hand, the focus on discourse, rather than the inexistent which is revealed to us through an event, is not only a philosophical dead end insofar as there are things that evade discourse, but also leads to a strategic impasse; as Jodi Dean describes with her experience of Occupy, people often stick to the discourses and identity politics they know, 'as if we were just the same assortment of individuals with opinions and views as before, rather than a collectivity so threatening as to incite [an] overwhelming and violent police response.'[29] What Dean is effectively describing is a situation where that which is unfashionable within discourse (such as class) is proscribed, and established discourses, that existed before any event, are adhered to.

I would argue here that the post-Marxist approach can achieve the opposite of what it sets out to do in practice. Instead of creating a hegemonic project of equivalences between various causes rather than focusing on one 'pure' class struggle, what can actually happen is that causes are diluted, while its participants are expected to pursue a new purity. Support for the working class is not enough—you must also have the right views on a range of other issues before you can be accepted into the fold, which partly explains the failure of the Labour Party in the 2019 General Election, led by a career backbencher and fellow traveller of possibly every possible cause a left-winger could support. The right, on the other hand, tend to get elected with a simple focus on lower taxes or cuts to benefits. While these things may be relatively easier to get elected on and to deliver compared to what the left might want, there is a lesson here for both parliamentary and evental politics of the left.

1.2.2 From Althusser to Poststructuralism

Laclau and Mouffe share with Althusser an anti-Hegelian stance, but they also oppose the *dialectical* materialism of Althusser. Laclau and Mouffe have argued that Marx remains in the field of idealism—the very idealism that he himself had rebuked in *The German Ideology*. Laclau and Mouffe regard Marx's theory of dialectical contradiction between the forces and relations of production as being itself a form of idealism. It is an idea of the laws of history 'which are not immediately legible in the surface of historical life.'[30] The historicist interpretation need not be the one we take from Marx, but the rejection of the dialectical materialism of Althusser rests on the critique of the idea that the economy is a determinant beyond all that is constituted discursively.

Laclau and Mouffe's displacement of the economy as determinant in the last instance reminds us of Althusser's displacement of history in his anti-Hegelian theory. As Jacques Rancière has argued, Althusser's systematic totality that disavowed history was a response to the 'bad totality' that he associated with leftism, which denies the autonomy of philosophy. Althusser maintained the autonomy of philosophy against economism in his earlier works, and then against history and 'leftism' in his later works. Andrei Zhdanov's view that philosophy is an ideology derived from historical materialism was a particular target for Althusser's dialectical materialism, as was Lukács's historicism.[31]

Althusser's attack on leftism has its precursor in Lenin's critique of the leftist rejection of participation in unions and bourgeois parliaments (in which the Bolsheviks took part before the formation of the USSR), and the leftist debate over whether the Communist Party could represent the proletarian class.[32] This critique of leftism, I would argue, in turn had its precursor in Marx's *Political Indifferentism*.[33] The theory of the subject that is found in Hegelian Marxists such as Lukács and Sartre, as well as Gramsci's 'revolution against *Capital*,' is also singled out for criticism. With the latter, the vanguard in the form of the Bolsheviks and others are seen not as 'Marxists' who follow Marx's *Capital* to the letter, but as living Marxian thought 'which represents the continuation of German and Italian idealism.'[34] This focus on praxis and experience forms a school of Marxist theory that Althusser sees as a leftist form of humanism and historicism. This humanist and historicist form of Marxism, as Althusser sees it, gives the proletariat the role of 'site and missionary of the human essence,' which is a departure from *Capital*. The political practice of the proletariat was seen as philosophy itself, as self-consciousness, most likely under the influence of the more Hegelian works up to *The German Ideology*.[35]

Althusser was also critical of the Hegelian interpretation of the base/superstructure model in Marx. For Althusser, the relation between the base and superstructure is not simply Marx's equivalent of the relation between civil society and the State that we see in Hegel's *Philosophy of Right*. In Marx we find 'determinant instances in the structure-superstructure complex which constitutes the essence of any social formation,' rather than simply finding that everything is determined by the economy in the last instance. As Althusser put it, Marx gave us 'two ends of the chain' ('determination in the last instance by the (economic) mode of production,' and 'the relative autonomy of the superstructures and their specific effectivity,' and it is our task to discover the relation between these.[36] It is also important to remember that Marx was a theorist of political economy, not merely an economist.

So rather than the economy alone being an essentialist determinant of social relations, superstructures have a relative autonomy, as does philosophy, in Althusser's view. But Laclau and Mouffe's dismissal of Althusser's take on the role of the economy as an essentialist and non-constitutive imposition upon all social relations leads them to diminish the importance of the economy altogether, and consequently relegate the importance of collectives formed around class. We can see how Althusser's notion of overdetermination is used selectively by poststructuralists.

Other aspects, such as the role of the economy and the privileged status claimed for Marx's philosophy, are looked upon with suspicion, however agreeable Althusser's anti-humanism and anti-historicism may be. In Althusser's works, 'Theory' with a capital 'T' is used to distinguish the dialectical materialism that is Marx's philosophy from conventional philosophy that Althusser calls 'ideological,' and he finds grounds for this approach in *The German Ideology*. Ideology is a form of 'practice' which, for Althusser, is the 'transformation of a determinate given raw material into a determinate product' by determinate human labour and determinate means of production. As social practice may transform social relations, ideological practice transforms its object, which is consciousness. There are various non-Marxist theoretical practices, but Althusser takes Theory to be the Theory of practice in general, the practice of transforming the ideological product into 'knowledges,' or scientific truths.[37] What Althusser means here is that the various ideological practices, which are the concrete activities of politics, law, morality, and so on, are theoretical and philosophical practices that through Theory (or Marxist philosophy, the materialist dialectic) become properly understood and enter the realm of knowledge. However, Theory, or the materialist dialectic, is not to be applied externally as a formula or a law. Science must continually free itself from ideology, and the constant struggle against ideology can have its aims clarified by Theory, but it does not prescribe the strategy for this struggle.[38] This is, as Badiou puts it, a process without a subject that can only be grasped by 'militants of the revolutionary class struggle.'[39]

More will be said about Badiou's critique of Althusser in chapter 2, given that it signals a point of departure from a thinker who, as Bosteels argues, was not able to see in the events of May 1968 any significant truth, a position that Badiou's critique may well have been a response to.[40] However, we can see that Althusser's thought is an interesting bridge between Marxist and 'structuralist' theory, and poststructuralist thought. Poststructuralism sits uneasily with the idea of determination in the last instance. This means that even the aleatory materialism of Althusser's thought seems essentialist. As Warren Montag has noted, Althusser's system has been seen as one of multiple relations of force that ensure the economic determination in the last instance never arrives.[41] Or as Althusser himself put it, 'From the first moment to the last the lonely hour of the 'last instance' never comes.'[42]

Althusser's belief in conjuncture and opposition to any immanent teleology meant he disavowed notions such as 'late capitalism' that Ernest Mandel and Fredric Jameson had worked around (not that this of itself makes them teleological thinkers). Concrete situations and the conjuncture of relations of force and structure took the place that history had occupied in many a Marxist's theory. Althusser went far beyond a simplistic understanding of social relations that merely related to a contradiction between relations of production and forces of production, but that does not mean the economy ceases to be a determinant common to all social relations. For a number of authors, Montag explains, Althusser's thought then boils down to one thesis, which is that ideology interpellates individuals as subjects. The subject is never a given in Althusser, as it was for Lukács and other Marxian thinkers, and has been seen by a number of authors as unprecedented in Marxian thought, for which the subject has usually been already constituted but deceived by ideology rather than constituted by it.[43] Lukács's proletariat comes to be when it becomes conscious of itself and its commodification, or the reification of its value by others as a commodity, and in true teleological style becomes the last example of class consciousness in history.[44] While I do not think that the realization of one's value as a worker is not a viable platform around which to form a political collective, Althusser's 'interpellation' of the subject, where ideology becomes the unconscious relation between man and the world, offers a more sophisticated understanding of the subject that pre-dates poststructuralism.

However, Choat argues that Althusser is not simply a structuralist; Althusser shares much with poststructuralism, such as his anti-humanism and admiration for Jacques Lacan. His 'structuralism' involves a flirtation with the structuralism he sees in some of Marx's formulas, but Choat maintains that Althusser radicalized Marx and replaced the dogma present in some Marxian theory with his definition of philosophy as class struggle in theory. Marx is thus politicized through his view of philosophy not as a whole, but as a system of positions likely to relate to the class struggle. Philosophy works in conjunction with class struggle rather than being a form of disinterested speculation, and is thereby politicized. Furthermore, Althusser's symptomatic reading of Marx that pays attention to the silences in his thought also suppresses aspects of Marx that did not accord with his materialist principles.[45] This much should be well known from his famous division of Marx's works into the 'Early Works' of 1840–1844, the 'Works of the Break' of 1845, the 'Transitional Works' of 1845–1857, and the 'Mature Works' of 1857–1883, the 'epistemological break' of *The German Ideology* being of particular importance, moving away from humanism and towards a more scientific approach.[46] At the same time as Choat urges us not to see Althusser simply as a structuralist at odds with all that is poststructuralist, Choat is also in agreement with Newman that Jameson's association of poststructuralism with postmodernism is inadequate, although essentially Choat's concern is that too close an association of postmodernism and poststructuralism obscures and prevents us from analysing the latter's relationship with Marx.[47]

Newman opts for the use of the word 'poststructuralism'—rather than 'postmodernism'—as a strategy or series of strategies that resist the totalities of modernity and its essentialist categories, and its absolute faith in rational truth. This does not mean, however, that poststructuralism has transcended modernity, but that it operates *within* the discourse of modernity while at the same time exposing its limits.[48] This is markedly different from Callinicos's view that poststructuralism and postmodernism both originate in the collapse of Hegel's system. Jürgen

Habermas, taking a stand against postmodernism, famously argued that modernity was based on a refusal to 'borrow the criteria by which it takes its orientation from the models supplied by another epoch; it has to create its normativity out of itself. Modernity sees itself cast back upon itself without any possibility of escape.'[49] The relationship between poststructuralism and Hegel will be touched upon in the next chapter; but here it is worth raising again how postanarchism seeks to retain an (unstable) universality against postmodern particularism. Poststructuralism and postanarchism are often critical of dialectics, but neither assume that modernism has collapsed and given way entirely to postmodernism. Newman also sees in Althusser something approaching the anarchist perspective that allows for the autonomy of the political through his use of overdetermination, and notes Callinicos's rejection of Althusser's dialectic, since this does not allow for what he sees as the classical Marxist approach in which there is a Hegelian dialectical synthesis of social practices back into an original unity.[50] We will see in the next chapter how poststructuralism does retain aspects of Hegel, but also how Badiou draws on Hegel to take us beyond Althusser.

Laclau's scepticism of any particularism based on permanently fixed identities has been influential on postanarchism.[51] The universal, for Laclau, does not exist as an outside to political practice, but is integral to its practice in the sense that there are universal limits to the constitution of identity. As we have seen, Laclau is sceptical of Marx who, while he talks of the universal dissolution of capitalist society and its class system, also has, Laclau would argue, the domination of one particular part of society (the bourgeoisie over the proletariat, but with an expanding proletariat which will come to dominate) as a condition for universality. According to this view, designations such as classes, ethnic groups and so on are particularities of little use once we take the non-essentialist approach that Laclau offers, with such identities being at best the name for 'transient points of stabilization.'[52] Newman notes the resemblance between Laclau and Mouffe's post-Marxism and aspects of anarchism, which is not acknowledged in their works—however, he argues that the hegemonic project central to the post-Marxist is unsuitable for horizontalist modes of radical politics today.[53]

1.2.3 *The Poststructuralist and Postanarchist Critiques of Marx*

Todd May, in his *Political Philosophy of Poststructuralist Anarchism*, distinguishes between three types of political philosophy—formal, strategic, and tactical philosophy. May sees formal philosophy as that which operates between one of two poles—that which *is* and that which *ought to be*. Within the latter category he places John Rawls and his theory of a just society that all rational people would choose behind a 'veil of ignorance' (but which still involves participants being aware of how life is in the world under current conditions), as well as the neoliberal theorist Robert Nozick who, May argues, pays little attention to what is, but rather purely to what ought to be. These two 'formal' philosophers are not very relevant to the discussion here, but May does identify Lukács as such a philosopher, since he distinguishes between the 'what is' that is history and the reification of value through commodity fetishism, and what ought to be, which is the development of the proletariat as the last form of class consciousness in history.[54]

Being less critical of Marx than he is of Marxism, May identifies much of the latter with strategic political philosophy, which also concerns itself with the tension between what is and what ought to be. However, Marxist strategists treat the tension between the 'is-pole' and 'ought-pole' in a dialectical manner, with May giving us the example of Lenin and his argument that the state will wither away. The bourgeoisie redistributes some of its power in Marx's analysis of events between 1848–51 in France in the name of democracy, but in reality does so to retain power. Lenin sees this dialectically, as a stage on the path towards revolution and the eventual withering away of the state. For May, however, there is no such dialectical synthesis that resolves the tension between the is-pole and ought-pole, and he proceeds to make a number of criticisms of Marxism.[55] For example, he points out the pitfalls of 'reductionism' in the base/superstructure model, which supposes that transformations at the level of the mode of production are sufficient to transform all power relations in society, adopting the Foucauldian view that power relations in society are dispersed and decentred. May also disputes Marx's theory of a falling rate of profit over time, pointing to improvements in workers' living standards as evidence of the effectiveness of unionization, against assumptions made by Marx that living standards will decline.[56]

The focus on a central site of power in this picture of Marxism is but one interpretation—power is also dispersed through various values and social relations, and this is also the target of Marxian analyses. Having criticized the strategic aspect of (so-called) Marxism, May's concern that there may never be a route from Marx to a 'just' society is a peculiar one, and may actually be an enduring strength of Marx's thought. Excessively prescriptive and strategic interpretations of Marx are critiqued, on the one hand, but welcomed, on the other, when Marx's theory of the falling rate of profit is seen to be inaccurate in the light of an improvement in profits and workers' conditions in the twentieth century.[57] However, this does not necessarily prove or disprove a theory, and May should welcome a theory that is open to interpretation by political theorists. Economists have also long argued over this point in Marx. Nobuo Okishio's 1961 'disproof' of Marx's law of the tendential fall in the rate of profit as a result of technological advances continues to be a matter of debate, and is something that Marxist economist Andrew Kliman has critiqued at length in defence of Marx.[58]

May sees the reductionism of Marxist analyses and the failure of their revolutionary predictions as an invitation to another kind of thinking, which he calls 'tactical.' May associates this with anarchist thinking, and believes tactical thought can retain Marxists' ethical commitments 'while jettisoning the philosophy they constructed to realize them.' Anarchist thought, according to May, could be seen as a forerunner to poststructuralist thought, and both forms of thought reject representational intervention, as well as rejecting the strategy (or the idea) of the concentration of power. Instead, there is a recognition of multiple struggles around multiple sites of power and domination, so a tactical approach is taken that seeks to understand and recognize the plurality of such struggles, rather than following a strategy of replacing one concentrated form of power—say, the bourgeois state—with another concentrated form of power—the workers' state. Where traditional anarchist and poststructuralist thought differs, however, is over the essentialist aspects of the former, which sees human essence as 'good' and uses this essence to build a case for a peaceful life without the state. This is an essentialism that has been criticized by poststructuralist thinkers as being an aspect of strategic thought—something that May seeks to redress through the tactical and anti-essentialist thinking of Deleuze, Michel Foucault and Jean-François Lyotard. For example, instead of looking at power as always repressive, poststructuralism sees this as only one mode of power's operation—power can also be, as Foucault would put it, positive and productive. Poststructuralists focus on the relation between power and knowledge because our relationships are immersed in, and partially a product of, this relation. Seeing power as wholly repressive is a 'political' or strategic interpretation.[59]

Newman's postanarchism draws on a wider set of thinkers, including Max Stirner, Jacques Derrida and Lacan, as well as Deleuze and Foucault, to consider the 'place of power.' Marxism, he argues, neglects various sites of power in society, because it reduces social phenomena to the capitalist economy. Similarly to May, Newman is critical of the economic reductionism he sees as central to Marxian theory, pointing to Foucault's critique of Marxism as neglecting the problem of power. While Foucault (like most poststructuralist thinkers) was not an anarchist, both Foucault and the classical anarchists are said to share a mutual suspicion of the Marxist and Leninist model of the 'Revolution,' in which state power is seized by a new class, rather than destroyed as a structure—thus amounting to no more than a 'changing of the guard.' It is also too simplistic to see the bourgeoisie as having a monopoly on power, while neglecting the multiple sites of power that run through the social body, such as the prison, the family and psychiatric discourse, for example.[60]

The 'place of power' has, for Newman, existed in various symbolic positions over the centuries, such as in the body of an absolute sovereign in Hobbes. Foucault, however, in rejecting the sovereign locus of power, sees it instead in terms of a war of force relations. However, this approach seems to be missing an abstract symbolic dimension, or a reference point around which this war of force relations can orient itself. As an alternative conception of antagonism to Foucault's, Newman introduces the notion of antagonism as partial indeterminacy and fixity, following the logic of the Lacanian real.

For Lacan, identity is only partially constituted, and fundamental to this partial constitution is that it lacks something—there is a lack between the subject's symbolic identity and the subject itself, resulting in a surplus of meaning. What is lacking is what cannot be symbolized, or what Lacan calls the 'real.'[61] There is always an absence in the symbolic order (that is, signs, signified and signifiers), pointing to an unsymbolizable element, whose very presence is indicated by its absence from this order.[62] Newman stresses that the lack is not an essentialist core of the subject, and Lacan's terminology helps us to go beyond poststructuralist thought on difference and plurality to construct a notion of political and social identity built around its own impossibility and emptiness.[63] Claude Lefort's notion of the 'empty place' of power is then invoked, so that the Foucauldian dispersion of power amongst a series of force relations in society is what enables society and identity to be constituted. This partial fixity and partial indeterminacy is the result of the imperative of various political actors and identities to fill the empty place of power, while failing to eliminate the contingent aspect of identity—no one can claim to fill the place of power absolutely, as new identities will always emerge.[64] For Newman, the empty place of power provides an ontological basis for anarchism as the horizon of politics.[65]

Despite their differences, comparisons between Marx and poststructuralist theorists have often been made. As has been noted, instead of focusing on political economy, poststructuralist thinkers broadened their inquiry to include other forms of power, often with the same targets as Marx. Foucault, for example, drawing on Friedrich Nietzsche, would argue, at least in the 1970s, that the ruling classes impose an interpretation on discourse, knowledge and categories of truth, which would later enable the bourgeoisie to present its reign as the result of a long narrative of progress and enlightenment.[66] While the approach taken by poststructuralist thinkers towards the critique of power appears to be different from that which Marx took, its blueprint may in part be found in Marx. Choat has written of the similarities between Marx and poststructuralism, and therefore postanarchism. Choat has argued that the post-Marxism of Laclau and Mouffe draws derivatively on Marx through Marxism, without providing detailed analyses of Marx's works. Looking primarily at Lyotard, Foucault, Derrida and Deleuze, Choat argues that these thinkers, along with Marx, have created a materialist philosophy of intervention rather than reflection. In doing this they welcome the unknown rather than what is already known, the creation of new values that we see in Deleuze that will disrupt the present order and established values. Choat also follows Althusser's symptomatic reading of *Capital*, where the reader should pay as much attention to Marx's silences and what goes unsaid as to what he does say.[67]

As far as postanarchism is concerned, Choat sees the value in reading classical anarchist thinkers through poststructuralist analysis, but not at the expense of Marxism (or rather, at the expense of all of the various possible Marxisms). Instead of Marx's theory being limited by 'economism,' Choat sees Marx as broadening the scope of political power by emphasizing economic conditions over the state, and not as reducing political power to the economy in a move that is equivalent to the classical anarchist reduction of power to the state. Marx goes beyond the efforts of classical economists by demonstrating that what are believed to be the neutral fields of production, distribution and exchange are really relations of domination, in contrast to the opposition classical economists make between an apolitical market as a natural harmony, and the artificialities of the state.[68]

1.3 Marx, the Performative Proletariat and Communism

1.3.1 Class as an Analytical Concept

We are concerned here with collective subjectivity as a challenge to capitalism, but we must first explain how class remains relevant. The radical collective Tiqqun sees the notion of class struggle as a strategic straight jacket from another age.[69] Nevertheless, class remains relevant for The Invisible Committee, who are associated with the Tiqqun group. They note that work includes two contradictory dimensions, consisting of both exploitation of labour through the appropriation of surplus value, and participation in the common and cooperative task of production. The former explains indifference towards managerial rhetoric, while the latter, it is argued, explains indifference towards Marx these days, given that workers appear to be cooperating with their exploiters (although this view ignores the dynamics of why it is that people comply with capitalist norms). However, while the idea of exploiters and exploited is present in their work, there is a 'non-class' to be added to the bourgeoisie and proletariat: it is 'those who take no sides: the petty bourgeoisie.' They are the neutrals in the relation between the bourgeoisie and the proletariat, the small business owners, minor bureaucrats, managers, professors and journalists, 'middlemen of every sort' who 'make up this non-class in France.'[70]

The existence of a growing middle class, albeit one that has been 'squeezed' in recent years, has been used to discredit Marxian theory on class, and has been met with various explanations. Erik Olin Wright has pointed towards a number of these explanations, including Nicos Poulantzas's view that the middle class is a segment of some other class rather than an expanding bourgeoisie, such as the 'new petty bourgeoisie'; or that it is a new class entirely, perhaps a managerial class of sorts. The rise of managers has also led to attempts to replace the concept of exploitation under capitalism with that of domination, although a wholesale replacement of the concept of exploitation with that of domination does not withstand scrutiny. A manager may both dominate and be exploited, dominating those he or she manages, but be only semiautonomous, given that he or she is also exploited for their labour. For Wright, the concept of domination should not be adopted at the expense of the concept of exploitation, as the former does not necessarily mean that the interests of the dominated are different to those of the one who dominates. The concept of exploitation, on the other hand, maintains that there are objective interests that the exploiter is pursuing in exploiting someone (appropriating surplus value, for example).[71]

Wright defines the term 'class exploitation' using three criteria. First, the material welfare of one group depends causally on the material deprivations of another. Second, the causal relation in the first criterion involves the exclusion of the exploited from access to certain productive resources, and this is usually backed by force of law (although not always), such as property rights. Third, the causal mechanism by which the second criterion leads to the first criterion (that is, the role exclusion from access to certain productive resources has in the material deprivation of a group) involves the appropriation of the fruits of labour from the exploited by those who control the productive resources.[72] Wright, as one of the leaders in the field of analytical Marxism, went to far greater lengths than can be outlined here in developing an analytical understanding of class. For much of his career he viewed Marxian class analysis as superior to rival sociological approaches, especially Weberian approaches, although Wright later drew on a wider range of analytical tools. However, the Marxian tradition remains a valuable body of ideas for Wright, including the identification of exploitation and domination as fundamental to class division (between capitalists and workers) in capitalist society, while most sociologists ignore these notions of exploitation and domination, or explicitly deny their relevance.[73]

Wright affirms his view that domination and exploitation are useful terms, with the latter term coming under especial scrutiny by sociologists who might view this term as a moral judgement. Reiterating his position in earlier works, domination is the ability to control the work of others, while exploitation refers to the acquisition of economic benefits from labour by those who dominate, so all exploitation is domination, but not all domination is exploitation. A manager in the civil service might be an example of the latter, and the middle class is a class Wright obviously acknowledges, which might include the better educated, those who dominate, those who spend their money in a certain way, and so on.[74]

So analytical Marxists, and policy makers in governments for that matter, will consider the wide range of class divisions in society. Marxian theorists, however, retain the concepts of exploitation and domination. Individuals seen as middle class may not be in a dominant or exploitative position, and are likely to be dominated and exploited themselves. Or they could dominate others in the workplace, but not exploit them. When an individual exploits labour, Marxian theory would tend to categorize them as bourgeois, with the appropriate capital to extract value behind them. An individual in the middle class may or may not be an exploiter or exploited, or bourgeois or proletariat in Marxian theory, and it is this divide between the exploiter and exploited, or bourgeoisie and proletariat, that has characterized the non-analytical Marxian philosophy that I am most concerned with here. Of course there are those who are not analytical Marxists who draw on the concrete economic position of the exploited, but the focus is on that moment or event in which workers become a collective political subject, and all the nuances of dry class analysis become academic and irrelevant in that moment.

1.3.2 The Becoming of the Proletariat

While this analytical understanding of class remains important, and we can see that it is still possible to discern a divide between the exploiter and the exploited, or bourgeoisie and proletariat, much of what Marx and Marxian theorists have written has depended on the subject seeing for themselves what their place is in the totality of social relations. Neither Marx nor many Marxian philosophers consider class in as much depth as an analytical Marxian like Wright does, although Marx does not leave us simply with a clear-cut exploiter/exploited, bourgeoisie/proletariat divide. We see, for example, the aspiring bourgeois in the shape of the artisan, but in the midst of the communist event (whichever interpretation one wishes to follow in Marxian theory), the collective political subject that is the proletariat sees social relations as broadly divided along exploiter/exploited lines. It is a broadly performative notion of class, crystallized in the act of identifying oneself as belonging to a class in a moment of crisis.

Michael Hardt and Antonio Negri see the continuing relevance of the proletariat, even though the industrial working class that it was previously associated with no longer has the privileged and prominent position it used to enjoy. In *Empire* they correctly define the proletariat as 'a broad category that includes all those whose labor is directly or indirectly exploited by and subjected to capitalist norms of production and reproduction.' The proletariat is within capital and sustains capital, according to Hardt and Negri, and this is what defines it as a class. While there is an analytical aspect to this understanding of the proletariat, it is through the immanence in practice of what Hardt and Negri come to call the multitude within global capital that the seeds of global capital's destruction are sown. With the power of capital encompassing the globe like never before, this Empire will, according to Hardt and Negri, find the deterritorializing power of the multitude to be both its sustenance and the force that makes its destruction necessary.[75]

This follows what Negri saw earlier in his career as the objectification of *Capital*, and the need to put the subject in the driving seat rather than the analysis of the intellectual. To get beyond the impasse he thinks he sees in *Capital*, Negri invokes the conceptual armoury in the *Grundrisse* as a means to bring the subject back to the fore, to 'liberate the revolutionary content of the Marxist method,' a method that explodes the binary dialectic by making 'worker subjectivity... the revolutionary class, the universal class.'[76] Negri notes a tension in the *Grundrisse* towards the world market (*Weltmarkt*), with the global spread of capitalism and the real subsumption of world society under capital creating the conditions for revolutionary subjectivity.[77] In *Multitude*, they explain the necessity of providing a new (or a more developed) social theory suitable for the contemporary social reality, as Marx would appreciate, while acknowledging that Marx may already have anticipated the theoretical challenge faced by them.[78] For Badiou, however, the idea that the multitude is both the power behind global capital and the force paving the way for its destruction is optimistic, arguing that with Hardt and Negri we get the old and questionable adage, 'the worse it gets, the better it gets.' Badiou sees in the multitude the new 'petit-bourgeois proletarians' whose convergences do nothing to challenge the dominance of global capital.[79]

We will see in the next chapter how Badiou's philosophy is built around an ontology that works with truths, rather than producing them, which is a similar position to that which Marx maintains: truth is a result of material change and events, and philosophers should work with these truths to change the world rather than only interpret it.[80] Marx undoubtedly privileges the proletariat as the agent of change, but Badiou, more so than Negri, describes the rarity of the event and the appearance of truth, even if he does not consistently wed this to Marxian theory in the same way Negri's subject is. The situation where the subject emerges and declares fidelity to a truth event is, however, an important aspect of Marxian theory. Considering the notion of truth in Lukács's and Walter Benjamin's thought, Žižek writes that while Marx often takes the terms 'proletariat' and 'working class' to be synonymous, a tendency can be discerned towards the term 'working class' being used as an analytical term belonging to the domain of sociological or conventional knowledge. The term 'proletariat,' however, suggests an operator of truth engaging with the new—a subject working with new demands in a revolutionary struggle.[81]

So the terms 'proletariat' and 'bourgeoisie' can be described at length analytically, as can terms such as 'cognitariat' used by Franco Berardi to describe the shift of the proletariat's work towards mental labour, and then the shift of mental labour to abstract labour—a kind of office-based proletariat that can have its labour exploited while on the move with contemporary information technology.[82] However, we have seen how Giddens' thoughts on the 'third way' of the 1990s label the proletariat as not working class at all, but rather enterprising human capital.[83] Not only is labour seen as capital, but capital can also include savings in a bank under the contemporary vernacular of the corporate world (and those it influences), instead of wealth that is used to accumulate more wealth through the extraction of value from others (as an employer or rentier capitalist, for example). As I have said above, such analytical nuances are left to academia and the corporate world, or to ideology, while the theory of the subject we are concerned with is a collective political subject not constrained by such analytical concepts. 'Proletariat' is a useful term that we may apply to a certain kind of political subject, but the Marxist subject is not created by such concepts, instead emerging performatively through an event.

1.3.3 *Performative Communism, Non-Philosophy and Non-Class in Marx*

As I have already mentioned, Marx does not simply reduce everything to the economy, but analyses the economy to reveal its political content. We have also seen how class is still relevant. But even though what may be analytically understood as the working class or the potential proletariat *may* be the most likely to challenge capitalism, we can argue it is the performative act that makes the collective political subject in Marx. The individual is still partially the product of his/her surroundings (including the economy) and ideology, but it is through the performative act that he/she is briefly released from these.

The position of Marx and Engels in *The Communist Manifesto* is well known. Political power was seen as the power of one class for oppressing another. For Marx and Engels, if the proletariat gets the upper hand in its contest with the bourgeoisie, and is compelled to organize itself as a class and 'sweeps away by force the old conditions of production,' it will also 'have swept away the conditions for the existence of class antagonism and of classes generally, and will thereby have abolished its own supremacy as a class.'[84] Engels, in his *Anti-Dühring*, later explained (more so than Marx) how he thought communism would be realized, arguing that the proletariat first seizes the power of the state and then transforms the means of production into state property. In the process, the proletariat 'puts an end to itself as the proletariat' as well as 'an end to all class differences and class antagonisms.' For Engels, there would be an end to the state, so that government is no longer used to keep any class subjugated, but becomes instead the 'administration of things and the direction of the processes of production.' The state then withers away, rather than simply being abolished.[85] Lenin's preferred road to communism was to use the state, organized by the party as vanguard. For Lenin, the Paris Commune of 1871 'appears to have replaced the smashed state machine "only" by fuller democracy,' which involved the abolition of the standing army and the election of all officials; this was actually, for Lenin, a transformation of bourgeois democracy into proletarian democracy. In the case of the Paris Commune, it was still necessary to suppress a particular class (the bourgeoisie), and in this sense the Commune failed. Such a 'special force' would no longer be required for the suppression of one class by another when the majority can suppress the oppressors (i.e. the bourgeoisie).[86]

While Marx did not have much to say about what communism would actually look like, it is clear that a theory of the subject and of class consciousness is important for understanding its realization. The passage in Marx's works often referred to when seeking a definition of his view of communism is that contained in *The German Ideology*, co-written with Engels, which envisaged the emancipation from the division of labour:

> In communist society, where nobody has one exclusive sphere of activity but each can become accomplished in any branch he wishes, society regulates the general production and thus makes it possible for me to do one thing today and another tomorrow, to hunt in the morning, fish in the afternoon, rear cattle in the evening, criticize after dinner, just as I have a mind, without ever becoming hunter, fisherman, shepherd or critic.[87]

For Marx, where communism is discussed in the works before the epistemological break that Althusser identifies, and where such discussion is more obviously present on the surface of his work rather than buried in his analysis of political economy in *Capital*, communism remains at the more humanist and essentialist level. Communism is '*positive* transcendence of *private property*, as *human self-estrangement*, and therefore as the real *appropriation of the human* essence by and for man; communism therefore as the complete return of man to himself as a *social* (i.e. human) being—a return become conscious, and accomplished within the entire wealth of previous development.' This is a 'fully-developed humanism [that] equals naturalism; it is the *genuine* resolution of the conflict between man and nature and between man and man,' a communism where 'the riddle of history is solved, and it knows itself to be this solution' [italics in original].[88]

This is a loftier pursuit than statecraft will allow, but history, according to Marx, will come to communism as a 'very severe and protracted process.'[89] This is, of course, before the epistemological break, and presents a humanism and utopianism that is marginalized in his later scientific works. Yet these in turn lacked practical guidance on how communism might be realized, providing an opportunity for Engels and Lenin to take up this task, and to leave a lasting and popular understanding of what 'communism' means.

As Lenin points out, the withering away of the state will take place '*after* the socialist revolution,' eradicating all forms of the state, democratic and/or bourgeois, noting from *The Communist Manifesto* that the organization of the proletariat into the ruling class involved 'the conquest of democracy,' but further noting that Marx did not have a utopian vision here (nor a practical vision) as to what would happen after the revolution. As Lenin writes, 'he expected the experience of the mass movement to provide the answer to the question as to what specific forms this organization of the proletariat as the ruling class would assume and as to the exact manner whereby this organization would be combined with the most complete and consistent 'conquest of democracy.' Lenin's own view, which is evident from what took place in the USSR, was that the bourgeoisie would still need to be suppressed, which is a task the Paris Commune failed to carry out, since it transformed bourgeois democracy and the suppression of the proletariat into a 'fuller democracy'; as we have seen, that was no longer a state 'in the proper sense,' and therefore not equal to the challenge of eradicating the bourgeoisie.[90] The vanguardist position of Lenin is well known, and it is true that the spontaneity of the masses can benefit from direction, requiring a 'high degree of consciousness' from those directing (social democrats, for Lenin)[91]—but we also know in what direction Lenin was heading with his vanguard.

It is frequently noted that Marx's elaboration of what he meant by 'class' trails off soon after it begins towards the end of volume 3 of *Capital*, leaving room for interpretation of Marxian notions of class that continues to this day. For an anarchist such as Mikhail Bakunin, the organization of the proletariat into the ruling class would mean there would still be another proletariat subject to this new state, that one class would still dominate another. One response found in Marx's notebooks was that such domination by the proletariat was a means of forcibly hastening the transition towards a classless society while 'the economic conditions from which the class struggle and the existence of classes derive have still not disappeared.'[92] This is one basis for a particular interpretation of the 'dictatorship of the proletariat' in Marx's political writings, and while I do not want to focus on the argument that Lenin's or Engels's interpretation of Marx is incorrect, or that their political strategy is wrong, I do want to draw upon the aspects of Marx that have inspired writers since to think about the creation of subjects. Marx's best-known references to the 'dictatorship of the proletariat' (in the letter to Joseph Weydemeyer[93] and in the *Critique of the Gotha Programme*)[94] may well provide solid evidence for some that Marx sought a straightforward dictatorship that is little more than a changing of the guard. However, the 'dictatorship of the proletariat' is not a term with a consistent meaning across the twelve loci that Hal Draper identified in the works of Marx and Engels. The appearance of this term comes to an end in their works in 1891, with Engels pointing readers towards the Paris Commune of 1871 as an example of the dictatorship of the proletariat.[95] Such an example is far from the type of regime established by Lenin in the USSR.

Marx knew the difficulties that the practice of communism entailed. The working class did not expect miracles of the Paris Commune, Marx wrote, having 'no ready-made utopias to introduce' by decree of the people. The Paris Commune was for Marx an example of 'impossible' communism' in which the 'class property which makes the labour of the many the wealth of the few' was to be abolished. The Commune wanted to expropriate the expropriators and turn the means of production, land and capital away from the exploitation of labour and towards being 'mere instruments of free and associated labour,' according to Marx's record of events. This communism may seem impossible, but so was the capitalist system for Marx.[96] A convincing and consistent strategy for the realization of communism is lacking in Marx's works, and, even if this is not by design, it means Marx's thought is open to various strategic or performative responses.

Marx did not do away with philosophy altogether, and we have already seen how Althusser's 'Theory' as the Marxist philosophy or materialist dialectic is distinct from philosophy as ideology. As Étienne Balibar has written, Marx did not attempt the exit from philosophy that he hinted at in the *Theses on Feuerbach* (that is, that philosophers have only interpreted the world instead of changing it).[97] Instead, there is something *performative* in the philosophy of Marx—there is more than one way to change the world (capitalism changes the world, and alternatives must be sought), but saying is doing and doing is saying, with philosophy being active and forever evolving according to the situation.[98]

Marx may have appeared to be an anti-philosopher at one stage, but Balibar sees Marx as having developed a non-philosophy more than simply an anti-philosophy. By non-philosophy, Balibar means a philosophy that falls short of (conventionally understood) philosophy by drawing conclusions without premises (such as Marx's claim that men make their own history, but not of their own free will), and which goes beyond philosophy by showing that instead of being an entirely autonomous field, it is partly determined by social relations, including class struggle. Oscillating between this 'falling short' and 'going beyond,' philosophy after Marx is, for Balibar, no longer as it was before. Having perhaps set upon the path of anti-philosophy, Marx ended up developing a non-philosophy that is not a closed system 'identical to itself,' but one which is permanently open.[99]

This reminds us of other critiques of philosophy as a self-sufficient system that have been developed, notably in the non-philosophy of François Laruelle, who sees in the philosophies of difference of Nietzsche, Martin Heidegger, Derrida and Deleuze an internal analysis that does not look beyond their philosophies of difference to a non-philosophical One beyond.[100] Laruelle maintains that one of the essential principles of non-philosophy is that it does not identify with a philosophy, and therefore does not make decisions or create divisions. Any claim to philosophy 'must be verified from without by *a science for philosophy* that will unmask not so much the vague and doxic claim of philosophy to be a science, as its narcissistic and specular pretention to be, precisely, a philosophy—and the right one' [italics in original].[101]

Laruelle identifies with non-Marxism, arguing that the use of philosophy by Marxism has always been non-philosophical in practice, even if this practice has drawn on philosophical tools. Laruelle's aim is to impoverish the philosophy of Marxism and to make the various neo-Marxisms irrelevant through a universal non-Marxism, not seeking to replace certain aspects of Marxism with new philosophical formulations, but instead to stress the importance of a real-without-philosophy.[102] Laruelle's point is that philosophy is its own enemy, and non-philosophy seeks to explain how. Furthermore, complementing earlier concepts of a non-class in Marxian thought, Laruelle develops a notion of the non-proletarian, which is not understood analytically as immanent to the proletariat, but as immanent to its cause, or 'in-the-last-instance,' with the aim of thinking 'the subject without the exteriority of the proletariat ... but not without a relation to the capital-world and its conjectures.'[103] In other words, it seems that the non-proletariat is, for Laruelle, linked to an event. Laruelle's non-philosophy has gained traction in recent years amongst some of those interested in the recent speculative turn in philosophy (with so-called speculative materialism) and its relation to a critique of capitalism.[104] However, Quentin Meillassoux has argued that this 'real' outside of philosophy is another form of what he calls 'correlationism.'[105] More will be said on correlationism in the final chapter (and Badiou does not escape criticism on this front), but the contention that the non-philosophy of Marx did much to revitalize philosophy, turning philosophy towards a critique of itself, has been vindicated in the second half of the twentieth century, including with the advent of poststructuralist thought.

My intention is to draw on Marx as a proponent of non-philosophy, where philosophy critiques real events and real events critique philosophy. Marx is also not destined to be a historical determinist; nor must the dictatorship of the proletariat be assumed to be a settled matter, especially the relationship of the few appearances of this term in his political writings with the 'philosophy' of Marx. The proletariat could be seen as a political subject that comes to be because its components are broadly after the same thing (representation, or to present themselves and their demands, and so on), the appearance of a group based on a new collective subjectivity rather than through discursive similarities based on points of commonality between constituted identities. The nature of the proletariat has never been a settled matter for Marx or Marxian theorists, but it is usually seen as the class that serves as a precursor for the classless society. As Rancière has written, Marx and Engels should probably not have written the *Manifesto of the Communist Party*, logically speaking, when the question of 'what communist party?' and 'what proletariat?' was not one for which there is an easy answer. The strategic direction they took was one of both the formation of an as yet non-existent class (the proletariat) and its dissolution, a 'non-class' that would become a One.[106]

So there are a number of aspects to Marx's works that will later be related to Badiou and postanarchism.

First, what constitutes the proletariat is not a settled matter in Marx's works, nor for many Marxian theorists. For the Marxian theorist Moishe Postone, Marx's analysis does not point towards the self-realization of the proletariat as the true subject of history, but towards emancipation through the abolition of the proletariat and the labour it performs.[107] Contrary to the claims of the post-Marxists, Marx does not see the proletariat as having an essentialist core. We could instead use 'proletariat' as one name among many for a political collective which emerges as a new subject that declares fidelity to a truth in social relations, without us having to determine an absolute strategic end-point (or have any strategy at all, as post-Marxists do). We also do not have to see the lack of resolution on the strategic role of the proletariat in Marx's writings as necessarily a weakness in his philosophy—it can also be its strength.

Second, and related to the first point, the dictatorship of the proletariat and communism in Marx's works are open to interpretation. Capitalism may be seen as a totality, but whether or not this totality will ever be replaced absolutely as Marx apparently believed (but again, without a fully developed strategy), there are nevertheless events, whether they be the 'impossible communism' of which Marx spoke when discussing the Paris Commune, or events as understood through Badiou's theory of the event, for example. There are, throughout history, attempts to challenge capital by political subjects who have in common their need to sell their labour. Such a political subjectivity is one that has emerged through an event, under certain conditions, with the exploitation of subjects cutting across the various identities and particularities of participants. Various names may be given to such a subject (such as 'proletariat,' or 'non-class') and its purpose, but what is discernible is that such events occur when material circumstances mean there is a widespread appetite for such action, whether it be the May 1968 riots in Paris, the Watts Riots in LA three years before, or the more recent occupations and riots across Europe and the Arab Spring. There are also other interpretations of communism, such as the theory of communization that emerged in the 1970s that rejected the transitional form of the dictatorship of the proletariat we saw in Lenin where workers remain workers, exploited for their labour. Furthermore, opposing the Leninist party-state model with other organizational forms (democratic councils, for example) fails to resolve the problem that *Théorie Communiste* considered through 'communization.' Instead of a transitional period where a workers' state would retain exploitation and the capitalist content of the state, communization would be characterized by immediate communist measures and the destruction of all capitalist categories, including 'exchange, money, commodities, the existence of separate enterprises, the state and—most fundamentally—wage labour and the working class itself.'[108]

Third, the non-philosophy of Marx that both subordinates philosophy to real events and directs philosophy towards understanding such events gives the political subject a performative role. The creation of the collective political subject remains a rare event, following Badiou, and one in which philosophers and strategists (be they humanist, Marxists, post-Marxists or anarchists) do not have much of a hand in creating, although they are often, for better or worse, influential after the event.

In the next two chapters, what Badiou means by 'event' will be discussed alongside a comparison of some of his key terms with those deployed in poststructuralist and postanarchist thought. Badiou salvages the term 'communism' and the lessons of the Paris Commune from popular imagination (from misconceived phrases like 'Communist Party' or 'Communist State,' 'an oxymoron that the phrase 'Socialist State' attempted to get around')[109] and from the interpretation of the likes of Lenin. Following a comparison of Badiou's works with poststructuralist and postanarchist works, a comparison between Marxian thought and Badiou's thinking will help tease out further those aspects of Marx that remain useful for postanarchist thought.

2

Postanarchism and Badiou's Early Dialectical Materialism: From Sartrean to Post-Althusserianism to Ontological Anarchism

> For the rest, saint Gilles, saint Félix, saint Jean-François occupy the same niche in the maniacal Cathedral of chimeras ... All these audacious revisions, which it claims to be making against 'totalitarian' Marxism-Leninism with the fiery novelty of the marginal masses in dissent, are word for word what Marx and Engels, in The German Ideology, had to pull to pieces—towards 1845!—to clear the ground for a finally coherent systematization of the revolutionary practices of their time.[1]

In drawing parallels between Badiou and postanarchism, we can see in postanarchism not only similarities with some of Badiou's work, but also with aspects of Marxian thought that Badiou has drawn on and have much to offer postanarchism. These include the performative (in the sense described in the last chapter) nature of subjectivity, the widening of the theory of power beyond the state (or states, for Badiou), and an advocacy of a politics of direct presentation, rather than representation. Underpinning these traits is the idea that multiplicity is the rule, and the One (and states) is the exception: for Badiou, there is a void on the edge of every situation; and for Newman the state conceals an empty place of power.[2] The previous chapter challenged the antagonism between Marx and (post)anarchism as one founded on a particular interpretation of Marx that often associates his work directly with Lenin or the USSR, or at least with a certain version of the dictatorship of the proletariat. Badiou's relation to Marxian theory will be considered more closely in the fourth chapter, but in this chapter we will see that while Badiou draws on Marx throughout his career and avoids the kind of confusion discussed in the previous chapter regarding the relation between poststructuralist thought and Marx (largely by avoiding any association with poststructuralism), he helps us to bridge the gap between dialectical materialism and postanarchism.

Badiou has passed through a few stages in his long career, from Sartrean philosophy to Althusserian theory, and to a post-Althusserianism openly at odds with poststructuralism and anarchism. If we take Badiou's criticism of Deleuze, or his criticism of poststructuralism and anarchism, at face value, the potential importance of his dialectical materialism to postanarchism is obscured. This is despite the fact that Badiou, like Deleuze, refers to his system as an affirmative dialectic, as we will see. A closer look over the next two chapters will reveal how Badiou's thinking is neither structuralist nor poststructuralist in the strict sense, but provides an ontological (or what could be called 'operational') understanding of states that complements the tactical (and in Newman's work also ontological) approach of postanarchism, without the strategic approach that has been associated with 'Marxism.' In doing so, we will be better placed to consider how Badiou relates to Marxian theory, and finds common ground between Marxian theory, communism and anarchism, ultimately making class relevant today for Marxists as well as anarchists.

2.1 Philosophical Anarchism

Before addressing Badiou's criticism of anarchist thought, I would like to place postanarchism and Badiou's thought in context with regards to philosophical anarchism. We have seen how, for Newman, anarchism is the horizon of politics and all forms of power, being the ultimate nightmare for the sovereign tradition.[3] Newman also refers to the 'anarchist invariant,' which is 'the recurring desire for life without government that haunts the political imagination.'[4] As I noted in the previous chapter, Badiou's theory of the event and his understanding of communism also assume that the state, in whatever its present form, is temporary, and an event against the state will be desirable for those included in (and counted by) the state, but not belonging to it. Badiou shows that the state's legitimacy cannot be assured, and that it will be called into question. Newman, in a similar way, develops an ontological approach that starts with anarchy—that is the non-legitimacy of power—and which implies that all power is always open to contestation.[5]

The approach whereby the legitimacy of the state is the overarching question for all philosophical inquiry into the state, rather than simply advocating its destruction once and for all, is one associated with philosophical anarchism. Magda Egoumenides, in focusing on political obligations and whether we can be obliged, on a philosophical level, to obey political institutions, has argued that 'philosophical anarchism' emphasizes a critique of political authority, without necessarily demanding that the state be abolished. While there are many who are both political and philosophical anarchists, a philosophical anarchist, she argues, is often nonpolitical. Egoumenides's critical philosophical anarchism studies what she sees as the best moral theories that might form the basis for justifying political obligation, and then sets about deriving from their failure a constructive account of how 'there is no general political obligation and that in this respect political institutions remain unjustified.' The question for critical philosophical anarchism is whether political institutions should exist at all, and the onus is then on institutions to continually justify themselves, which is a task that becomes increasingly more difficult over time. One of the points that Egoumenides makes is that critical philosophical anarchism, through providing a critical analysis of political obligation, can appeal to anybody, and not just political anarchists. The questions asked of the moral justifications for political obligations are of use to all political scientists.[6]

Egoumenides remains sceptical of any form of political obligation, including John Horton's defence of associative political obligations, which includes obligations towards a group even when membership is not voluntary. Horton is seeking here to defend at least some form of political obligation, and non-voluntary membership would include the family (although Egoumenides argues that obligation in this sense can be built around gratitude towards one's parents rather than a non-voluntary obligation).[7] Much of Egoumenides's argument follows Horton's work, including the idea that philosophical anarchists need not be political. Furthermore, in defence of anarchism, Horton argues that 'anarchists need not, and mostly do not, subscribe to the absurdly perfectionist account of human nature with which they are sometimes saddled by their critics,' with many being under no illusion that human nature is essentially good, and that life without the state will always be harmonious. Indeed, Horton notes that while anarchists prefer life without the state, they are not opposed to other forms of political organization on their terms.[8]

However, something that all anarchists share, according to A. John Simmons (with whom Egoumenides agrees on this point), in addition to opposition to the state, is a commitment to voluntarism, with all non-voluntary political obligations being illegitimate.[9] We can see how philosophical anarchism, before we even get to postanarchism, provides moral antecedents for the ontological approach later taken by Badiou, even though he distances himself from anarchism. John P. Clark has noted how Badiou lends support to historical events (at least those he considers to be events) which, after a time, detaches politics from contemporary possibilities, a trait which Clark notes is present in Murray Bookchin's work as well, using historical phenomena to present a vision of how contemporary society ought to be.[10] However, within anarchist thought it is not Bookchin whose work Badiou's most resembles. Despite the potential for fidelity to an event to become associated with ideological constructs (which I deal with in the fifth chapter), the similarities between Badiou's thought and that of postanarchism, and in particular Newman's thought, should not be overlooked. By considering Badiou's thought in this way, we see how his selective reading of Marx and Marxian thought can help bridge a divide between anarchism and Marxism.

2.2 Badiou Beyond Marx

While Badiou's relation to Marxian theory is a complicated one that has changed through the various phases of his long career, he has been largely consistent in standing in explicit opposition to aspects of poststructuralist and anarchist thought. In his Marxist-Leninist pamphlet *Theory of Contradiction*, published for the *Union des Communistes de France Marxiste-Leniniste* (UCFML) in 1975, Badiou has Lyotard, Guattari and Deleuze in particular in his sights, mirroring Marx and Engels's choice of words in *The German Ideology*, where they critiqued 'Saint Max' Stirner's views on property and communism at length.[11] Badiou has been critical of Deleuze throughout his career. In another UCFML publication during his Marxist-Leninist phase, *The Flux and the Party*, Badiou would write that 'Deleuze would like to be to Kant what Marx is to Hegel, Deleuze flips Kant upside down: the categorical imperative, but a desiring one; the unconditional, but materialist; the autonomy of the subject, but like a fluid flux.'[12] This critique continues into Badiou's later 'politics without a party'[13] phase during which he distanced himself from the state and Marxist-Leninism, arguing in *The Clamor of Being* that Deleuze presents us with a theory of a permanent One and of 'one single event for all events.'[14]

For postanarchists like Saul Newman and Todd May, Deleuze (and Stirner) has been particularly influential, and yet this school of thought converges with Badiou's thought on a number of points. For example, the place of both the singular *and* the universal in philosophy, so important for Badiou, is a question that Newman has considered. For

Newman, the question needs to be *how* to theorize the universal after postmodernism, without basing it on a universal notion of the human subject, and without developing a notion of hegemony that still sees the state as the domain of politics.[15] And as we will see, the event, for Badiou, is both singular and universal.[16] Yet while Newman and others associated with postanarchism (such as Benjamin Noys)[17] have engaged with Badiou's works, Newman has noted Badiou's dismissive attitude towards anarchism.[18] At the same time as stating the importance of a 'politics without a party' for emancipatory politics, Badiou also dismissed anarchism as a 'vain critique' or 'shadow' of communist parties.[19]

This apparent hostility towards anarchism perhaps sits well with Badiou's long engagement, temporally at least, with Marxian theory, Leninism and Maoism, and increasingly throughout his career with communism. As Alberto Toscano has noted, Badiou's relationship to Marxism has been complicated and incomplete, with Badiou claiming in *Metapolitics* that Marxism does not exist, in the sense that it must refer to the history of political singularities.[20] In other words, because of the rupture and foundation that takes place between Marx's works and Lenin's, and between Stalin and Lenin and Mao and Stalin, there is no continuity and linear development in Badiou's view. Instead, Badiou believes that 'Marxism' [is] the (void) name of an absolutely inconsistent set, once it is referred back, as it must be, to the history of political singularities.'[21] So while there are many theorists who draw on Marx and may call themselves 'Marxists,' there is no such thing as one 'Marxism,' it being an operation that names a political singularity, in Badiou's view. This much is evident from the various 'crises of Marxism' as it has responded to various conjunctures, which Stathis Kouvelakis has written on (and notes the more polemical 'deaths of Marxism' that are usually proclaimed by those external to the Marxian canon).[22]

Toscano's analysis of Badiou's thinking of politics, and the stages in his works that include the end of his Maoist or Marxist-Leninist phase and the beginning of the 'destruction' and 'recomposition' of Marxist politics in *Can Politics Be Thought* (which preceded his best known work *Being and Event)*, includes some of the markers that demonstrate Badiou's convergence with postanarchism. The political, Toscano notes, is seen by Badiou as the transcendental illusion linking the social bond and a sovereign authority, while what Badiou is interested in is separating politics from the political.[23] In other words, politics (as opposed to the political) is what is better known in Badiou's most famous works as that which is associated with truth and the event, not with the official politics of the state. This distancing of politics from the state is certainly not alien to Marxian theory, although anarchist theorists tend to appear more united when it comes to their opposition to the state. For postanarchists, however, any strategy that 'simply' involves abolishing the state is as short sighted as the Leninist or Maoist seizure of the state. Badiou and postanarchists accept that there is such a thing as the state, without assuming that its existence in all its forms will cease one day, and without proposing a strategy to abolish it. For Badiou, any state, as a One, is an operation that cannot last forever in any case, as we shall see, but like postanarchists he sees politics as something separate from the state.[24]

For Newman, postanarchism is both 'political' and 'anti-political.' The political, for postanarchism, is an engagement with power and antagonism whether within or outside the state, while the anti-political is an ethical approach that seeks to transcend power and sovereignty. Newman takes liberalism as an example, it being neither sufficiently political because it subordinates the autonomy of the political to universal human rights and 'neutral' market exchanges, nor sufficiently anti-political because it does not challenge the state as the guardian of the political. Postanarchism makes explicit this 'politics of anti-politics' that can be found in anarchism.[25]

So there is common ground between Badiou and Newman, and the way in which they consider 'the political' and 'politics,' and 'the political' and 'the anti-political,' and yet Badiou's approach towards such questions has often had a Marxist tone. Badiou's complex relationship with Marxism, Maoism and anti-capitalism has been addressed in recent years not only by scholars such as Toscano and Bruno Bosteels,[26] but by Badiou himself. Maoism and communism have been addressed at length by Badiou, even in recent years in the *Logics of Worlds*,[27] *Polemics*,[28] *The Communist Hypothesis*,[29] as well as in papers given at conferences on the 'Idea of Communism' in London and New York in 2009 and 2011 respectively.[30] Whether Badiou is a Marxist has been less clear cut. In *The Rebirth of History*, Badiou recalls how Antonio Negri used him as an example of those who are communist without being a Marxist, to which he replied that it is better to be a communist without being a Marxist than a Marxist without being a communist, reasoning that everyone, including those who govern in the interests of the bourgeoisie, are Marxists without being communists, being obsessed with stock market wobbles and negative economic growth. Badiou therefore reluctantly calls himself a Marxist, which for him is 'the organized knowledge of the political means required to undo existing society and finally realize an egalitarian, rational figure of collective organization for which the name is "communism".[31]

This by no means gives closure to the question of whether Badiou is a Marxist, or what kind of Marxist—these questions will be considered in chapter 4. What is clear is that Badiou engages with Marx and Marxian theory, but does so in a way that enables us to draw parallels between postanarchism and Badiou, and subsequently to further the case that Marx still has much to offer postanarchism.

2.3 Badiou, the Performative, and the Operational

The performative nature of Badiou's theory draws clears comparisons with postanarchist thought. As theories that respond to events, they focus on the negative and subtraction (that is, that which is missing or is unacknowledged by the regime of power) rather than resolving ongoing ethical dilemmas, for example, once and for all through positive and authoritarian demands with no basis in an event. Their approaches instead feed into ethics, but an ethics lacking absolutely stable universal criteria where Newman is concerned,[32] and an ethics that opposes false universalities with no basis in an event (such as Nazism) where Badiou is concerned.[33] Anarchism, as Koch has noted, is 'the only defensible normative position' if knowledge cannot be externally validated, as it is the action of the state against individuals that needs to be justified, and not resistance to the state.[34] Badiou expresses this idea far more systematically, albeit by drawing on ontology. The contingency within the state is expressed as an operation in Badiou's most famous works, and in making a comparison between Todd May's three types of political philosophy (formal, strategic and tactical), we might call Badiou's system an *operational* one. In other words, Badiou 'simply' considers how states exist as operations, that is, temporarily and contingently. The onus is on any of us who wish to apply formal, strategic or tactical philosophies to the lives of others to justify such an approach, bearing in mind that all states, which includes all Ones and not just nation states, are temporary operations whose continued existence is never guaranteed.

We have seen how May views anarchism as a forerunner to poststructuralism, and poststructuralist anarchism as a tactical type of philosophy that recognizes multiple struggles and a dispersal of power. Furthermore, he also sees the tactical philosophy of poststructuralist anarchism as capable of retaining the ethical commitments that what he calls Marxists have pursued, but without the formal or strategic approach they constructed in this cause.³⁵ Badiou's system is also tactical, but the operational aspect of his work underpins the tactical and performative aspect of his philosophy. The operational nature of his system does not call on us to establish Ones as the outcome of any political strategy we may have, but recognizes that Ones come into existence as operations whether we like it or not. In the grand scheme of things, this might suggest that the seizure of state power may be both strategically and tactically viable if such a One were bound to be temporary.

Neither postanarchists nor Badiou advocate such an approach, although the case with Badiou may be less certain, as we will see when looking at his relation to Marxian theory in chapter 4. The operational character of Badiou's philosophy does suggest, however, that whatever we would like to happen, the vanguardist movement against the state that May sees as strategic will only ever be a temporary operation, as will the state and states, and not an absolute commencement of an eternal state (or the end to the dialectic).

2.4 Badiou's Tussle with Postmodernism

To the reader who simply places Badiou in the Marxist camp, a comparison between his thought and poststructuralism may remind them of the old debates between Marx and the anarchists. While some of Badiou's thought may appear difficult to square with anarchist thought at first, Badiou has developed into a post-Althusserian thinker who, while not a poststructuralist, shares with poststructuralism the view that politics is contingent and takes place on unstable ground.³⁶

It is not possible to simply oppose, for instance, anarchism to Badiou's more 'scientific,' or at least mathematically rigorous, approach to politics. Lewis Call notes that while the early anarchists were critical of what they regarded as the 'scientific elitism' of Marxian thought, they were not opposed to science per se, but simply to the idea of a 'government by scientists,' as Bakunin put it. Bakunin thus called for a revolt of life against science to keep science in its place, renouncing its political aspirations to rule over society.³⁷ Badiou's understanding of science as one of the four conditions for philosophy is at odds neither with anarchism/postanarchism, nor poststructuralism. The truth, for Badiou, is 'in-human,' insofar as 'a truth is not at all reducible to anything whatsoever which takes the form of a human capacity or property, in the sense of the human animal.' Badiou continues: 'To claim that it does is to remain within the legacy of Aristotelianism,

Kantianism and analytic philosophy....'[38] There is no hero of the event, since ontology demonstrates for Badiou that the event is not. Since the axiom of foundation in mathematics prohibits self-belonging as a contradiction of the Idea of the multiple, the event does not exist for ontology. But this does not mean, Badiou argues, that the event has not taken place—it just does not exist for ontology (or mathematics). Badiou evokes the axiom of *choice*, which as we will see in the next chapter forces ontology to think intervention in its being given the undecidability of the event.

So Badiou uses mathematics not because it enables us to impose an order on humans, nor because it enables humans to understand themselves completely. Mathematics is used by Badiou to demonstrate how there are events that do not conform to what might have been seen as a consistent system. Proving or disproving Badiou's theory on mathematical grounds will neither prove nor disprove his theory's applicability to human behaviour (unless someone can prove that mathematics and human behaviour are inexplicably linked), but Badiou's use of mathematics has enabled him to move away from the automatism he saw in the philosophy of language and the formalism of the 'linguistic turn.' Badiou acknowledges that when he wrote *The Concept of Model* he had a mechanical conception of a mathematics that could reveal the 'secrets of thought' because of its a-subjectivity, but he began to distance himself from this conception, instead seeing mathematics' ability to reveal the secrets of thought as being due to the type of thinking that it is.[39] In other words, Badiou is not applying mathematics because it is an a-subjective science capable of turning us into automatons under its guidance, but instead uses mathematics to think about events, contingency, multiplicity, universality, and so on as an autonomous field beyond the state.

Badiou should also not be seen as an adversary of poststructuralism and postanarchism simply because of a perceived modernism—and a proclaimed anti-postmodernism—in his works. As Newman notes, in any case, poststructuralism is not the same thing as postmodernism. Poststructuralism refers to a strategy and series of strategies that resist the totalities of modernity and its essentialist categories, as well as its absolute faith in rational truth; it does not transcend modernity as such, but rather operates within the discourse of modernity while exposing its limits.[40]

Badiou perhaps does the very thing that Newman finds objectionable, or maybe that is the impression one gets when reading Badiou's critiques of 'postmodern' and poststructuralist thinkers. In art, Badiou sees postmodernism as that which abolishes universalism and supports the 'total exhibition of particularisms.' The 'postmodern,' for Badiou, is that which 'bears witness to the unlimited and capricious influence of particularity.' The difficulties associated with particularism and identity politics are well known, and the two types of particularity that Badiou identifies in art should be familiar, with one being ethnic, linguistic or sexual (among other things) particularism, and the other being 'biographical particularity, the self as that which imagines that it can and must 'express itself.'[41] In other words, Badiou sees particularism as self-indulgent identity politics, at odds with his conception of politics as a collective act.

Peter Hallward sees Badiou's conception of art as broadly modernist, focusing not on an aesthetic process, but the consequences of artistic events and truths.[42] Badiou's philosophical and political course may also be understood as modernist, with universality a key component alongside singularity (the singular event is of universal relevance), which may well lead the casual reader to assume that Badiou's system is inimical to poststructuralism. Badiou has certainly been critical of the language games he sees in Ludwig Wittgenstein's work, and Lyotard's 'postmodern' philosophy is condemned for much the same reason, so focused as it is with philosophy as a discipline in search of its own rules, as Hallward notes.[43] Although Newman usually refers to the bulk of the works he draws on as poststructuralist (with Stirner an obvious exception), he does not flinch from using the term 'postmodern,' possibly because the unsettled nature of the term makes it ripe for developing a politics suitable for contemporary times. Newman maintains that universality is thinkable under the conditions of postmodernity, and that postmodernity can even renew radical politics. However, for this to happen, Newman insists that universality must be rethought, and like Badiou he views the singular event as being at the same time the event of universality.[44]

Universality, Badiou argues in his *Eight Theses on the Universal*, must have its grounds in the singular event, through the subtraction of particularities, but not as the supposition of existing particularities (or identitarian politics), even though identity will play its part. The singular event and its universal relevance, and the fact that there is a rupture in the whole, will be challenged with the universality of the state and the law that refuses to accept any lack in the whole—what Badiou calls 'evental revisionism.'[45] So while Badiou has been critical of thinkers who might be considered postmodern or poststructuralist, we can identify a number of similarities between Badiou's post-Althusserian thought and what we find in postanarchism.

2.5 Badiou's Journey Towards Post-Althusserianism

Hallward notes two important shifts in the young Badiou's thought during the 1960s. According to Hallward, Badiou went from being an admirer of Sartre's treatment of the relation between subject and structure in *Critique of Dialectical Reason* (which will be considered in the fourth chapter when Badiou's relation to Marxian thought is looked at) to being a confirmed follower of Althusser by the end of 1966, having taught what Hallward describes as a 'broadly Althusserian course' at the École Normale the previous year.[46] Zachary Luke Fraser has described how Badiou's works between 1966 and 1969 affirmed his fidelity to the Althusserian project at every opportunity. Fraser specifies four works in particular which mark Badiou's Althusserian period: 1966's *The (Re)commencement of Dialectical Materialism*, 1968's *The Infinitesimal Subversion*, 1969's *Mark and Lack*, and *The Concept of Model*. This last work was prepared and delivered as lectures shortly before and after the events of May 1968 in Paris, the first lecture being delivered on 28 April 1968, and the second lecture due to be given on 13 May, when the events of May 1968 were underway.[47] May 1968 marks, unsurprisingly, the second shift in Badiou's thought, Badiou's 'road to Damascus' that he recalls in *Theory of Contradiction*, and would come to be characterized, as Hallward notes, by the rejection of Althusser's relation of science and ideology, replacing the theory of ideology understood as an imaginary representation with a theory of ideology whereby ideology is exactly the way things look from the perspective of exploiters or the exploited.[48]

This view of ideology, set out in Badiou's 1976 essay *Of Ideology*, arguably appeals less to the Marxist notion of false consciousness than Althusser's notion of ideology does, although Badiou, quite rightly, does not see it this way. Badiou argues in *Of Ideology* that the philosophy of the exploiters masks the interests of the class it legitimizes behind a veil of the universal, although bourgeois ideology is usually transparent, especially in the way it defends property, free enterprise and parliamentarianism against 'totalitarian collectivism' and 'single party dictatorship.' Badiou extends this point to argue that the exploiting class also defends its class interests in philosophy.[49] Unlike with Althusser's understanding of ideology, then, Badiou does not see a process without a subject so much as a process that can be discerned, even if, later in

Badiou's works, challenging this ideology is tied to a theory of the subject that involves collective political action. Badiou recalls how Marx saw the reduction of ideology to the real kernel it expresses as insufficient. Ideology needs to be understood through the materialist and historical situation to which it relates. As Badiou says, 'to seize ideology as a process, and not as a closed, imaginary mechanism, that is Marx's scientific directive, whose direction Althusser reverses.'[50] So the events of May 1968 caused Badiou to shift away from Althusser, while Althusser himself was unable to see any significant truth in this event; thus, a clear line was drawn between them according to Bosteels.[51]

Althusser and Badiou clearly relate to Marx in different ways. What Badiou has retained from his Althusserian period is his dialectical materialism, albeit of a different kind. In *The (Re)commencement of Dialectical Materialism*, his 1966 review of Althusser's *For Marx*, the first thing Badiou states is that 'Althusser's work is attuned to our political conjuncture,' a clear signal of Badiou's commitment prior to May 1968.[52] Badiou here provides a neat summary of the role dialectical materialism has in Althusser's thought, and its relation to historical materialism. It is well known that Althusser turned his back on Hegel, famously noting the 'epistemological break' of 1845 where Marx turned away from Hegel and his works became ever more scientific.[53] We know that Marx developed a materialist conception of history, but did not explicitly refer to this as 'historical materialism,' nor as 'dialectical materialism.' His post-epistemological break works contain this dialectic, but there are only rare and brief hints at such terminology in his works, such as the notes on materialism and dialectics in *A Contribution to the Critique of Political Economy*.[54] Historical materialism would be the term later used and defended by Engels,[55] and Sartre and Lukács, among others, would later place an emphasis on historical materialism. Althusser was well aware that Marx never wrote a 'Dialectics,' despite talking about doing so, although we know, according to Althusser, where to find it—in Marx's theoretical works such as *Capital*. Dialectical materialism is, for Althusser, the Theory (or Marx's philosophy (*the* philosophy), or science) that unearths knowledge against ideology, as described in the previous chapter.[56]

Badiou elaborates on Althusser's dialectical materialism and its relation to historical materialism in his 1966 piece, identifying Adam Smith and David Ricardo as the ideological other of Marx, and not Hegel. Badiou is clarifying the fact that Marx was not in a strict sense Hegelian in most of his works before the epistemological break, drawing on and critiquing his works (*Critique of Hegel's Philosophy of Right* is referred to), while economists such as Smith and Ricardo get the same treatment in Marx's post-epistemological break work, *Capital (Critique of Political Economy)*. The difference between Hegel and Marx would then become the difference between the Marxist science of historical materialism and what Althusser called 'dialectical materialism,' following what Badiou calls a 'perhaps questionable tradition' in the use of this term. Dialectical materialism would be 'the discipline within which it is possible in principle to pronounce the scientificity of this science' (that is, historical materialism). The distinction between historical and dialectical materialism in Marx's post-epistemological break works then becomes a key part of Althusser's theoretical strategy.[57] So the science of history is key to Marx, provided it is approached scientifically. In other words, *history as an ideological construct* is to be discarded, but *history as the production of knowledge* revealed though the science of dialectical materialism is interior to the latter. There is almost an echo of this position in Badiou's post-Althusserian period, writing in *Theory of the Subject* that 'history does not exist,' but only historicizations.[58] Badiou is distancing himself here from any Hegelian sense that history is teleological or comes to an end with an absolute ideal being realized; he would later affirm this stance against the 'vulgar Marxist' view of history.[59]

Yet this is perhaps just an echo of Althusser's approach towards history, given Badiou's later understanding of ideology. The process through which historicizations appear involves the subject far more in Badiou's theory than it does in Althusser's, and the logic of how things appear is something Badiou covers later in *Logics of Worlds*. Furthermore, Badiou's later works draw partially on Hegel, as we shall see. To the Althusserian Badiou of 1966, ideology is not the real relationship of humans to their conditions, but just the way in which they live these conditions. Science produces knowledge and transformation, while ideology is a system of representation that produces an effect of 'recognition' and a process of 'repetition,' creating an illusory feeling of the theoretical.[60] This concern with representation would retain a prominent position in Badiou's later work, concerned as it is with how events present themselves and appear in a world, and postanarchists, in their own way, will come to focus on the problem of representation over presentation. We have seen how in *Theory of Contradiction* and *Of Ideology* Badiou came to see ideology as the way things actually appear, or the almost transparent appearance of bourgeois philosophy over the exploited.

Two articles that Badiou published in the *Cahiers pour l'Analyse*,

'Infinitesimal Subversion' (summer 1968) and 'Mark and Lack' (winter 1969), appear after the events of May '68, but do hint towards a change in direction. Hallward remarks how Badiou was drawn to the formal rigour of mathematics and logic with the *Cahiers pour l'Analyse* and the fact that despite this, the category of subject was still present, albeit not within the structure of a state or discourse.[61] The focus on structure may here be associated with Althusser, but there is a hint of the subjectivity to come in Badiou's work that is beyond this structure. In 'Infinitesimal Subversion,' Badiou argues that Lacan's 'real' for a domain of fixed proofs is defined by the impossibility of any constant occupying constructible places.[62]

Badiou is borrowing from the field of mathematics when he refers to constructible places, but he could just as well have said that the symbolic and imaginary in Lacan's system cannot be occupied by any constant, as the real would reveal this to be impossible. The impossible would appear to be a place that cannot be occupied by a constant, or set in stone with the expectation that no real will interrupt it. A variable, therefore, may come to occupy the place of the impossible so that it can designate its impossibility, and what Badiou calls the 'infinity-point' will thereby inscribe itself as a constant. Badiou defines the infinity-point as that which, in a domain of mathematical objects, is a supplementary mark that both occupies an unoccupiable place, but is governed by all the initial procedures found in a domain of mathematical objects that are defined by various axioms. So 'the infinite is the designation of a beyond proper to the algorithm of the domain: the marking of a point that is inaccessible according to the algorithms themselves, but which supports their reiteration.'[63] The infinity-point is, however, excluded from the domain, insofar as the marking of the infinity-point is 'the becoming-constant of a variable in the impossible place whose impossibility it indexes,' which also marks the infinity-point's exclusion. The mark that the infinity-point's variable makes, Badiou argues, is what Lacan would have called the 'hallucinatory position' of the infinity-point, hiding what is really an exclusion.[64]

We will see how exclusion is an important category in Badiou's later theory of the subject, and the infinity-point precedes the more developed void of *Being and Event*, as well as the undecidability of the event. In light of Badiou's continual use of mathematics and his critique of Hegel, it is interesting to note here Badiou's objection to Hegel's 'poisoned chalice of "qualitative" relation,' and his debasement of multiplicity and an enslavement to speculation. Speculation, Badiou argues, requires the supremacy of quality, and the 'relative discrediting of algorithmic or inscribed thinking: i.e. of structural thinking.' Quality, continuity, temporality and negation are seen by Badiou as the 'oppressive categories of ideological objectives,' while 'number, discreteness, space and affirmation: or, better, Mark, Punctuation, Blank Space and Cause: the categories of scientific processes.'[65] In Badiou's post-Althusserian period, we see the now more familiar lexicon emerge that includes terms such as 'undecidable' and 'void,' but the possibility of the impossible remains, and interesting parallels with Marx's political work and its relation to Badiou's communism can be developed further, especially given how Marx saw the Paris Commune as an example of 'impossible communism,' but one that must remain possible nevertheless.[66]

Hallward sees in Badiou's 1969 article for the *Cahiers pour l'Analyse*, 'Mark and Lack' (again, written before the events of May 1968) a pivotal moment in French structuralism. Here, Badiou reaffirms his commitment to the separation of ideology and science by way of mathematical marks that are self-identical, but with the caveat that this rule applies only to mathematical marks rather than the objects to which they refer. Philosophy (that is, ideology in the Althusserian sense, rather than the philosophy of Marx) tries to intervene in science so that its marks apply to the subject, where the subject is actually lacking in science. Philosophy has a radical lack of any lack, and as an ideological practice it tries to locate a subject in science, a stance that Badiou rejects. For Hallward, it is 'hard to imagine a more emphatic assertion of the inviolable autonomy of science as a weapon against ideology and its subject'; but the events of May 1968 interrupted the author to the extent that 'Badiou's subsequent reorientation from scientific closure to a philosophy of perseverance... involve[d] an affirmation of the subject in precisely the place where science had excluded it.'[67]

So the subject remains outside of the structure for Badiou at this point, with science autonomous from ideology. Indeed, in 'Mark and Lack' Badiou's affiliation with Althusser is evident enough, defining 'philosophy' (that is, non-Marxian philosophy) as the 'ideological region specializing in science' by giving science a signifier. For Badiou, there is no signifying order capable of enveloping the discourse of science, and yet this is what philosophy seeks to do, as much as 'historical materialism' claims to explain on its own the hold ideology has over the subject. Ideology operates within philosophy understood in this way, and insists on marking its lack. In other words, as Badiou explains, philosophy is 'compelled to mark, within its own order, the scientific signifier as a total space.' Science cannot receive this mark, however, and what philosophy claims to be science is actually the lack of science. Science is 'pure space [l'espace pure], without inverse or mark or place of that which it excludes.' In science, lack is not lacking, but philosophy tries to show us the opposite by marking the lack, the 'figure of Being gnawing at itself, haunted by the mark of non-being,' and thereby 'philosophy exhausts itself trying to keep alive its supreme and specific product: God or Man, depending on the case.' Science does not lack anything that is not already signifying, with marks substituted for one another indefinitely, instead of attempting to mark a lack permanently in the way that philosophy does. Science is 'the movement where we never risk encountering this detestable figure of Man: the sign of nothing.'[68]

So Badiou came to turn against Althusser and saw ideology as laying bare the role of the bourgeoisie, and while Badiou in his Althusserian years saw the subject as coming from outside of the structure, in his post-Althusserian years he sees the subject as something that the structure includes, but which at the same time does not belong to the structure—the subject is not counted by the state. Any state is a temporary One. As Bosteels has written, Badiou weaves a line in his Maoist years between an excessively structuralist or 'right-wing' approach, and an excessively 'left-wing' or 'anarchist' approach. The latter includes Deleuze and his students, who Badiou sees as the flip side of conservative structuralism, 'anarcho-desirers' who end up opposing dialectical materialism with structuralism (unintentionally, of course) and ideologies of desire.[69] This charge of unintentional structuralism is an early indication of Badiou's later critique of Deleuze, which I will come to.

We can see how the language used in 'Mark and Lack' develops during Badiou's post-Althusserian years, with phrases such as 'pure space' preceding the more systematic use of particular terms in Badiou's later works. For example, the notion of 'pure space' may be a precursor to that of 'space' and 'space of placement' in *Theory of the Subject*, while the later uses of 'inconsistent multiplicity' and the 'void' more systematically demonstrate the lack which Badiou had been describing in his Althusserian years. The relation between ideology and science in Badiou's work will be considered further in chapter 5.

2.6 The Early Development of Badiou's Dialectic— Hegel Beyond Hegel

For all Badiou's (sometimes critical) references to Hegel, he reinterprets Hegel to complement his theory in a way that is not at odds with an anarchist ontology (including a notion of the partial fixity of truths), while also eschewing any theory of consciousness or a Hegelianized Marx, such as that found in Sartre. For example, we can draw comparisons here with Sartre's event and its collapse back into seriality; but Badiou more systematically explains how such an event leaves its mark in the symbolic order through the continued actions of subjects to the event. Indeed, as I discuss in the final chapter, Badiou is well aware that aspects of his thought may be described as metaphysical, while stepping beyond metaphysics—a 'metaphysics without metaphysics' as he calls it in *Metaphysics and the Critique of Metaphysics*.[70] For now, I will look briefly at how Badiou draws on Hegel in the early part of his post-Althusserian period, before setting out his theory of the subject in more detail.

The *Rational Kernel of the Hegelian Dialectic*, published in 1978 (which, as Tzuchien Tho explains in his introduction, is within the 'red years' of 1968 to 1979,[71] when Badiou turned more towards political thought compared to his earlier formal and mathematical work) gives an insight into the different ways in which Badiou and Sartre draw on Hegel. While the relevance of Sartre's thought for Badiou's is dealt with in the fourth chapter, the relation of Badiou's thought to Hegel's is important in distinguishing his thought from Althusser's (seen as anti-Hegelian), and for making a case that even the most dialectical materialist aspects of Badiou's work are not incompatible with postanarchist thought.

Despite the hidden Kantianism that Žižek sees in Badiou's thought,[72] Badiou draws far more on Hegel, although an argument might be made that his metaphysics without a metaphysics in some respects provides an antidote to the antagonism between Kant and Hegel's thought. Kant and Hegel are well known as adversaries (to Hegel's mind at least), with Kant famously maintaining that the 'thing-in-itself' cannot be understood exactly for what it is, but exists objectively only insofar as it exists in the world of ideas (for us humans) through a transcendental understanding built on a priori knowledge (a knowledge of things as they appear for us, not as they really are).[73] The basis of Hegel's critique of Kant was that the thing-in-itself, which Kant argued cannot be known from experience, is posited by 'spirit,' by the subject, which means that the thing-in-itself cannot be out of bounds for the subject. Spirit is embodied, as the thread flowing through all subjectivity, and is not something separate from the world (or *Geist*, or God). The subject encounters others in its thought, and is in that respect finite; but as a self-positing spirit it is not separate from *Geist*—it is part of the absolute Idea. Where Spinoza spoke of substance, Hegel spoke of spirit, the 'actual,' the essence that has being in itself, which 'wins its truth only when, in utter dismemberment, it finds itself...Spirit is this power only by looking the negative in the face, and tarrying with it.'[74] Badiou, however, turns towards inconsistent multiplicity and mathematics, and against Hegel, who saw mathematics as a subordinate science.[75]

The *Rational Kernel of the Hegelian Dialectic* is a critique of Zhang Shiying's thoughts on the rational element of Hegel's philosophy, written with two of Badiou's contemporaries, Joël Bellassen and Louis Mossot. It is a reading of Hegel that impressed the then Maoist Badiou, who had turned against Sartre's placing of the affective subject at the centre of the experience of the world.[76] Sartre's view of being not being its own foundation was a departure from Descartes, who deals with this sense of doubt by positing an idea of perfection, a proof of the existence of God that serves to occupy the cleavage between the being that his cogito can conceive and the being that he is.[77] This stems from Descartes' well known dualism, his '*I think, therefore I am*,' and his view that he was a substance whose essence consisted of thinking, and depended on no material thing, so that his 'I' was distinct from his body. The fact that he had doubts upon reflection led him to believe that there must be something of greater perfection, of certainty, which could not emerge from nothing, so it must emerge from God.[78]

Descartes' famous methodical doubt was seen by Sartre as an action, a 'transcendent object of reflective consciousness,' opposed to Sartre's view that beginning with a reflective and transcendental *I* is the death of consciousness.[79] Sartre's pre-reflective cogito is the condition upon which consciousness reflects upon itself, becoming conscious of itself through consciousness of a transcendent object, not by being the transcendental itself. But this is the starting point for consciousness, and does not imply a subject for Sartre, which comes later. There is a lack of certainty here for Sartre's consciousness, without a completeness and self-sufficiency that would lead to closure from the possible: 'My I, indeed, *is no more certain for consciousness than the I of other men*,' where the *I* 'is no longer in any way a *subject*, nor is it a collection of representations; it is quite simply a precondition and an absolute source of existence' [italics in original]. He considered this work sufficient 'to enable us to establish philosophically an absolutely positive ethics and politics.'[80]

What such a politics might look like is given shape in the *Critique of Dialectical Reason*. For Sartre, 'Marxism is History itself becoming conscious of itself,' and he sets out to critique dialectical reason '*through ourselves*,' not as empiricists would, but in terms of the dialectic as lived experience, as situated experience—'no one can *discover* the dialectic while keeping the point of view of analytical Reason ... while remaining *external* to the object under consideration' [italics in original].[81] Badiou was disappointed that Hegel in France (in the 1970s) had become 'a tragic idealism against a scientific idealism.' A Hegelianized Marx had become, in the works of Sartre, aligned with the latter's notion of the transparent *cogito*, which for Badiou meant that Marx had become reduced to the idealist aspects of Hegel, while Hegel has ceased to be that Hegel which was influential to Marx, the Hegel of *The Science of Logic*. We have already seen how Badiou had by this point moved beyond both Sartre, and then Althusser, as early influences, and this movement is neatly encapsulated in *The Rational Kernel of the Hegelian Dialectic*. As Badiou notes, the anti-Hegelian Althusser failed to include within his theory those aspects of Hegel's thought that are valuable to Marxian thought, while Sartre drew on Hegel the idealist rather than the rational kernel of his thought. In other words, *The Science of Logic* was absent in both Sartre (who Badiou called 'the Descartes of the *cogito*') and Althusser ('the Descartes of the machine'), the latter seen as the more 'menacing' by Badiou for mingling with the scientific and technological 'revolution' of the French Communist Party, while the former was more aligned with the Maoists whom Badiou favoured.[82]

What Zhang Shiying is keen to draw from Hegel is the difference between the idealist aspects of his dialectic and the rational kernel. He outlines two fundamental characteristics in Hegel's philosophy. One is the 'concrete' within Hegel's philosophy, which is the internal unity between qualities. Hegel referred to a bouquet of flowers to illustrate his point. Were a quality such as 'colour' to be abstracted from the bouquet, colour would become abstract, but things in the world are concrete unities of different qualities, there being nothing abstract in the world (that is, no quality without relation to other qualities), and such an abstraction would lack sense. Hegel argued that this is why truth is concrete—it does not exist in isolation. The term 'concrete' should not, however, be enough to perturb poststructuralists on its own, for the second fundamental characteristic that Shiying outlines is that of truth always in development, with truth containing contradictory elements. Reality is not fixed, and truth is a movement and a process.[83] In other words (which remind us of Laclau's influence on postanarchism), reality and truth consists of a partial fixity of qualities and their relation to each other, which is liable to change.

Shiying continues, explaining how, despite Hegel holding thought as primary and being as secondary in his idealist system, the rational kernel exists as the interior to this idealist philosophy. For all the idealism in Hegel's philosophy, there also exists the unity of the laws of thought and laws of objectivity.[84] This is discernible in the four types of judgement in the three major parts of *The Science of Logic*: 'essential judgement' in the Being stage; 'reflective judgement' and 'necessary judgement' in the Essence stage; and 'conceptual judgement' in the Concept stage. The last, especially, illustrates the rational kernel of Hegel's system. Essential judgement enables us to see if a rose is red just by using sight, without any knowledge of the essence of the rose, so this is a stage of Being and rather straightforward. 'Reflective judgement' would involve stating that the roses are useful, for example, which relies on an understanding of the roses' relation to other qualities, and knowledge of the particularities of the rose. 'Necessary judgement' would then state that roses are plants, for example, and considers more closely the particularities of the roses, beyond what might be called value judgements. These two types of judgements (reflective and necessary) relate to the Essence stage. Finally, there is the 'conceptual judgement' in the Concept stage, which considers whether a concrete thing corresponds with its concept, and to what degree (for example, whether a bouquet of roses really matches the concept of the rose, and if they are beautiful, whether they really match the concept of beautiful).

More than just considering whether a statement matches an idea, Hegel is considering the concept of the object, and had 'unconsciously reflected the dialectic of objective things themselves; therein resides the 'rational kernel' of Hegel's dialectic and it[s] great historical merit.' As Shiying sums up, Hegel's dialectics were unusable in their existing form, which is why it was so important that Marx and Engels's rejection of Hegel's idealism revealed the dialectic beneath—albeit a dialectic of objective things that Hegel had only guessed at.[85]

This might seem academic, but Badiou's interest in Zhang Shiying's work (early in his career) stemmed from the consideration of the relation between Marxism and Hegel that was taking place outside of academia. Such consideration was tied to the struggles of the Cultural Revolution, as well as Badiou's own 'militant philosophical preoccupations.'[86] Badiou also sets himself apart from both Sartre and Althusser (as well as Deleuze) in revisiting the Hegel of *The Science of Logic*, and thereby introduces us to some of the ideas that will underpin his theory of the subject. The aim of Badiou, Bellassen and Mossot (an early student of Badiou's) was to demonstrate that the principle that the 'one divides into two' is a subtle and new interpretation of the dialectic that overcomes the 'vulgar Stalinist interpretation.'[87] Drawing on contemporary interpretations of Hegel's dialectic and its relevance to dialectical materialism, Badiou is able to root his interpretation in contemporary Marxian debate without discarding Hegel (as Althusser claimed to do), or giving us a more idealistic Hegel (as Sartre did), or drawing on Hegel in such a way that it leads many to think he has been discarded (as happened with Deleuze).

The well known objection Hegel had against Kant is reiterated by Badiou. That is, Hegel rejects the founding of thought on the idea of an inside and an outside. The exterior and interior are the same for Hegel, but for Badiou they are only indiscernible in the all, or whole, in Hegel's system. What actually happens is that the one is partitioned and becomes two, even if Hegel prefers to focus on this two becoming one again as the contradiction is resolved. Following Lacan's example of the Möbius strip, the interior and exterior is discernible at a particular point in the band, but not globally as the band twists itself in full circle so that an object on the interior of the band at a particular point will eventually find itself on the exterior after one lap. So globally there would appear to be no exterior and interior. The band needs to be cut to release its torsion and reveal the distinction between the inside and the outside that is locally hidden.

2.7 The Subject and the State in Badiou's Early Dialectic

Badiou explains his use of the Möbius strip more clearly by referring to the proletariat, which is an internal part of capitalist society exploited for its labour, as well as a force for the destruction of capitalist social relations as the revolutionary class. Strict inclusion or exclusion of the proletariat is not possible within capitalist society, so the real of this divide between the proletariat and bourgeoisie is hidden in the whole of the Möbius strip.[88] The same example is given in *Theory of the Subject*, in a lecture delivered in 1975 (the book was published in France in 1982). In language almost familiar from his *Cahiers pour l'Analyse* days, Badiou tells us that for 'the materialist dialectic ... there where space provides for neither place nor lack of place, it is the Subject ... that one comes across .... It is then that every subject surpasses its place by force, inasmuch as its essential virtue lies in being disoriented.' It is the Möbius strip that for Badiou illustrates so well the fact that *splace* and *outplace* are parts of the same band, with the outplace included in the splace, much as the proletariat is included in the capitalist system.[89]

In explaining these terms, we see how Badiou shares something with poststructuralists without being one, and with postanarchists while virtually refusing to acknowledge any similarities with their thought. The notions of 'splace' and 'outplace' that Badiou introduces in his theory of the two eschew all essentialism in not privileging any one thing, and in simply observing how relations operate. Splace and outplace are translated by Bosteels from the French 'esplace' and 'horlieu.' Splace is used to denote the 'space of placement' of a thing, the structure similar to 'state' (of a situation) in *Being and Event*, and outplace is used to denote the a-structural force from outside of that which is placed. Bosteels arrives at 'outplace,' as in 'out of place' or 'out of site,' to distinguish the term from the eventual site in *Being and Event* which he feels Oliver Feltham's use of 'offsite' fails to do; and outplace better captures the sense of something that is outside what is there, with hints of a 'nonplace.'[90] These terms, splace and outplace, operate as dialectical opposites (the outplace against the splace is the dialectic), as do the terms place and 'force.' Force is much like the event we see later in Badiou's works, and is here 'what overdetermines the exclusion from any place in which the outplace lies revealed.' Like the event, force is universal, acting as the 'non-numerical quality of the whole,' and yet does not function according to the regime of the splace.[91] Force is not counted in the splace, just as a group may not be counted by a regime, but may reveal itself as part of the whole that is governed by a regime, yet not according to the regime's rule (so not, for example, by the ballot box, which would not be an option for force).

So to return to Badiou's non-essentialist treatment of space, the contrary of something is not to be understood merely as something else, but the space of its placement. In other words, as Badiou explains, something, A, is placed as a pure being, and its being-placed denoted as A_p. It is the space of this placement, that which designates the index, that makes possible a contradiction in the 'space of placement,' rather than A_p simply contradicting another A_p.[92] So, rather than assuming a Spinozan substance, or an essentialism whereby some things are assumed to be more important than others, things exist in relation to other things; this 'something' (A) not existing in relation to an absolute One, but in relation to other things and a 'space' that is at that moment the temporary operation of a One. While something may be placed as pure being, it is where it is placed (the space of placement, or 'splace') that really matters. The space of placement is not an essentialist One, a permanent structure (of society) that cannot be changed, and nor is that which is placed in this space—these relations are procedural rather than permanent. A contradiction does not lead to a synthesis creating a One, but a One, as part of a process of subtraction, divides into two.

Badiou illustrates the dialectic throughout *Theory of the Subject* with reference to the bourgeoisie/proletariat pair. The dialectic is described as 'the outplace against the splace' in the 'sawdust-filled arena of the categorical combat,' the a-structural force from outside against the space of placement (splace). By way of demonstration against what might be called structuralism, Badiou argues that the determination of the determination is necessary if what is new in the dialectic is not to be annulled by relapsing into the splace. By this (and using the Cultural Revolution by way of illustration), he means the positive newness of the proletariat, a force or event from the outplace, determines the determination that is the splace, or in this instance the bourgeoisie (although here, with a Maoist hat on, it is the people who revolt to designate the new bureaucratic bourgeoisie—of the Cultural Revolution—as the 'global determination of the revolutionary antagonism itself'). This determination of the determination is what Badiou calls torsion, a process whereby 'force reapplies itself to that from which it conflictually emerges,' rather than the new simply relapsing into the place (splace), which Badiou argues is the principle of structuralism wherever it appears.[93]

For all Badiou's references to the proletariat, Marx, and Maoism throughout his works, he observes operations in what could just as well be an a-political manner (just as, dare we say, the social scientist would). Badiou clearly finds Maoism to be more fertile ground for political theory than anarchism. In *The Century*, Badiou writes that the Maoist approach in 1966 and 1967 in particular was one supported by a minority of the party leadership, and more closely aligned with the leftist approach. The Maoist approach is interpreted by Badiou as one in which the state 'must not be the policed and police-like end of mass politics, but, on the contrary, that it must act as a stimulus for the unleashing of politics, under the banner of the march towards real communism.'[94]

Whatever one makes of Badiou's interest in Maoism during his red years and beyond, we can see in *The Century* some common ground with postanarchists in his desire to extract the real from the reality that surrounds it. Indeed, Newman sees in Lacan's discussion of the lack/the limits of representation and the real not just repressive social structures, but the fact that individuals are only partially constituted through such structures; Lacan's notion of the real shows us a way out of absolute subjection given there is always a lack in the symbolic order.[95] This lack is what Badiou calls the subtractive path, with a passion for the real that avoids the slide into terror, the aim being to subtract reality from its unity 'to detect within it the minuscule difference, the vanishing term that constitutes it.' Badiou continues, 'What takes place *barely* differs from the place where it takes place. It is in this 'barely,' in this immanent exception, that all the affect lies.' This subtractive politics, Badiou notes, is an approach evident in Marx and Engels, who reject the reality of the family and nation-state that surrounds us in favour of the real of a proletariat that would be negative, not predicated on anything, and therefore a universal conception.[96]

We can start to see how Badiou frames dialectical materialism, as he sees it, in a way that should not only be palatable for postanarchists, but also provides a bridge between a certain dialectical materialism and Marxism. I have already mentioned the longstanding conflict between Marxists and anarchists, one that seems, at least on the surface, to continue with Badiou. Postanarchist theorists have engaged with Badiou's ideas, but in Lacan they find a common influence. To take one of the less obvious examples in Badiou's works, the concept of the real echoes Badiou's stance to a degree in *Mark and Lack*, insofar as philosophy attempts to mark this lack with a concept of man, God, and so on, but science refuses this mark of the lack. There is such a thing as lack in science, but it cannot be marked in the way philosophy has often attempted—science is not lacking signifying marks, but these marks are substituted for one another indefinitely, as we have seen above. Similarly, we have seen how, for postanarchism, the real as that which is lacking is only lacking in the symbolic order, following Lacan. The real itself is not lacking, but just not present in the symbolic order. It is not for philosophy to mark this lack of a lack, and in this way both Badiou and Newman avoid an essentialist core to their works. For Newman, political and social identity should be built around its own impossibility and emptiness, with a notion of the outside that does not become a place.[97]

Of Badiou's three major works, *Being and Event* is arguably the best known, and the most systematic illustration of his theory of the subject. Having looked at Badiou's development into a post-Althusserian thinker in the earlier stages of his career and the relevance of his dialectic to postanarchism, we are now in a position to take this further and consider the relevance of this work to postanarchism.

3

Being and Event and Postanarchist Ontology: Inevitable Intervention Against Inevitable States

The previous chapter introduced Badiou's early materialist dialectic, as well as charting the development of his thinking from Sartrean, to Althusserian, to post-Althusserian positions. We saw that while Badiou has been dismissive of poststructuralism and anarchism, there are a number of traits he shares with postanarchism. These include a non-essentialist understanding of place and the way in which individuals relate to each other in an ontological rather than phenomenological sense—an example from *Theory of the Subject* was discussed towards the end of the previous chapter,[1] while Newman retains the concept of subject but sees it as 'empty,' with no essentialist baggage but considered in the context of its relation to a structure(s).[2] In addition, both have a shared interest in reviving the notions of singularity alongside universality. For Newman, the relevance of universality is an important question after the advent of postmodernism,[3] while Badiou's concern is with how universality and communism can retain their relevance after state communism's collapse and its continuing association with the state or 'criminal enterprises.'[4]

Given the pivotal position that *Being and Event* occupies in the works of Badiou, and having considered Badiou's earlier works in the previous chapter, this chapter aims to give a concise description of its key terms and relevance for postanarchism. In addition to this, the dialectic we see in Badiou's works will be seen to be an affirmative one, despite Badiou's focus on it being a subtractive dialectic. Although Badiou has described his work as a confrontation with the dialectic,[5] he continues to describe his work as a materialist dialectic, and even an affirmative dialectic in which the generic (or truth) really concerns a positive complexity of differences.[6] Understanding the key terms of *Being and Event*, and Badiou's more developed dialectic, is key to understanding his relation to postanarchism, as well as to Marxian theory, which will be considered in the next chapter. As I will emphasize, an ontological approach is important, from the point of view of both Badiou and postanarchism, for understanding the subject's place in society and his or her role in politics. It is for the subject to make a decision in relation to an approximate truth as to how to challenge, and even attempt to fill, the place of power, even if this can only ever be temporary.

3.1   *Being and Event* and Badiou's Dialectic

We saw in the previous chapter that in *Theory of the Subject* there is no Spinozan substance, no absolute One, under which everything exists. There is placement under a One, but this is a procedural rather than permanent One, much like any arrangements put in place by humans, including states, are ultimately temporary. There is no Hegelian finitude in Badiou's dialectic, so multiplicity is the default, but a (finite) One is possible nonetheless. For Hegel, spirit is finite and finds its truth within the infinite, albeit a limited infinity. With the negation of the finite in the process of becoming under the infinite absolute, Hegel is actually speaking of a *finitized* infinite that ends in synthesis.[7] As we have seen, there is no absolute or end-point to history for Badiou. For Badiou, if 'Hegel makes a circle, it is because he always seeks a single time'[8] under an absolute One. The dialectical method at work in *Theory of the Subject* is evident right up to the more recent *Logics of Worlds*, which rejects any notion that the world is the totality of existence in and for itself, or that there is such a thing as a single world. Instead, 'it is of the essence of the world not to be the totality of existence, and to endure the existence of an infinity of other worlds outside of itself.'[9] There are, in other words, many worlds, a theory of multiplicity rather than an absolute One, which is always an operation rather than a totality with no beyond.

Being and Event, published in 1988, is, I would argue, the best exposition of Badiou's system. Sandwiched between the two more obviously dialectical of Badiou's three major works, the materialist dialectic is still discernible throughout. Bosteels has identified a knowledge/truth dialectic in Badiou. While Bosteels sees in *Theory of the Subject* and *Logics of Worlds* a richer exposition of the dialectic of the subject, he notes what he calls a 'post-Maoism' throughout his work—not simply that which comes after Mao Zedong, but a return of thought to the lessons of Maoism.[10] Bosteels argues that the 'dialectical rapport' between truth and knowledge is where Badiou's debts to Maoism are really to be found, especially in *Being and Event*. Furthermore, Bosteels notes that after Badiou abandons the Maoist vocabulary, learning from truths (in art, science, love and politics) outside of philosophy becomes Badiou's aim, just as learning from the masses was Mao's aim. Instead of serving the people, as Mao would have it, Badiou is 'serving the truths.'[11]

3.2 The Regime of Presentation

It is in *Being and Event* that I maintain we see the common ground with postanarchism set out most rigorously, with notions of multiplicity, presentation/representation and inclusion/belonging. There have been attempts within the more ontological anarchist approaches to theorize something along the lines of Badiou's theory of the event—perhaps most famously with the post-anarchy of Hakim Bey and his theory of the Temporary Autonomous Zone (TAZ) developed in the 1980s. This approach does share something with Badiou's approach, with its frustration that revolutions are usually seen as failed revolutions unless they impose the same or even a more oppressive state upon their people than existed before. The TAZ, on the other hand, is not an end in itself, and does not engage directly with the state, preferring instead to undertake guerrilla operations before the state can crush it, and before it can relocate elsewhere. Bey's style of writing, however, certainly cannot be described as rigorous, and he describes the TAZ as 'almost a poetic fancy.'[12] It does seem to me, however, that Badiou has also been grappling with a poetic fancy, with notions such as undecidability, which is key to his work, as well as the broader applications of his theory (to love and art, and not just to science and politics) and the lessons he draws from Stéphane Mallarmé. It is the way in which Badiou makes the theory of the subject a rigorous one that makes him interesting, while also maybe explaining why he loses those with whom he might share common ground.

Badiou illustrates much of his theory with set theory, with mathematics presenting nothing but presentation itself (the multiple, which is prior to the One). Truth is linked to the four generic procedures already mentioned—love, art, science and politics. Politics, the generic procedure of most interest to us here, is a collective act. The being of truth is a generic multiple (it is universal), and truth is a subtraction from knowledge, and in this sense indiscernible, unnameable, and unpresentable. Despite truth being indiscernible to knowledge, Badiou contends that it can be demonstrated that truth can be thought. Instead of referring the four generic procedures to representable conditions, utilising the tools that knowledge already provides us with, Badiou proposes, with the category of the generic, 'a contemporary thinking of these procedures which shows that they are simultaneously indeterminate and complete; because, in occupying the gaps of available encyclopaedias, they manifest the common-being, the multiple-essence, of the place in which they proceed.' A subject is manifested locally, supported solely by the generic procedure, and is a finite moment of this manifestation.[13] In other words, a singular and universal event brings to the fore the incomplete nature of knowledge, ideology or the symbolic order, and it is for the subject to take a gamble or wager over what to fill this gap with, as we will see. While this generic procedure might be temporary, it is down to the subject to defend the consequences of an event, whatever they turn out to be.

Against the primacy of the One, Badiou defines the multiple as the regime of presentation, and the One, in respect of presentation, an operational (and temporary) result. Presentation itself is of direct relevance to the operation that is the count-as-one, and the multiple is the regime of this presentation. 'Being' presents itself, rather than being presentation itself, so being is neither multiple (the regime of presentation) nor One (an operational result of presentation).

In a development from his earlier term *splace* (the space of placement), Badiou's more formalized mathematical approach uses the term 'situation' for any presented multiplicity, the place of taking-place. Every situation has its own operator of the count-as-one, what Badiou terms 'structure,' which prescribes the regime of the count-as-one for a presented multiple. Something belongs to a situation when it is counted as one in a situation. This is, however, an effect—the One is not, and cannot present itself (unlike being), since it is only an operation. The situation, or the structured presentation, has a duality of multiplicities that is established in the count-as-one, with inconsistent multiplicity before the count-as-one, and consistent multiplicity after. Inconsistent multiplicity draws our attention towards presentation as a multiple once we see that a being-one emerges as a result, an operation, while consistent multiplicity consists of several units of multiples, 'several-ones' (which could be social movements, religious and cultural groups, and so on). Inconsistent multiplicity is therefore a key term in *Being and Event*—it is pure presentation understood retrospectively, once we are aware of it, as the non-one. We should also note the term 'state of the situation,' whereby the count-as-one structuring a situation is in turn counted-as-one, a one of the one-effect.[14]

In the politics of the state, we can see how there are numerous count-as-ones in society, that are again counted-as-one by the state and thereby included, for example, in the count-as-one that is the United Kingdom—a finite One, like any state, that will one day cease to exist. As with anarchist theory, there is no primacy of the state. The state is the exception. As with postanarchist theory, however, there is no natural law against the state, nor for it. States come and go as operations, and this much can be witnessed throughout history without the aid of philosophy, I would argue.

Nothing is presented in the situation that is not counted, which is why inconsistency is not presented. Inconsistency is not under the law of the count, and its presupposition, as pure multiple, is that the One is not, prior to the count. That which is presented must be under the effect of the structure. In the parlance of *Being and Event*, Badiou needs a new term to account for what is not presented. The term 'nothing' is considered, to name the immediately unperceivable gap between consistency and inconsistency. Nothing, taken by itself, is for Badiou 'the name of unpresentation in presentation.' Given that 'something' (which is not an 'in-situation-term') has not been counted when the One results, this being necessary for the operation to count-as-one, the nothing is really the operation of the count but, as source of the One, is not counted itself—it does not belong to this operation, but this exclusion is vital for the One. (This reminds us of how the empty place of power has a pivotal role in the postanarchist understanding of power—those in power may wish it was not there, but all power depends on being able to find, and fill, this place at the base of systems of power.)

The nothing is as much structure and consistency as pure multiple and inconsistency, naming the undecidable of presentation that is unpresentable, or that is subtracted from presentation. This suture to the being of the situation is then termed the 'void' by Badiou, rather than nothing. For Badiou, 'every structured presentation unpresents 'its' void, in the mode of this non-one which is merely the subtractive face of the count.' Void is the term used because the nothing corresponds to the global effect of structure where everything is counted, while not being counted (as one) is also local in its occurrence. Void, as the name of being/inconsistency according to a situation, indicates that no term is presented, and the nothing is not located structurally. For ontology, then, a situation must present everything that falls under its law, the multiple-without-one.[15]

'Belonging' and 'inclusion' are deployed by Badiou as two possible relations between multiples in set theory, where belonging is the counting of a multiple as an element in the presentation of another multiple (a social group, for example, that is counted and clearly exists for the state), and inclusion is where a multiple is a sub-multiple of another multiple (or a social group that is included in the state as a collection of individuals that go almost unnoticed in the presentation that is the state). Badiou's elaboration on this point arrives at the excess of inclusion over belonging, where in set theory *'no multiple is capable of forming-a-one out of everything it includes'* [italics in original]. There will always be some element that is included but does not belong in the One. The void, too, is included in everything, but nothing, including the void itself, belongs to the void.[16]

In a practical sense, as far as inclusion and belonging are concerned, the state (a One), for Badiou, is concerned with inclusion, but is indifferent to belonging: 'Any consistent subset is immediately counted and considered by the State, for better or worse, because it is matter for representation.'[17] A social group may belong, but the state is not concerned to make this so. If it is not presented, it is simply represented. In Badiou's parlance, 'singularity' is a term which is presented, having a presence and demanding attention, but not represented, which takes us beyond the state being blithely indifferent to a group, towards a political collective that emerges from an event, and in its newness is not represented (it presents itself despite not having representation—'normal' is a term which is both presented and represented, and 'excrescence' is a term which is represented but not presented).[18] Badiou will later describe, in his logic (of appearance), how the proletariat is subtracted from the sphere of political existence. The multiplicity of the proletariat can be analysed, but the rules of the political world that govern appearance means that it does not appear in this world.[19]

One important historical example of this relation of inclusion but not belonging was the plight of subject populations living under colonial domination. During the Great Famine in India of 1876–78, in which around 5 million starved to death,[20] the viceroy, Lord Lytton, arranged a huge banquet to welcome Queen Victoria as Empress of India. Natives were dying due to Lytton's insistence that the free market should not be interfered with, giving clear orders that the price of food should not be reduced to ease the famine. Lytton was following Adam Smith here, and the logic (and ideology) of the free markets. The native population was clearly counted and included under the regime, but evidently did not belong and was considered disposable. The famine appears to be missing from academic texts on the history of the nineteenth century,[21] and I would argue that it does not feature in the dominant ideology today of what it is to be 'British.'

3.3 Undecidability and Intervention

Central to Badiou's event is the undecidability of its belonging to the situation. In order for there to be an event there needs to be a 'site,' which is 'a situation where at least one multiple on the edge of the void is presented.' For Badiou, there is a problem in deciding whether the event belongs to the situation. If it does, it would be a One (an 'ultra-one') that is under the count-as-one, since it presents itself in this situation, but in that case it would be separated from the void by itself—it is the ultra-one because it counts as both the presented multiple and the multiple presented in its own presentation (which was not previously presented), so it is counted twice. If, however, the event does not belong to the situation, only the void can be subsumed under it and no other presentable multiple responds to the name of the event (although if this were the case, Badiou argues that the French Revolution could be proven not to have existed if it is only a pure word). The choice, therefore, is to decide whether the event belongs to the situation, and for an intervention to decide: 'By the declaration of the belonging of the event to the situation it bars the void's irruption. But this is only in order to force the situation itself to confess its own void, and to thereby let forth, from inconsistent being and the interrupted count, the incandescent non-being of an existence.' Badiou argues that ontology demonstrates that the event *is not*, since self-belonging is prohibited in ontology for being against foundational finitude (Badiou refers to the axiom of foundation). According to this axiom, something cannot belong to itself, isolated from other things; but this is why Badiou argues that a choice needs to be made. An event occurs, and a decision needs to be made as to whether its existence should be acknowledged, which is an acknowledgement that there is a void in the situation. It is a *wager* to decide that the event belongs to the situation, given that it is the essence of the event to be undecidable in relation to its belonging to the situation. The wager should not be legitimate (in a legal, statist sense), however. If it were, it would be part of the structure, a 'legitimate' action, like voting, because it is already recognized by the state.[22]

Badiou uses the term 'intervention' for any procedure which recognizes a multiple as an event, although as we have seen, such recognition can mean a multiple composed of elements of its site that are represented as well as itself, and a decision that the multiple is a term of the situation and belongs to it. But then there is nothing but a term of the situation, a legitimacy of the 'event.' This poses a problem for Badiou similar to Nietzsche's Eternal Return—the 'event' will simply be a recurrence, and nothing new at all.[23] The wager that is the intervention is unpresentable and ontologically 'illegal' or illegitimate because we would not have an event if it were presentable and legal—it would comply with the regime of the count-as-one if that were the case. The naming that is part of the event's consequences is also illegal and unpresentable, there being no absolute commencement or a primal event that can be legally presented, or acknowledged by the state (which Badiou calls 'speculative leftism,' probably, in my view, because to see an event as an absolute commencement, such as the permanent establishment of a 'communist' society, would have to be speculative in the conventional sense, betting on the permanence of a new society). Badiou makes the point that the event requires us to follow its consequences, not to rest on the glorification of its occurrence, and this requires fidelity to the event, conserving its consequences that cannot be discerned by structure and remain undecidable.[24]

3.4 The Subject and the Approximate Truth

This leads us to the subject's relation to truth, for which Badiou uses the term 'confidence' to denote the subject's belief in a truth, but this belief draws in part on knowledge, with the operator of fidelity discerning relations between the name of the event that has been wagered, and multiples of the situation; so this discernment is an 'approximate truth.' Rather than the subject receiving some untainted truth, the subject is committed to the consequences of an event, but is not the event itself. The subject is tasked with discerning a relation between the situation and the truth, and not with leaving the event alone (or living without relation to the situation themselves). The subject has to contend with a common knowledge that does not recognize the event, and the act that is involved in the wager and what it should mean in practical terms. Meaning, for the subject, is in the 'future anterior'—that which is not just external to knowledge, but which means nothing to knowledge at present. The names in the subject-language that follows the event and intervention are not just terms of the situation (since the subject and the language they use exist in a situation), but also names with referential meaning which exceed the situation, this meaning existing officially should the event come to have existence or presentation in a count-as-one (that is, within a state).[25]

Badiou introduces a 'fundamental law of the subject,' which states that if a term of a situation exists that belongs to the generic part of the subject-language that is the truth, as well as maintaining a particular relation with the names at stake in a statement of the subject-language, this is because the statement of the subject-language will have been veridical for the situation in which the truth has occurred. In other words, part of the subject-language relating to the truth event will relate to terms that are already acceptable to the state. Such a relation is determined by the encyclopaedic determinants (knowledge) of the situation, so it is possible to know if a statement of the subject-language may be true in a situation in which a post-eventual truth is deployed, it being sufficient to verify only one term of such a statement that is related to the indiscernible in the situation: 'If such a term exists, then its belonging to the truth (to the indiscernible part which is the multiple-being of a truth) will impose the veracity of the initial statement within the *new* situation.'[26] We can see here why Žižek views this etching into the symbolic order as a kind of Kantianism, but I would argue that Badiou's theory of the subject is directed at events rather than categorical imperatives, and could just as well be compared to a Sartrean event. Indeed, despite Badiou's view in his post-Sartrean years that Sartre combines the worst of Hegelian and Marxian interpretations, they still share a privileging of the subject's decision-making capacities over ontology.[27]

'Forcing' is the term Badiou develops from this fundamental law of the subject, through which a term of the situation forces a statement of the subject-language, so that its veracity is equivalent to its belonging to the indiscernible that results from the generic procedure; forcing a statement with a positive connection to the event to be true in the new situation. Forcing is, for Badiou, verifiable by knowledge, although the term that forces a statement (that is, the truth of the event) is not verifiable by knowledge as to its belonging to the indiscernible (so the means (forcing), if not the message (truth), are verifiable by knowledge). Whether it belongs is down to the chance of enquiries, of interventions. The subject is a finite instance of a truth which possesses the capacity of indiscernment, forcing the undecidable to exhibit itself as such, on the substructure of being of an indiscernible part. It is thus assured that the impasse of being is the point at which a subject convokes itself to a decision, because at least one multiple, subtracted from the language, proposes fidelity to the names induced by a supernumerary nomination the possibility of a decision without concept.[28]

Only the subject has the finite capacity of indiscernment, free from relations. We will see in the next chapter how Badiou's earlier work is explicit in its Marxian tone, with the bourgeoisie/proletariat and splace/outplace dyads, but the knowledge/truth dyad in *Being and Event* again places this work in the Marxian canon. The knowledge (or ideology in an almost Althusserian sense) of the bourgeoisie and truth of the proletariat have been prominent in Marxian theory, and we will see how Badiou's system as it relates to the proletariat (among others) avoids the essentialism that postanarchism also seeks to avoid (in anarchism as well as Marxism).

There being no hero of the event, and the event occurring not through the sole efforts of a subject (who, rather, declares fidelity to the consequences of the event), we see a problem in Badiou's thought that is familiar to us from much of Marxian theory. This is the problem of how a subject is to know whether an event is actually an event (of the kind Badiou describes), and whether conditions are actually right for revolution. In the heat of the moment it is likely to matter little to the subject whether an event would be called such by Badiou (or whether they really are a subject)—what matters more is the practical matter of having significant support. A philosopher such as Badiou would only study the event after the fact, working with its consequences. And Badiou, I argue, is far from being a vanguardist. He writes about historical events such as the Paris Commune of 1871 or the events in Paris in May 1968, but he frequently refers to other revolts throughout his work, such as the revolt against changes to employment law in France in 2006, or the occasional riots in French suburbs sparked by police harassment. Both these movements he sees as 'proof of a form of existence that is irreducible to the games of the economy and the State.'[29] What we take from Marx and Badiou is the impossibility of prescribing a fixed communist politics that is consistent with their thought, but I maintain that this should be a strength. We will see how Badiou's thought relates to Marxian thought, but if Badiou's thought is Marxist, it is of the performative kind described in the first chapter, a communism lacking prescription.

3.5 Badiou's Operational Theory and Postanarchism

Anarchist Alejandro de Acosta has argued that the enduring interest that philosophers have had in anarchism may be due to it never having been a 'successful' theoretical system. Such attempts are 'happily incomplete,' and anarchism is 'an untimely echo of how philosophy was once lived, and how, indirectly and in a subterranean fashion, it continues to be lived.'[30] We have established that both poststructuralist and Marxian theory can be performative in the sense that they work with material change, and that Badiou's system is also performative as a dialectical materialism that works with truths without claiming to create them. But for all the apparent rigidity of Badiou's philosophical system, it is its engagement at the operational level that enables it to apply to situations and events, to see contingency as the default and to work with truths. It does not prescribe a form of politics or society, instead explaining how every One is an operation, an operational result in the regime of presentation (the multiple). We see how that which is not already presented through an operational result (a One) comes to be presented through an event, but how the subject-language that follows an event is not completely verified by knowledge. Part of the event and the subject's fidelity to the event will be etched into knowledge or the symbolic order, but incompletely. For what looks like a complete philosophical system, Badiou's theory has incompleteness at its core.

Badiou contrasts his approach to Deleuze's philosophy: an important influence on postanarchism. Deleuze should not, however, be used as a wedge to be driven between Badiou and postanarchism. Rather, what I believe it helps illustrate is that there is more than one way to arrive at a position similar to postanarchism, with Badiou moving from his Sartrean, to Althusserian, to post-Althusserian phases, inflected with Marx all the way, and largely by-passing poststructuralism to inadvertently make a significant and valuable theoretical contribution to postanarchism.

Deleuze is usually taken to be a philosopher of the multiple (or multiplicity) and singularity. To take one example from his many works, in *Difference and Repetition*, when Deleuze spoke of being confronted with two identical elements with the same concept, he urged us to distinguish between these elements, between repeated objects and a secret subject that is the real subject of repetition. The problem Deleuze wanted to tackle was that of difference being already mediated by representation. Rather than different elements being united and made the same under a concept, the two forms of repetition Deleuze describes enable us to see the singularity of the Idea rather than being constrained by a representation of elements as being the same.[31]

Badiou argues that Deleuze is actually a philosopher of the One, rather than of the multiple. The image of Deleuze as 'at once, radical and temperate, solitary and convivial, vitalist and democratic' is challenged. It is, according to Badiou, a mistake to see in his writings the 'anarchizing ideal of the sovereign individual.'[32] There is no shortage, of course, of those who defend Deleuze against Badiou's charge. The postanarchist Todd May, for example, argues that Badiou overstates the case, arguing instead that Deleuze is a philosopher of the One *and* the Many.[33]

Jon Roffe argues that, on the other hand, Deleuze rejected the One-Many dyad; but that was not with the aim of affirming the One *above* the Many, as Badiou suggests. What Badiou fails to acknowledge, Roffe argues, is that the entire One-Many dyad is replaced with the concept of substantive multiplicity. Furthermore, Badiou only used the word multiplicity in *The Clamor of Being* where it can be easily changed for the word multiple, erasing a decisive term in Deleuze's works. Badiou routinely asserts, Roffe continues, that the conflict between his thought and Deleuze's is based upon the status of multiplicities, and yet 'the theme of multiplicity is *everywhere premised by a critique not of the relative subordination of the One to the Many, but by rejecting this dyad outright*' (italics in the original).[34] Roffe notes that Deleuze is consistent on this point, referencing two works twenty years apart, starting with the work that introduced his interest in the concept of multiplicity, *Bergonism* (published before *Difference and Repetition*). Between this work and *Foucault*, which followed twenty years later, and which Badiou discusses himself, Roffe argues that there is no divergence in the way Deleuze understands multiplicity. In both these works, Deleuze argues that the One-Many dyad must be replaced with a concept of substantive multiplicity. Roffe acknowledges that this theory of multiplicity may be insufficient, but the important point is that it is not to be seen as the pre-eminence of the One in the way that Badiou imagines.[35]

The common conception that Deleuze is anti-Hegelian and anti-dialectical is also challenged by Roffe, and the repetition of this view by Badiou is attributed by Roffe to the power of cliché. The dialectic is present in Deleuze, but it is the Platonic dialectic that Deleuze seeks to refute and develop into something applicable to the virtual (but not the actual). Referring to *Difference and Repetition*, Roffe quotes Deleuze's definition of the virtual Idea: 'The problematic or dialectical Idea is a system of connections between differential elements, a system of differential relations between genetic elements.' In other words, as Roffe explains, the virtual Idea is characterized by 'an irreducible multiplicity, a differential dialectical system,' and yet 'Badiou's account of the virtual... [is] a unary emanative One.'[36] Deleuze's theory is instead one of multiplicity, and an affirmative dialectic rather than a negative one. He sees negation as difference, but seen 'the right way up,' difference is affirmation, an act of creation that must also be created, and yet representation fails to capture this affirmative world of difference. Representation has a single centre, and 'mediates everything, but mobilizes and moves nothing.'[37]

This affirmative dialectic of Deleuze's may seem at odds with Badiou's way of thinking, but the division of the One into two is also affirmative in this sense. The differential dialectical system that Deleuze describes does not seem far removed from Badiou's insistence that truth has no identity, other than that from a difference. In place of the becoming of Deleuze's system, for Badiou 'the being of all things is the process of its division into two,' measured against the place that it exceeds and the structural system.[38] This description of the division of One into two in *The Rational Kernel* neatly encapsulates the affirmative aspect of the dialectic in Badiou's system, against what may seem to be the more structuralist aspect when compared to Deleuze. Badiou has in recent years referred to an affirmative dialectic, affirming here that the generic in his work is really a complexity of differences rather than the pure absence of being. The generic in Badiou's dialectic is not reducible to pure nothingness (and the void is never pure nothingness), unlike the pure nothingness of class in 'classical dialectics.'[39] Badiou remains, however, at odds with Deleuze in his own assessment of their relation, and with a number of those who favour the poststructuralist approach.

Simon Critchley, who favours the tactical anarchist approach towards the state over 'Marxist' approaches, sees politics as 'the manifestation of 'dissensus,' the cultivation of an anarchic multiplicity that calls into question the authority and legitimacy of the state.'[40] Critchley claimed to feel uneasy about ontology in a debate with Badiou, expressing concern that it gives too little agency to the individual to express their subjectivity. For Critchley, genuine political subjectivity is rare, but his suspicion is that an ontological analysis of the individual or society restricts the individual's subjectivity. Badiou's response, as one would expect, is that ontology acknowledges that there are constraints on any individual, and that we cannot simply choose to ignore the structure and structures within which individuals exist (or are included).[41] This is the post-Althusserian Badiou who, as we have seen, does not support the view that there is a process without a subject, but that there is nevertheless a process against which subjectivity emerges as the exception. That is to say, there are operations of the One, but there nevertheless occurs an exceptional event to which the subject may pledge fidelity. This is a position more usually associated with Marx. It is not that Marx claimed that the proletariat were essentially the agents for change and revolution, but he did think that circumstances were likely to afford the proletariat the opportunity for revolution. It was possible in Marx's time to define the proletariat analytically, and I have argued that it continues to be so, as we saw in the first chapter with Erik Olin Wright. However, the proletariat is also a performative category—a potentiality for acting, given the right conditions.

Postanarchists have not turned their back on ontology, but there is a suspicion towards Badiou. There is certainly a preference in postanarchist thought for Deleuze's ontology of difference and multiplicity, rather than Badiou's ontology of the event. Yet, in drawing on Deleuze, Newman is acknowledging the constraints placed on the individual, albeit in a less formally structural sense than Badiou. The 'state form' in Deleuze and Guattari's work, for example, is compared to the 'ruling principle' of the state that concerns anarchists. The state is an abstraction (or 'abstract machine') that appears in many forms throughout history. What is important for Newman is not the form in which the abstract machine appears but its function, a similar line of critique to that which anarchists directed at Marxists for focusing too much on the state, and not enough on its 'fundamental operation and function.' Furthermore, while Marxists would argue that the state develops from the dominant mode of production, Newman maintains that the state is not to be attributed to a mode of production, but instead that what Deleuze and Guattari call the 'eternal state,' which takes many forms, is actually what accumulates the forces of production, turning them into a mode. It is nevertheless the case that these two thinkers associate the modern state with capitalism, which both 'deterritorializes' desire by breaking down state-coded structures so that commodity relations and fetishism are in the ascendant, while 'reterritorializing' through the state where it serves to protect capital against the free flow of forces that capital takes advantage of only up to a certain point.[42]

For Badiou, instead of there being many forms the state may take, there are many states. As with Deleuze, so for Badiou the state is not built on an economic mode of production. It has been noted how Marx deepens the analysis of the state to include economic and social relations through a materialist conception of history rather than narrow the study of the state to a single, sovereign place of power. Deleuze claims to be in agreement with the anti-historicist approach of Althusser when he considers the idea of multiple, differential relations between the mode of production and property relations which are 'established not between concrete individuals but between atomic bearers of labour-power or representatives of property.'[43] The economic instance is not a narrow conception of these relations, but is constituted by a social multiplicity, or by varieties of these differential relations. For Deleuze, these relations may be 'incarnated in the concrete differentiated labours which characterize a determinate society,' such as the real relations between the juridical, political and ideological, and the actual relations between capitalists and labourers, but these are not already given. Instead, the 'economic' is never given, but designates in the present a 'differential virtuality to be interpreted, always covered over by its forms of actualization.' The economic is 'the social dialectic itself—in other words, the totality of the problems posed to a given society, or the synthetic and problematising field of that society.'[44] The actualizations, whether historicist or ideological, can only be temporary maskings of the dialectic, according to Deleuze. Badiou expresses this more succinctly through the way in which being and structure mask pure multiplicity; but both analyses provide insights for anarchist and Marxian theory.

Newman has drawn parallels between anarchism and Badiou's work, notably his analysis of the state and advocacy of a politics without a party. While Badiou does discuss Engels and Mao in *Being and Event*, I would maintain that he is referring to the state as an operation, something that is an ontological inevitability, rather than the instrumental way in which some Marxists would use the state. It is not that the state should or should not be used for political ends, but that the state just is, as are all Ones.[45] Badiou's frequent references to figures in the history of Marxism and the way in which his position has shifted through his career makes it difficult to know what his strategic and tactical approach towards the state is. Indeed, there are contradictions in Badiou's works that Newman notes: for example, the view in *The Flux and the Party* that the state is a construction, and any rupture with it requires another construction if it is not to end in failure and massacre, as happened with the Paris Commune of 1871.

While Badiou has distanced himself from anarchism, we have seen how he is on very similar ground to Newman when he seeks to salvage the term 'communism' and the Paris Commune from being too easily associated with the 'socialist state' or 'communist party.'[46] Badiou came to this position after *The Flux and the Party*, which was written during his association with the UCFML, although he has since distanced himself from the state and the strategy of Leninism.

For Newman, as we saw in the last chapter, what makes the political event possible is that political and social identity is built around its own impossibility and emptiness in the sense that identity is only partially constituted and built around a lack that does not appear in the symbolic order, drawing on Lacan as well as Laclau and Mouffe. The tactical approach is then to recognize common ground between different groups in the name of a common cause.

We see something similar in Badiou, albeit with little mention of common, non-class based, causes or hegemonic projects. In Badiou's description of operations of the One, we have seen that there are many count-as-ones that are then again counted by the state in the process of including these Ones. Of course, Badiou's description of the state of the situation has its differences, and Badiou's tactical approach, as far as he has expressed it over the years, does not mirror the post-Marxist or postanarchist approach to politics. However, both theories are suited to societies where power is dispersed rather than limited to a more Hobbesian structure where power might be challenged by symbolically cutting off the sovereign's head, and there are few situations or states in which such a critique would be useful today. Both theories have also, as we have seen, arrived at their positions taking different routes. However, Badiou's theory of inclusion and belonging is relevant to both theories. Both are concerned with understanding political and social groups that emerge from events but are not recognized by the state, these states being inevitably temporary ontological structures, for Badiou, and symbolic orders with a lack at their core, for Newman. These points will form a crucial part of the next chapter as I look at how Badiou's understanding of the state relates to Marxian theory and his understanding of communism.

4

No More Heroes: Badiou, the Proletariat, Communism and Permanent Revolution

'I too am a Marxist...'[1]

Badiou's association with Marx's thought is well known but often taken out of context, and referring to Badiou as a 'Marxist' without qualification is likely to be problematic for many. In this chapter, I argue that Badiou's thought nevertheless shares certain traits with Marxian theory, most notably the view that we exist in circumstances not of our own (direct) making, and furthermore, that events (and truths) are not entirely of our own making either. The proletariat, of which Badiou continues to say so much, is, however, not developed around an essentialist understanding of class. For Badiou, truths reveal themselves, and subjects have to make a decision whether to declare their fidelity to a truth that can only be known approximately (sharing with Sartre the importance of decision).[2] The proletariat is important for Badiou, in a pre-eventual and analytical sense, but he does not privilege this class *essentially*, and nor does he believe in a socialist event to end all events. This much Badiou shares with certain anarchists.

Badiou's long engagement with the left is partly responsible for this confusion. Badiou's view on the Paris Commune of 1871, for example, has shifted since his association in the 1970s with the *Union des Communistes de France Marxiste-Leniniste* (UCFML) and his more recent works. In The *Flux and the Party,* a UCFML publication, we have seen how Badiou leans towards Leninism and his appraisal of the party, with its 'apparatus, hierarchy, discipline, [and] renunciation' as essential, working with the aspiration of the masses for the 'non-state' and communism, the party being its 'iron hand.'[3] This is in marked contrast to Badiou's later 'politics without a party' where he calls for an end to the model of the party or multiple parties; however, this is with the qualification that this should not lead one to lapse into 'the figure of anarchism,' as we have seen.[4]

Badiou's problematic and ambivalent relation to anarchism, and postanarchism in particular, was considered in the last chapter, and his more recent work, as we saw, has been an attempt to salvage the term 'communism' from its association with the 'socialist state' and the 'communist party.' In particular, in *Being and Event*, Badiou dismisses the 'absolute commencement' that he associates with speculative leftism (that is, a revolution to end all revolutions, believed to be the precursor to a permanent communist settlement).[5] This distancing from Leninism opens up an opportunity to consider Badiou's 'Marxism' in a new light.

In particular, we will see some common ground between Badiou's theory and those aspects of Marxian theory that are not reductionist (the well-worn charge that Marxian theory is an economism). Badiou understands the proletariat as a performative identity and category for the emergence of a new collective subject, without relying on a teleological historicism or a narrative of the withering away of the state.

The event, for Badiou, is an abstraction from the circumstances surrounding it. It dispenses with essentialist relations and imposes itself back onto the situation. While the event is aleatory, Badiou identifies, under the present circumstances, the proletariat as a likely subject and the 'factory' as a likely event-site, but it is for subjects to declare fidelity to an event. There is no solid ground in Badiou's system to say that the proletariat will be the revolutionary subject, but the proletariat, or parts of it, can certainly be identified analytically, before an event, as being included in a situation but not belonging to it. It can therefore be seen as a *potential* (but not necessarily actual) revolutionary subject. Badiou is aware that his position in *Can Politics Be Thought* is likely to lead to the charge that while he has abandoned Marxism in its 'substantive historicization' and turned it towards a politics of non-domination, he has reintroduced 'the empirical worker in the final instance,' but Badiou takes the view that it is impossible not to consider the position of the worker in pre-political situations.[6]

However, Badiou is otherwise dismissive of any identification of a subject before an event, perhaps because he sees this as an essentialism given the tenuous grounds on which such identifications are made. Badiou's criticism of postmodern particularisms should be seen as a rejection of the identification of subjects as part of a hegemonic project before an event, based on thinking forms of power under the present state and leaving it intact rather than challenging it with anything new. Badiou's non-essentialist subject, which includes the proletariat (and which is present in his work right up to the present day) may be active before the event, but it becomes a collective subject in the wake of the event, injecting meaning into what would otherwise be a rather a-subjective event. Badiou's communism is one where the subject persists in weaving the event into common knowledge, rather than collapsing into seriality afterwards, as in Sartre.

In Sartre's notion of seriality, a fused group acts in unity after breaking from the totalized series of 'not-beings' (or the everydayness of social relations to which most people give little regular consideration) before inevitably dissolving back into seriality.[7] For Badiou, the hope is that some aspect of the event leaves a trace, rather than accepting seriality and almost admitting defeat. Badiou understands Sartre's attempt to theorize Stalinism in this way, in the sense that the choices intellectuals face are historically situated, and one of those choices may be to support seriality (or Stalinism).[8] Badiou, however, seeks to keep a trace of the event alive through the commitment of those claiming fidelity to the event, making its consequences exist maximally in the more recent *Logics of Worlds*.

Badiou does not dismiss difference, and we see how recently he has described the proletariat (and the generic) as based on a complexity of differences, but one focused on equality that cuts across identity.[9] Badiou does not seek to create (potentially false) universalities before the event, and we can say that there is never always already such a thing as a communist. The appearance of the subject is performative, and history, in accordance with Badiou's understanding of Marxism, is not pre-determined. Unlike Sartre's notion of History and totalization, Badiou's theory of the subject is perhaps better described as a non-continuous totalization, the event leaving a trace if its subjects work to make this happen, but without a thread necessarily linking all events throughout history. Like Marx, Badiou works with truths and does not create them (thereby not privileging the philosopher). Furthermore, I maintain that the proletariat in Marx is not predestined to be a collective subject, but becomes one through situations imposed on society by the capitalist mode of production.

4.1 Anarchism and Marxism—
The Narrow Divide that Badiou Crosses

4.1.1 *The Anarchist Charge against Marx and the Proletariat*

To expand on the ground covered in the first chapter with a focus on class, the reading of Marx and Marxian theory presented here will necessarily be a selective one, drawing on those aspects that are compatible with, and useful for, Badiou and postanarchism, rather than claiming to draw on an orthodox Marxism, whatever that means.

The sometimes antipathetic stance of anarchists and postanarchists towards class is something that Benjamin Franks has discussed. In particular, Hakim Bey and Bob Black are noted for denouncing 'leftism.'[10] Bey denounces the 'outdated baggage of Leftism' and calls for an emphasis on the 'practical, material & personal benefits of radical networking' in his laughable, but probably influential, *Special Communiqué* in which the Association for Ontological Anarchy discusses a 'post-anarchism anarchy.' Lamenting the fact that the 'anarchist 'movement' today contains virtually no Blacks, Hispanics, Native Americans or children... even tho [sic] in theory such genuinely oppressed groups stand to gain the most from any anti-authoritarian revolt,' Bey then seeks to discover how such agents may be enlisted to his cause.[11] While having wide appeal is no bad thing, it reminds us of how Marxists 'simply' isolate an agent they call the proletariat and invite them to follow their programme for freedom, or so that particular anarchist narrative goes, and this particular post-anarchy anarchist is inviting objectifiable groups ('Blacks, Hispanics...') to free themselves with the anarchist programme.

Although Badiou's message on the role of the proletariat in politics has been mixed, and erred on the pessimistic side in a 1997 interview with Peter Hallward, he consistently opposes the particularism of new social movements. This may be territory best avoided by a white male, but Badiou states that his concern with those who focus on oppression as a woman or a black person is whether 'this identity, in itself, [can] function in a progressive fashion—that is, other than as a property invented by the oppressors themselves.'[12] Badiou is quite neutral over who becomes a subject, but sceptical about pre-eventual identities, whether based on race, gender or class, even if they can be looked upon as possible event sites. Similarly, for Newman, while a proletarian class consciousness is no longer a viable means to challenge the state, neither is 'identity politics.' Neither are written off entirely by Newman (and I will come onto his views on the contemporary proletariat), but as with Badiou, identity politics poses no challenge to neoliberalism. Such a politics 'risks falling into an essentialist trap where one is in a sense imprisoned within one's own subjectivity, whose interests and desires have been carved out for it by power.'[13]

Having endured decades of being overshadowed by Marxism, Bob Black also celebrates a 'post-leftist anarchism' now claimed to be in the ascendant. The ideology of Marxism, for Black, is now merely 'a campus—and mostly a faculty—phenomenon,' parasitic upon feminism and 'racial nationalisms,' and now merely an 'Oriental despotism' that is unthinkable as a model for the West.'[14] However, Franks notes that part of the reason for this distancing of anarchism from class discourse and leftism has been the perceived Leninist and Stalinist monopoly on the discourse of class oppression, and the consequent desire to avoid anything with Leninist overtones. In doing so, postanarchists risk ignoring economic and class oppression, and 'start to prioritize certain elitist forms of resistance and agents of change.' Instead, according to Franks, postanarchists point to nomadic subjects, who are not bound by place or past experience, and are more likely to be economically independent, privileged identities.[15] In simple terms, it could be seen as a way to subvert the materialist dialectic through relying on those who think they are free from the economic and social relations that shape their lives, although I would maintain that any academic writing on anarchism is clearly not economically independent or entirely privileged if they have to sell their labour to make a living

4.1.2 In Defence of Marx and the Proletariat against 'Ontological Essentialism'

The proletariat is referred to throughout Badiou's works, yet as we have seen, his more robust and systematic theory avoids privileging *essentially* any one agent. Through a selective, but by no means revisionist, reading of Marx, we saw in the first chapter that the proletariat need not be understood essentially as the class destined to be the agent of revolution, but that it nevertheless exists and can be a key agent against economic oppression. We have seen the performative Marx that Étienne Balibar identifies[16] in the *Theses on Feuerbach*, which argues that the world changes through means other than philosophy, and that while people are products of their circumstances, people also change their circumstances.[17] We have also seen how Balibar sees in Marx a 'non-philosophy,' which does not eschew philosophy, but does go beyond philosophy by showing us that it is not an autonomous field that can change the world on its own.[18] In a similar way, Badiou does not look to philosophy to produce truths, but instead to seize truths.[19]

Marx's view of communism following the Paris Commune of 1871 is problematic in itself, noting that it seemed both impossible, and yet had to remain possible if something is to replace capitalism.[20] In the works of Marx, the dictatorship of the proletariat and communism are questions that remain unsettled, the bulk of his work being an analysis of capitalism and a materialist conception of history, not a political programme. Given this, it is easy to see how communism best functions as the horizon of politics, as an assumption that all states are illegitimate and that we should be free to organize our lives the way we want, while coming up against the ontological impossibility of such a communism on most occasions.

Perhaps this gives us a basis for making Marx more relevant in the field of postanarchism. Of course, this project needs to be qualified by the fact that it is a selective reading. There are also concerns with the ontological approach amongst postanarchists,[21] exacerbated by the presence of ontology in Badiou's work as well as in the works of Lukács and Sartre, even if the latter's *Critique of Dialectical Reason* retains ontology in all but name. Badiou's project is, however, different in nature to that of those Marxian theorists who have placed the proletariat as the essential agent in their vanguardist strategy.

As I have suggested, there is a critique of ontological essentialism in postanarchist thought, aimed at both classical anarchists and what is taken to be 'Marxism,' but this does not mean that an ontological approach is inimical to postanarchist theory. The question here is whether any Marxian theory of the proletariat as agent, and of communism as a practice, must be guided by an ontology that is incompatible with postanarchism, and more particularly whether Badiou's relation to Marx and communism can revive the proletariat as an agent without the essentialism with which anarchists take issue.

4.1.3 *An Anarchist Proletariat*

Class has by no means been dismissed as a category by all postanarchists, and we have already seen Franks' concern over the tendency of anarchists to sometimes look towards privileged individuals as agents, something that we will see Badiou aims to avoid in a manner which postanarchists should be sympathetic to. For Call, pop culture can help to take postanarchism 'out of its bourgeois ivory tower and broadcast it into living rooms around the world,' with *Buffy the Vampire Slayer* used as an example of 'a classical anarchist assault on the military-scientific complex, followed by an all-out post-anarchist attack on the Symbolic' accessible to those workers who do not read much Lacan.'[22] Whatever the merits of engaging workers through their television sets, direct action around class itself continues to be referred to by those associated with anarchist thought. David Graeber, in his account of Occupy Wall Street, wrote that it became 'increasingly unclear what the difference between financial power and state power really is,' and this is why Occupy Wall Street called themselves the '99 per cent,' challenging the concentration of power in the hands of business and government. In calling themselves the 99 per cent, Occupy Wall Street 'managed to get the issues not only of class, but of class power, back into the centre of American political debate.'[23]

The Occupy movement was an example of the proletariat as performative, in the sense that it was in a time of economic crisis that significant numbers of people started to see themselves as the 99 per cent against the wealthy 1 per cent. I am avoiding referring to the 99 per cent against the 1 per cent as necessarily the proletariat against the bourgeoisie, as we cannot claim that all those involved in the various Occupy movements saw themselves in this way. Nevertheless, such a resonance can easily be found in Marxian theory. We have seen how the analytical Marxist Eric Olin Wright describes the complexity of class, acknowledging in his later work a middle class that is defined by the way it spends its money as well as by the more conventional yardsticks such as education and domination in the workplace. Yet we have also seen in Olin Wright how domination in the workplace is not always exploitation, while exploitation is always domination.[24]

Office managers may dominate staff without exploiting them for their labour (that is, without profiting from their exploitation), and understood through analytical Marxian theory, society still consists of bourgeois exploiters and the exploited proletariat. Perhaps the office manager in a dominant position will consider themselves 'bourgeois' because someone reports to them, but they are not exploiting them for their labour. That is done by the bourgeois exploiter, who exploits both these workers, albeit paying them different salaries. I would argue that this is also the case for both private and public sectors, or what Marx might call productive (because it creates surplus value for the exploiter) and unproductive wage labour (which eats into the stock of surplus capital in an economy) respectively.[25] The latter is useful and adds value to society, and labour is exploited in the same way from the point of view of the worker, but this does not create surplus value as understood by a capitalist. Beyond Marxian circles, terms such as bourgeois and proletariat may have taken on a different meaning, and the idea of a labour aristocracy has been replaced with the idea of the middle class. However, with Occupy we saw people from a wide range of backgrounds and varying levels of wealth join forces against the exploiters. This is where the analytical Marxian analysis is put into practice and morphs into the performative Marxism that Balibar sees in Marx.

Newman does not agree with the use to which the proletariat was put by 'orthodox' Marxian theory, nor with the idea of the proletariat as the principal revolutionary agent led by the vanguard party; but he does not dismiss the proletariat out of hand. Referring to what he calls a process of 're-proletarianization,' with increasing levels of poverty, precarity and worsening conditions for exploited labour around the world, Newman argues that, while 'proletarian' may not be a sufficient category with which to analyse political subjectivation today, nevertheless, 'if we are to understand—as Marx himself did—proletarians as those who are excluded from the fruits of the wealth they produce and whose deprivation is the necessary structural feature of capitalism, then we can certainly retain this designation.'[26] Indeed, the analytical category of the proletariat is a broad and complex one because it concerns forms of exploitation that affect a great proportion of the populations of most states. We have already seen this broad analytical Marxian definition in the three criteria by which Olin Wright defines 'class exploitation.' To briefly recap, these three criteria are: that the material welfare of one group depends on the material deprivations of another; second, that this first causal relation involves the exclusion of the exploited from access to certain productive resources; and, third, that the second criteria achieves the first through appropriating the fruits of labour from the exploited by the exploiters.[27] So we are using a broad understanding of 'proletarian' from an analytical perspective, which has little to do with one's job title, and everything to do with social relations and one's actual position in relation to the exploiter. And in times of crisis, the performative proletariat is all the broader, with agents identifying with the exploited for any number of reasons, without regard to what Marxian theorists or philosophers have said, even if their analysis may be the correct one.

This broad understanding of class exploitation demonstrates that Marxian theory is far from missing the big picture (and can include faddish terms such as 'precariat'). The global poor, underemployed, casually employed and those excluded from employment deserve as much consideration as a disciplined and united working class for Newman, while also arguing that the proletariat may never have been the uniform group some may have seen it as, noting workers rebelling against the coercion of the factory and Rancière's insights into the literary and 'bourgeois' passions of many workers in the nineteenth century. Newman's principal condition for any category for understanding political subjectivation is that it not be essentialist.[28] This is not a dismissal of the proletariat, but of a particular definition in some of Marx's political texts (and I would say sketchy by comparison to his theoretical work). It is not at odds with the non-essentialist, performative notion of the proletariat that I have been developing thus far, and nor is it necessarily at odds with the way in which Badiou understands the proletariat as subject.

Although Badiou's theory of the event and the subject is based on a fundamental antagonism with the state, this does not prevent subjects from supporting state-based measures to get what they want. It would be premature, however, to place Badiou on that side of the 'double movement,' identified by Karl Polanyi, which acted as a countermovement against the increasing marketization of society and for social protection.[29] The countermovement against markets in the last century required state regulation, and Badiou's work, as we have seen, focuses on events against the state and states, although the era when the state acted to regulate the market with the aim of social protection has long since seen its zenith in the West, at least on its current trajectory, and for the time being. When Badiou does engage with contemporary politics, his critique of the state is always associated with a critique of neoliberalism, especially in Greece and France,[30] and Badiou does campaign for certain protections from the state with *Organization Politique* and their campaign for workers' rights.[31]

What is interesting, however, is that in the political conjuncture Badiou finds himself in, his theoretical attacks on the state align him with those he might identify as particularist. These would be the third movement to Polanyi's double movement that Nancy Fraser identifies. If demands for social protection against the markets is often led by organized labour, Fraser contends that the latter cannot form the backbone of the former, given it is dwindling in size as more people find themselves in less stable and non-unionized employment. The third movement of which Fraser writes seeks emancipation from the state, and consists of those movements that are anti-racist, anti-war, feminist, and so on; and yet these groups, while not being economic liberals, were wary of the domination of the state that social protection could lead to. By not being attuned to the challenges posed by free markets, the 'hegemonic currents of emancipatory struggle have formed a "dangerous liaison" with neoliberalism, supplying a portion of the "new spirit" or charismatic rationale for a new mode of capital accumulation, touted as "flexible," "difference-friendly," "encouraging of creativity from below."' The emancipatory critique and the neoliberal critique of the state therefore converge, joining forces 'with marketization to double-team social protection.' The challenge now is how to reinvigorate the emancipatory movement and release it from its association with neoliberalism.[32]

4.2 Badiou's Communism

4.2.1 The Unheroic Proletariat and the State

While Badiou shares with postanarchism a tactical approach that does not prescribe a clear-cut strategy for what politics ought to look like, he also knows that Ones and states are an inevitable yet temporary part of the political landscape. This makes it possible to support political causes without eschewing contingency, given that this is how politics operates. It also raises the question as to what kind of Marxist Badiou is, and what kind of figure of the proletariat we see in his works.

I have argued that Badiou's reference to the proletariat when writing about political subjectivation suggests a non-essentialist proletariat, yet this continual reference point has been changing over his career. It is certainly possible to argue that the proletariat in Badiou's 1980s works and onwards is the result of his tactical concerns and its place amongst the operations of the state and states. In other words, instead of being an essentialist proletariat, it is the most likely or most prominent of political subjects at the time Badiou was writing. However, because of this there is much in Badiou's earlier works that may appear essentialist.

Hallward notes that for the Badiou in *Of Ideology* (1976) the proletariat is unique in attaining the purification required for subjectivation, since it was the first exploited class that both formed itself as a revolutionary subject and had no specific class interest, and therefore had to destroy itself as a class. Badiou is yet to move to a 'politics without a party' here, Hallward noting that in *Theory of the Subject* Badiou sees purification being achieved through the party as an organ that strengthens the working class and isolates them from the whole.[33] References to the proletariat continue to permeate Badiou's works, including his work on logic, invoking the proletariat in 2009's *Second Manifesto for Philosophy* as an example of a political collective whose social and economic being is not in doubt, but whose existence is in doubt until there is a transcendental change and the proletariat appears in the sphere of political presentation[34] Hallward notes that while the proletariat appeared consistently as the vehicle for political subjectivation in Badiou's earlier works, whereby Badiou equated 'the subjective process of becoming confident in oneself with the global process of historical struggle itself,' he later saw 'classical Marxism' as mistaking its object for its subject. In other words, the working class was mistaken for its continuous subject, which meant that Marxism was unable to consider other social categories and objects, and ultimately failed as a result. Noting the various ways in which the later Badiou draws on Marx, Hallward points to Badiou's rejection of a direct articulation of politics with economics, as well as his tolerance for a degree of reliance on the state, there being no single subject of history and no primacy of the class struggle, as positions that may cast doubt on his Marxism.[35]

Badiou's reliance on the state is perhaps ineluctable when it comes to the forms of activism he endorses and is directly involved in, especially with the *Organization Politique*. Here he shares with Žižek a certain 'pragmatism' when it comes to supporting social democratic reforms and making specific demands on the state. Žižek's sympathetic views on 'Obamacare' is a case in point.[36] Moreover, making demands on the state is not inimical to Badiou's theory. We have seen how all states are operational Ones, temporary yet inevitable. This does distinguish Badiou from Marx, although I have already discussed Marx's inconsistent approach towards the state and the dictatorship of the proletariat in his political writings. The works of Engels and Lenin are far more consistent on this point, and Badiou's earlier works do appear to follow the line that the state and the proletariat will disappear one day through a double vanishing. However, this does not, in my view, involve an essentialist view of the proletariat. The striking difference between *Theory of the Subject* and *Being and Event* is Badiou's abandonment of the party—but the proletariat is selected as the agent for a particular period of history, not as an essentialist agent for a teleological history.

So the party and the proletariat are not essentially always already at the vanguard of political subjectivation, but they can form a vanguard for a particular political conjuncture. Of course, this is the point Marx was making, and in *Theory of the Subject* Badiou discusses the destruction of the proletariat, illustrated by examples from the politics of Leninism and Maoism. The destruction of the proletariat is of course familiar within Marxian discourse. Lukács's worker, to take a well-known example, only becomes conscious of his existence in society as a proletarian once he becomes aware of himself as a commodity. The proletariat, by becoming conscious of its existence in society, uses this subjectivity to liberate itself as a class, but it can only do this by abolishing all classes. As Lukács puts it, 'its consciousness, the last class consciousness in the history of mankind, must both lay bare the nature of society and achieve an increasingly inward fusion of theory and practice.' Only this class, for Lukács, is capable of relating to the whole reality in a revolutionary way, whereas the individual confronting objective reality is capable only of a subjective recognition or rejection. Only this class can see through reified objectivity.[37] The proletariat can therefore be seen as acting subjectively, but only as a collective when it realizes a new objectivity by seeing through the reified objectivity under which it was subsumed.

The focus on the proletariat continues within Badiou's work, but he is not as inclined to link events to a realization that the proletariat have become reified as commodities. If there is an aspect of Lukács's work that Badiou comes close to, it is Lukács's view that being has ontological priority over consciousness, which he saw as the central thesis of all materialism. For Lukács, this meant that 'ontologically … there can be being without consciousness, while all consciousness must have something existent as its presupposition or basis.'[38] Badiou certainly shares more with Lukács in this respect than with the 'Hegelianized Marx' he saw in Sartre's work (after those years in which he might have counted himself as a Sartrean). As we have seen, this version of Marx was reduced to aspects of Hegel, but not those aspects that had been influential on Marx, according to Badiou.[39]

For the Badiou of *Theory of the Subject*, we see a more Maoist idea of the One becoming a Two, or of the revolution that is to occur after the initial seizing of the state apparatus. We have seen how Badiou does not believe in absolute revolution and an absolute commencement of a new society.[40] In this respect at least there are similarities with the Sartre of the *Critique of Dialectical Reason*. In *Theory of the Subject*, published in 1982, long after Badiou had moved on from being an admirer of Sartre, we see theoretical precursors of concepts such as the void and fidelity to the event. These terms were explored in the previous chapter. The 'clinamen,' in *Theory of the Subject*, helps illustrate how the event lives on through those claiming fidelity to the event, rather than a permanent and absolute One being established.

Borrowing the term from ancient atomism's description of the unpredictability of atoms, Badiou sees in the clinamen 'the outplace of an unlocatable, deregulated movement.'[41] We have seen how, for Badiou, the dialectic is the outplace against the splace, or that which is out of place against that in the space of placement. I have argued that what poststructuralists may find acceptable about this is that the splace is a non-essentialist way of describing the sense in which things are placed. The space of placement is not an essentialist One, nor a permanent structure, and relations between things that are placed are procedural, not permanent. That which is not recognized in the splace may force a change from the outplace, and the clinamen illustrates this force. The clinamen is 'outside time,' beyond the law, with 'neither past (nothing binds it) nor future (there is no more trace of it) nor present (it has neither a place nor a moment).' The clinamen 'takes place only in order to disappear, it is its very own disappearance.' As with atoms, so with humans, Badiou associating the clinamen with the subject and subjectivation, and the masses making history just as atoms, for Democritus, make the world.[42] The clinamen, as an unlocatable movement, and one that is unintelligible in the splace, disappears, but this 'vanishing term' also 'leaves behind this enormous trace that is the whole.' As a vanishing term, there is nothing comprehendible in the splace once it disappears, except the force which it grounded in breaking with the One.

As an example, Badiou explains that this clarifies for the Marxist the role of the mass movement, which 'is both absolute in terms of force and null in terms of place.'[43] The mass movement is a vanishing term, applying its force in the splace following an event. However, the relation of the mass movement to the splace and the state is of crucial significance. Badiou distances Marxism and the mass movement from state socialism here:

> The fact that one can describe the mass movement, its memorable lucidity, its invincible courage, its particular division, its suspicious-looking assemblies, its fraternal terrorism, does not authorize us to believe that therein lies a stable term of socio-political being. Any attempt to institute in a lasting way the forms of its creative impatience, or to define its state of affairs, changes the mass movement into its opposite. All that the Soviets after 1920 or the Chinese revolutionary committees after 1970 accomplish is the statist disappearance of their historical apparition.[44]

The mass movement disappears without a trace in what Badiou calls the 'vast stages of the historical splace,' but which might be called the grand narrative of these variants of state socialism at the time. The masses make history as a vanishing term that leaves a trace, and not as a movement that becomes synonymous with the state. For Badiou, it is 'according to the modality of their stable splacement that the masses are history, whereas it is in their appearing-disappearing that they make history.' Disappearing gives the mass movement its being, paradoxically making its existence all the greater.[45]

4.2.2 Antagonism and the Bourgeoisie

Theory of the Subject does not dismiss the state as a revolutionary tool, but hopes that Maoist politics (cultural revolutions) would be a better path towards a double vanishing of the bourgeois state and then the state itself, rather than leaving a 'rat's nest of bourgeois bureaucrats' which had so far been the experience of the masses in so-called socialist states.[46] We have noted how Bruno Bosteels sees Badiou's debt to Maoism manifest itself through a 'dialectical rapport' between truth and knowledge, especially in *Being and Event*, even though Mao may be more immediately evident in *Theory of the Subject* and *Logics of Worlds*.[47]

What should be clear is that Badiou sees his dialectic as instructive for Marxists, clarifying the role of mass movements in history, without there being an absolute end to the dialectic achieved through the state. This may be caveated in *Theory of the Subject* with the vanishing of the proletariat, but is clear that the state should not give the proletariat a stable socio-political being, and Badiou has since remained resolute in standing against any teleological sense of history or absolute or final revolutions through what he calls the 'vulgar Marxist' view of history.[48] Furthermore, there is no egotistical individual at the centre of the event, but mass movements and those who declare their fidelity to the event. As we know, there is no hero of the event, truth being 'in-human,' and the event does not exist as far as ontology is concerned. We see in *Being and Event* that self-belonging, as a new force not recognized by the state or states, is prohibited under the axiom of foundation in mathematics, so the event does not occur for ontology, except that it is still forced, by the axiom of choice, to think intervention in its being.[49] While events are not entirely of the subject's making, it takes a subject to make a choice over the undecidability of the event, and to declare fidelity to the event.

In *Theory of the Subject*, the proletariat exists wherever there is exclusion from bourgeois politics (or where there is an 'outplace' beyond the bourgeois splace). While Althusser resists any notion of the proletariat as consciousness, Badiou continually refers to the proletariat as a political collective, but one that is excluded from political presentation. The proletariat is also seen by Badiou as 'the political inducer of nonpolitics (of communism)' with the potential to break down the divide between the bourgeoisie and the proletariat, reminding the reader that the real of Marx is that there is no such thing as class relations. By this, Badiou means that there is antagonism between the bourgeoisie and the proletariat, as well as within class—antagonism is prior.[50] So as long as there are relations between classes, relations without antagonism are impossible.

Panagiotis Sotiris has, however, argued that antagonistic relations between classes do not appear to be the basic condition of their existence in Badiou's work, unlike in Althusser's theory of class relations. In other words, class interests may appear after an event, along with an antagonistic relation between classes, but they do not determine an event. Political choices are radically contingent in Badiou's work, and Sotiris cites 'Badiou's refusal to treat socio-economic analysis as an essential prerequisite of political intervention' as an example of the lack of any causal relation between empirical social reality and the event.[51] However, not being an 'essential' prerequisite, and not being able to predict events with certainty, does not mean that the proletariat is irrelevant, and that events are not tied to their predicament. For Badiou, events are unpredictable and aleatory, breaking with relations, but these relations (the relation of the outplace to the splace, for example, or the proletariat that is excluded from political presentation) do exist.

Badiou argues that the bourgeoisie does not make a subject, it makes a place—and in Marxism, the name 'proletariat' is reserved for the political subject of the real of revolutions, which Badiou argues is 'neither more nor less appropriate than the (dubious) word "unconscious"' in psychoanalytic theory.[52] 'Unconscious' and 'proletariat' may be less than ideal words for the political subject, but it recognizes an antagonism with the bourgeoisie that is repressed. As with the impossibility of the sexual *qua* relation in psychoanalysis, the 'real of Marxism' is that there is no such thing as class relations. Despite the aleatory character of the event, the proletariat and even the notion of the vanguard feature in *Theory of the Subject*. The object for Marxism is its subject, the political subject. Militant Marxists are lamp-bearers, inspecting 'the political place in order to discern therein the staking out of antagonism that will relay the promise and organize the future.' Vanguardism has its place, but it does not control force or the event, and the subject is still a rarity: 'Every subject is political. This is why there are few subjects and rarely any politics.' Furthermore, contrary to the view that Badiou disregards socio-economic relations (rather than simply not writing about them much), he aligns himself with the analytical aspects of Marx and the exploiter/exploited dyad, agreeing that the proletarian is 'whoever is separated from them [the bourgeoisie] and has at his disposal only his labour force, which he sells.'[53] The bourgeoisie and the proletariat have definite relations. With the distinction between the bourgeoisie as those who own capital, and the proletariat forced to sell their labour power, we have, as Badiou puts it:

> made a distinction governed by the rule of a structured set, in which 'distinction' is actually only a law of composition. What you have is *Capital*. Here the working class is even the most precious capital, since it is the only active principle of its regeneration. You may do away with the capitalists, all the while maintaining the law of capital...The workers, by contrast, cannot be subtracted from the overall configuration. From this we can infer that their initial distinction from the bourgeoisie, purely from the point of view of exploitation, of the extortion of surplus value, came down to the following statements of inclusion: the bourgeois world splaces class, capital is the place of the proletariat.[54]

Badiou argues that the bourgeoisie has not been a subject for a long time, but rather just makes the place, there being only one place and one subject at a time, 'for any given historicization,' and 'the proletariat exists everywhere where some political outplace is produced.' Drawing on Lacan, Badiou writes that 'The real of Marxism is the revolution. What does the revolution name? The sole historical form of the existence of the relation of class, that is, antagonism, which turns out to be *the destruction of that which did not exist*.'[55] In other words, the destruction of the exploitation whose presence the bourgeoisie denied

4.2.3 Beyond Particularism—Subjects Doing It for Themselves

Given Badiou's criticism of postmodern particularism, one could counter Badiou's position against identity politics with the accusation that these numerous references to the proletariat amount to just that. Alberto Toscano notes that Badiou's move beyond class as sole agent of change was based on a political judgement.[56] Unlike the politics of equivalence we find in Laclau and Mouffe, Badiou's work is concerned with the production of equality that is the generic truth of an event; and Badiou seeks to move beyond a self-referential Marxism and the working class referent, and towards a non-classist and non-systemic understanding of proletarian potential through a politics removed from the state. Badiou opposes the Marxian categories of totality and system, along with any notion of the Whole, and *Being and Event* can be seen as a response to the crisis of Marxist politics that Badiou was grappling with in the 1980s. From the 1980s onwards, Toscano argues, Badiou is committed to 'producing a metapolitical framework for thinking the persistence of communism as a minimal, universalizing hypothesis even in political scenarios where the name "communism" is anathema.'[57]

Badiou has described his work as a 'confrontation' with the dialectic, and as his thought has developed he has moved away from giving destruction a central place (as we have seen with the destruction of the proletariat in *Theory of the Subject*). Marxism in the twentieth century concerned itself with the absolute goal of class warfare, as Badiou sees it. Rather than renounce destruction, Badiou argues that the idea of absolute subjectivity being manifested through a war to end all wars no longer has any political intensity. More importantly, it does not hold in theory, being a 'last figure of the One.'[58] As *Being and Event* makes very clear, this is not possible given that all Ones are operational results in the regime of presentation. Interestingly, Badiou does make a comparison between the final 'triumph of generic humanity' that he sees in the communism of *The Communist Manifesto* with the proletariat as the historical agent of change, and truth as generic.[59] Truth for Badiou is generic, a singularity that is of universal relevance as a subtraction from the regime of presentation or knowledge. Truth may be indiscernible, but being generic it occupies the gaps of available encyclopedias or knowledge.[60] It is in this sense that Badiou's proletariat as subject may force itself after the event as belonging to the indiscernible and generic, rather than being the pre-determined historical agent of change.

So, for Badiou, particularly in his later works, the subject does not always have to be the proletariat. Toscano has provided one explanation for this: Badiou is primarily concerned with politics as the production of sameness or equality, rather than the respect for differences. The truth in Badiou's thought is generic, so the event requires 'an organized subtraction or separation from its manner of structuring and stratifying our experience of the world.'[61] We are not concerned with retaining existing identities and differences, but with the new generic truth with which to identify and free oneself from the splace or situation.

Despite Badiou's anti-essentialist approach and his view that the proletariat is not the sole agent of change, Toscano argues that Badiou equally insists that emancipatory politics cannot bypass workers.[62] Laclau and Mouffe, of course, do not bypass workers, but that is because they look for equivalences across numerous identities, which will inevitably include workers (as well as any number of conservative forces, provided an aspect of their discourse can find an equivalence in other discourses). If Badiou insists that workers be included in emancipatory politics intentionally, this goes some way to answering the claim that Badiou's system is so neutral it risks disregarding moral imperatives in favour of the unpredictable event, as Costas Douzinas has argued.[63]

Toscano argues that Badiou is aware of the potential incompatibility of his thought with the privileging of workers, but is also aware that a certain interpretation of his work could result in a 'pluralist idealism' that we see in post-Marxism. Badiou counters this, Toscano notes, with his 'pre-political situations,' in which the failure of the regime of the One is discernible through the complex of facts and statements arising from workers and various singularities. This is a Kantian refutation of idealism which, while leaving Badiou's system open to subjects arising anywhere, is in Toscano's words 'a merely negative *reductio ad absurdum* of the maximal claim of political contingency' [italics in original].[64] Emancipatory politics must include the oppressed and excluded, but it should also include the site or presentation of them as emergent subjects, or we remain at the level of state representation in which the excluded remain the excluded. For Toscano, this 'refutation of idealism does not simply attack (or literally reduce to absurdity) the 'new social movements' ideology according to which emancipation may take place anywhere, anytime, by anyone,' but 'also undermines any notion that the dominated may be represented in a political programme without partaking of political action themselves.'[65]

It is possible, therefore, to identify which actors and sites are likely to be capable of challenging the regime of representation according to Badiou's system, and this is through direct action rather than through any existing means of representation, such as through NGOs or political parties. This opens the door not only for a recognition of the potential of a non-essentialist proletariat (which, as we have seen, remains a broad social category in analytical terms, as well as performatively with movements such as the '99 per cent'), but also the Marxian (following Balibar) and Badiouan understanding of the proletarian subject as being a performative one taking matters into its own hands. In Marxian circles there often continues to be a distrust, or at least scepticism, regarding the role of NGOs. David Harvey, for example, acknowledges their achievements in the fields of women's rights, health care and the natural environment, but revolutionary change under capitalism by NGOs is impossible, being constrained by the political preferences of their donors. They also tend to have their anti-capitalist alternatives absorbed into the 'dominant capitalist practice,' even encouraging this, as reflected by their prominence in the World Social Forum.[66] NGOs thus become part of the same policy process, weighing up the political, economic and environmental consequences of their preferred policies with government policy advisers before arriving at a negotiating position.

Toscano provides further evidence of the continuing relevance of the worker in Badiou's best known work. The role of the worker and the site of the oppressed in Badiou's thought is not only given a meta-ontological solution in *Being and Event* that harks back to the problem Badiou was grappling with in his turn away from Leninism and his recomposition of Marxian politics in *Can Politics Be Thought?*; but *Being and Event* was also going to include a chapter on the factory worker. 'The Factory as Event-Site' was instead published in *Le Perroquet* in 1987, and continues Badiou's recomposition of Marxism with a dialectic of 'the void, which in the Marxist apparatus is connected to the specificity of the proletarian subject (having nothing to sell but his labour-power, the proletarian is the bearer of a generic capacity), and the site, which Badiou links to Engels's inquiries into the localized conditions according to which exploitation is organized and countered.'[67]

The proletariat involved in any event is both singular in its localized conditions and universal in presenting circumstances that cut across identities. Through Badiou's thought we identify an anti-essentialist proletariat as an agent that must be included in emancipatory politics. This is not to privilege the proletariat as the only actor in emancipatory politics, but acknowledges its universality where other social movements might marginalize the proletariat and the economy as important factors in subjectivation.

Badiou has also argued, in a 2012 lecture published under the title 'The Subject of Change,' that his view of the proletariat is not reductionist. Badiou seems to confuse matters here, having connected the proletariat to the void. Referring to *The Communist Manifesto*, Badiou notes that, on the one hand, Marx's aim of abolishing private property is an abolition of being by the 'active nothingness of the proletariat,' and takes exception to genericity (of the proletariat) being defined by its nothingness. Rather than a negative definition of the generic, Badiou sees the question for politics today as one involving a positive definition of the generic. So, on the other hand, Badiou sees in Marx a positive notion of communism, especially in the importance of internationalism, which demonstrates a will to go beyond the pure nothingness of the proletariat and work with differences in a positive way to identify the generic. Badiou argues that we 'can affirm that genericity is really a complexity of differences rather that the pure absence of being [...

and the] conviction of the new genericity is not reducible to the pure nothingness of a class as in classical dialectics.'[68]

It should be remembered, however, that the void is not the same as nothingness. Indeed, Badiou chose the term 'void' in *Being and Event* because when he uses the term 'nothing' he is really referring to that which is not counted by the One, rather than nothing at all. It still has as much structure and consistency as a pure multiple, but just happens to be excluded from the operation of the One because every presentation unpresents its void.[69] The proletariat as void is therefore not a nothingness, and its genericity is compatible with the positive complexity of differences and affirmative dialectic that Badiou puts forward.

4.2.4 Badiou, Totalization and the Clinamen

We have seen how, for Toscano, Badiou sought to recompose Marxism without categories such as totality, and it is true enough that totality is not a key term in Badiou's thought. Nevertheless, Badiou's description of the clinamen has some obvious similarities to Sartre's dialectic in the sense that a trace is left behind after the event. The notion of totality has been written about at length in post-war Marxian theory, and while it does not form the bulk of Badiou's work, he is clearly continuing this line of thought. This is important because it relates to what happens after an event and, as we shall see in the next chapter, the role of ideology after an event.

Although Badiou moved away from Sartre's thought from 1966, we can see the roots of his system in Sartre, even if Badiou's outplace, splace, void and event are a considerable advance in my view. For example, the 'project' we see in *Being and Nothingness* concerns not my relations with any particular object in the world, but my total being-in-the-world. We have a role in making ourselves, but we appear to be *made* more than we make ourselves, being born into a race, a class, and 'the history of the collectivity' of which we are a part, and we are not free to escape our situation: 'The history of a life, whatever it may be, is the history of a failure.'[70] What seems like Sartre's pathos is the early appearance of the failure and finitude that we see in his later dialectic. 'Totalization' in the *Critique of Dialectical Reason* becomes Sartre's dialectical word for the term 'project' of his earlier works, and as Fredric Jameson has written, totalization is a temporal word that can never lead to closure, but always designates a finitude similar to the 'modish notion of *singularity*' [italics in original].[71]

Sartre's notion of finitude is perhaps better compared to operations of the One in Badiou, rather than the question of the event and one's fidelity towards it. Sartre is also more forthcoming about his theory being an affirmative dialectic. It is within the framework of totalization that the negation of negation becomes affirmation. A break from seriality is, for Sartre, a political subjectivity that breaks with the everyday collective consciousness, and in eventually dissipating still leaves its mark on the totality of social relations (even though this is not marked enough, for Badiou).[72] Hallward seems to see in Badiou's *Logics of Worlds* a loose return to his Sartrean roots, although Hallward suggests—incorrectly in my view—that both this work and *Being and Event* are neither materialist nor dialectical.[73]

Sartre's dialectical reason is an advance on Henri Lefebvre's earlier work on dialectical reason, which he distinguished from Hegel's 'understanding' (a theoretical stage in the history of thought, which Lefebvre believed would unsuccessfully attempt to provide a coherent logic to the universe). For Lefebvre, alienation can be grasped through understanding, but it should be thought dialectically, with the philosopher thinking the 'minutiae of everyday life' in a universal and concrete way and not being detached from everyday life, so that dialectical thought becomes 'dialectical consciousness of life.' Dialectical reason for Lefebvre is a totality that is not immediately graspable, while non-Marxian philosophers act as if totality is already with us as a body of thought.[74] Indeed, Lefebvre disagrees with Lukács's view that totality is the bearer of the principle of revolution in science, since totality as a philosophical category is used by non-Marxists (including to attack Marx). Lefebvre subordinated the category of totality to 'dialectical negation' to attain, in his view, a totality that applies more to everyday life than to knowledge or society in general (with which non-Marxists preoccupy themselves).[75]

Rather than grasp totality as one would grasp an object (as non-Marxists would in Lefebvre's view), Sartre and Badiou are interested in the way in which an event impacts on the totality, leaving a trace that is difficult to discern. Although Badiou does not discuss totality as such to the extent Sartre did, his more recent work on how things appear in a world suggests ways in which we may grasp the consequences of an event. Badiou acknowledges the similarities with Sartre, as well as Heidegger, in arguing that 'to exist' must be relative to a world. We have seen this already with the earlier concept of splace, but in *Logics of Worlds* Badiou is much clearer that existence is a transcendental degree indicating the intensity of appearance in a determinate world of a multiple-being. If an x in a world has the maximum value in the transcendental, it exists absolutely in that world, while an x with the minimal value in the transcendental *inexists* absolutely, with degrees of appearance between these absolutes.[76] Where the event is concerned, a maximal existence for the duration of its appearance grants the site the power of a singularity. However, the force of a singularity rests not only in making itself exist maximally, but in making its *consequences* exist maximally.[77]

So both Badiou and Sartre view existence in relation to a world, yet Sartre's *Critique of Dialectical Reason* appears to focus on the more bread-and-butter concerns of Marxian thought. Scarcity and matter are key terms for Sartre in his *Critique*. Scarcity is described by Sartre as a lived relation of a practical multiplicity to surrounding materiality within that multiplicity itself, and is the basis for the possibility of human history, 'a fundamental relation of *our* History and a contingent determination of our univocal relation to materiality.' In other words, we are all shaped by our relation to scarcity of matter (such as material goods).

Scarcity, which we appear to produce more of and makes History possible (although other factors are necessary to produce History) sits alongside his other concepts of praxis, the practico-inert and the series. Sartre's concept of the series '*is a mode of being for individuals both in relation to one another and in relation to their common being* and this mode of being transforms all their structures' [italics in original]. '*The Other*' is a being common to all: 'every Other is both Other than himself and Other than Others, in so far as their relations constitute both him and Others in accordance with an objective, practical, inert rule of alterity.' In other words, unity is always elsewhere in the series, always in the Other for everyone. It is a genuine unity for Sartre, but 'the unity of a flight,' a totalized series of 'not-beings,' everyone causing the other to become incapable of acting on him or her directly, unlike what we would see in a Sartrean event. This follows Sartre's elaboration of the practico-inert, the praxis (or instrumental activity) inscribed in matter, instruments or machines and so on by past labour, and the order placed on matter by past labour orders humans—man is dominated by worked matter, and is the product of his product.[78]

Sartre is on more familiar Marxian territory here in squaring his existentialist philosophy with Marxism:

> Man makes History; this means that he objectifies himself in it and is alienated in it. In this sense History, which is the proper work of all

activity and of all men, appears to men as a foreign force exactly insofar as they do not recognize the meaning of their enterprise (even when locally successful) in the total, objective result.[79]

Circularity is part of the process of totalization, with the practico-inert that is the common work of the series becoming constituted and later worked on by the fused group which breaks with the series to challenge the practico-inert; but this freedom will come to disappear as inertia creeps into the group and praxis dissolves into seriality.[80] This form of finitude has a pivotal role in Sartre's totalization, with death as part of the human condition, a universal presence under which we make '*a history of mortal organisms.*' This universal presence, Sartre contends, makes individuals produce the death for others that they wish to avoid themselves, and is connected to praxis dissolving into seriality. Every group must necessarily die in the course of its own action, 'to vacate the premises—the theatre—of its functions *before* it has completed its role.' Death is History in transcendence, a finitude that is universal as groups are formed, die, and History made.[81] The event will have happened though, and found its way into the field of knowledge, even if this is not always easy to grasp.

We can see how this reminds us of Badiou's clinamen and event. Badiou's singular act in which 'subjectivation is immortal, and makes Man'[82] refers more to the finitude of the One and the lasting force of the event through fidelity, rather than an absolute dismissal of finitude. Indeed, Nina Power notes how despite the finite moment of each generic procedure in Badiou, like 'Sartre's universalising example of the group-in-fusion storming the Bastille, there is an atemporal, ahistorical structure to Badiou's political subject.'[83] The event for Badiou is of a different register to operations of the One, since the event does not exist for ontology. Operations of the One remain temporary, while the task for those claiming fidelity to an event is to ensure the event leaves a trace.

Žižek describes the post-eventual inscription in Kantian, rather than Sartrean, terms. For Žižek, the idea of communism for Badiou 'schematizes the Real of the political Event, providing it with a narrative coating and thereby making it a part of our experience of historical reality—another indication of Badiou's hidden Kantianism.' The event becomes intelligible through communism as a transcendental illusion that gives the sense that the event is part of social reality, or ideology. What is more interesting is Žižek's view that, in claiming that any history that goes beyond a particular world or situation is an ideological fiction, Badiou is completely renouncing Marxist historical materialism. Just as some historical materialists renounced dialectical materialism as a general ontology, Badiou aims for a dialectical materialism without historical materialism.[84] Žižek sees this as a dismissal of political economy. Political economy can give a sense of continuity between events, but Badiou does not want to see historicizations where there are none, or assume that political economy can provide a link between events unless that is really the case.

Despite barely mentioning capitalism by name in the two volumes of his *Critique*, humanity's relationship with matter is the continuous factor throughout history, according to Sartre. Badiou, on the other hand, while being open to any number of evental sites and disavowing a continuous interpretation of history, focuses on exploitation in the here and now, or exploitation under capitalism as a likely source of exclusion. As Nick Hewlett has explained, Badiou's theory of the Two demonstrates that he cannot explain history in continuous or evolutionary terms; instead he is a 'discontinuous philosopher.'[85] The proletariat and the site of their exploitation may be the most likely place an event will occur, but Badiou does not select subjects. Instead, he sees the philosopher's task as working with truths and events. Unlike those who focus on 'particularisms,' Badiou does not seek to create hegemonic projects before an event, but to recognize the generic and the struggle for equality where it occurs. In Marxian terms, perhaps Badiou is closer to Moishe Postone, for whom Marx's analysis does not point towards the self-realization of the proletariat as the true subject of history, but towards emancipation through the abolition of the proletariat and the labour it performs.[86]

Nina Power has noted how the 'collective' in the works of Sartre and Badiou has a different relation to the event. In Sartre's work it comes before the event to describe seriality rather than the fused group, unlike Badiou's collective, which arrives after the event. It is well known that Sartre was attempting to give his philosophy a more Marxian tone with his *Critique*, and this is a further difference that Power identifies. Sartre was concerned with explaining how the event must give way to terror and then seriality, and in this sense his work describes the 'communist' project under Stalinism. Badiou, on the other hand, wants to present the subject after the event to preserve its relevance. Power goes on to argue that Badiou's subject moves beyond the proletariat after *Theory of the Subject*, and is even removed from his later works (which we have seen is not really the case) in favour of a generic humanity. Furthermore, the collective, in both Sartre and Badiou's thought, is not necessarily pre-determined. It is 'not "Man" per se, with its biologistic and sexist implications, as the collective contains within it an active subjective element that counters any naturalistic definition.'[87]

Badiou does not identify the specific subject who precedes the event; the event constitutes the subject who chooses to declare his/her fidelity to it. Subjects, however, have a role after the event, and it is not just a case of letting the clinamen be. This role brings with it the problem of ideology, and whether subjects can avoid turning towards ideology when defending the consequences of an event.

One explanation for Badiou's distance from the concept of totality is perhaps explained by his Althusserian background. We have seen how Rancière views Althusser's anti-historicist totality as a reaction against the bad totality of 'leftism' and the denial of the autonomy of philosophy.[88] Philosophy, for Badiou, works with truths, and we know from Badiou's late Althusserian phase that it is distinct from ideology in not seeking to dispense with any lack by creating totalizing concepts such as 'God.' Badiou shares with Althusser a disdain for speculative leftism, which as Bosteels has put it, 'comes to represent an uncompromising purification of the notion of communism, not so much as the abolition but rather as the complete *tabula rasa* of the present state of things, including all classes, parties, and ideological apparatuses of the State.'[89] Badiou opposes any fixed idea of communism, as well as opposing any teleological idea of history.

Badiou has argued that the statement 'history does not exist' is crucial for Marxism, there being 'historicizations' but no pre-determined history.[90] In other words, there are what become historical periods, but no historicism, an approach similar to Althusser's. A historicization in this sense is similar to the One in *Being and Event*—the One, as with historicizations of particular periods, is an operation.[91] History does not exist for Badiou in the way it does for Sartre, but it consists of various events that are historicized, which goes someway to meeting Sartre's notion of totalization without being continuous. We could even say that Badiou puts forward a system of non-continuous totalization. We can also choose to challenge historical trends (and declare our fidelity to events), and Hallward has placed Badiou in a long line of thinkers (including Lenin and Lukács) who claim that access to the truth is achieved by going against the grain and the current of history.[92]

We have seen how Badiou moved to favouring a politics without a party, and his notion of communism continues to be opposed to the party and the state form of communism. Incidentally, Sartre saw the party as necessary in relation to the mass, since the mass, by itself, cannot create spontaneity. Instead, the mass remains serialized.

However, the party that brings the fused group into being out of the mass becomes reactionary and serialized once it is institutionalized, and then lags behind the fused group it brought into being.[93] For Badiou, the idea of communism has become associated over the last few decades with totalitarian states or totally forgotten, but he sees this reactionary period coming to an end.[94] We know that communism without a party is consistent, in the end, with *The Communist Manifesto*, and even before Badiou turned towards a politics without a party he was opposed to bureaucratic forms of organization. Although Sartre does not put it in quite these terms, his idea of the party is of a revolutionary, not a bureaucratic, one. If Lenin were around at the time, perhaps he would call Badiou a leftist for avoiding workers' bureaucracies, trade unions and elections during his time with the UCFML. Instead, Badiou favoured the Maoist view that political work 'was defined as work in factories, housing estates, hostels,' and 'was always a matter of setting up political organizations in the midst of people's actual life.'[95]

Despite the aleatory nature of the event, we have seen how Badiou has been committed to political causes, and to the proletariat within his theoretical work. We saw how Sotiris has described Badiou's thought as detached to an extent from social reality. However, the detachment of the subject from social relations in Badiou's event is not absolute, but a clear distinction between Badiou's dialectic and the more poststructuralist variety. In response to Hallward's interpretation that the process of subtraction in Badiou's thought leaves little room for a dialectic with social and historical factors, Badiou emphasizes the difference between his notion of the event and subtraction, and the view of Foucault, and more recently Negri, that power should be challenged on its own terrain, and that resistance and power are mutually constitutive.[96]

For Negri, modern political philosophy, such as that of Hobbes, is born from fear: 'Modernity is... the negation of any possibility that the multitude may express itself as subjectivity,' as Negri puts it in *Insurgencies*. No space is given to constituent power in modern political theory where Negri is concerned. Constituent power is seen as extraordinary where it presents itself, as an exteriority where it imposes itself (rather than being immanent), and 'when it triumphs over every inhibition, exclusion, or repression, it must be neutralized in the "Thermidor".'[97] In other words, modern political theory, for Negri, attempts to constitute constituent power where this is necessary, with the result that it loses the revolutionary intention of the multitude. Hardt and Negri see the multitude as being immanent within Empire, both constituting its ontological substance and acting as a point of resistance within. Empire provides the multitude with the conditions for its emancipation, according to Hardt and Negri: 'When the new disciplinary regime constructs the tendency toward a global market of labour power, it constructs also the possibility of its antithesis. It constructs the desire to escape the disciplinary regime and tendentially an undisciplined multitude of workers who want to be free.'[98]

For Badiou, 'multitudes' is 'only a pedantic word for mass movements,' and petit-bourgeois movements at that. He sees this as a 'historicism painted in fashionable hues,' and a politics of the One. Revolt is merely the manifestation of an immanent and constituent power against constituted power. Badiou's dialectic, on the other hand, opposes the One with a Two. However, although Badiou's event is one of subtraction, to say that it is aleatory and separated from social reality is to say that it is not linked essentially with social reality or history. There is a dialectic, but it is not essentialist. Furthermore, in Badiou's political activism with the *sans papiers*, he acknowledges that their struggle must face social reality, or government policy. Where the event is concerned, although we start with the affirmation of a principle or an abstraction (which Badiou sees as the foundation of all thought), he argues that the procedures of truth should not be reduced to abstraction. For Badiou, 'the whole question is to know how and at what moment the axiom[atic proposition] becomes the directive of the situation.'[99] An event, as a subtraction, has a non-essentialist relation with its circumstances, subtracting itself and then being imposed on the situation. To do as Foucault and Negri do, Badiou argues, is to enter into politics through thinking the forms of power that are already present, leaving the state intact.[100]

It is necessary to break with the state on one's own terms, and instead of one event that replaces the totality of capitalism with a new totality, Badiou allows for numerous events, such as the Paris Commune of 1871. That the Commune was short-lived does not make it any less an event. For Badiou, the 'communist Idea is what constitutes the becoming-political Subject of the individual as also and at the same time his or her projection into History,' bearing in mind Badiou's understanding of history.[101] The indiscernible multiple, or truth, that Badiou describes does not deliver any meaning (the void, or the proper name of being, is in-human and a-subjective), but there is a procedure whereby the subject effectuates a post-evental truth. The subject believes there is a truth, and as an operator of fidelity to this truth, sets about discerning connections and disconnections of this truth between multiples of the situation and the name of the event.[102]

In the Paris Commune the communards developed the commune on their own terms, as an operation of a One. However, if this is an attempted totality, practice showed how there was a One/Ones beyond this that it would have to contend with—no totality is absolute. As Badiou says, 'it is of the essence of the world not to be the totality of existence, and to endure the existence of an infinity of other worlds outside of itself.'[103] We know that all Ones are temporary operations that cannot claim permanent authority, yet they are also inevitable. In the present circumstances the proletariat occupies a site where events may well occur. It is a proletariat defined both analytically and through its own actions, performatively, in agreement with Marx and manifested recently through the 99 per cent. This does not exclude other evental sites, and Badiou is not privileging the proletariat as an essentialist agent. Instead, an evental site is likely to be where there is an excess of inclusion over belonging, and it is for the post-evental subject to declare fidelity to the event and give it meaning. Badiou may oppose absolute commencements of permanent Ones, but he could remain indifferent to those claiming to do this. After all, Ones are temporary, no matter what those who serve them may think. Badiou's communism is a continuous challenge to the state, and recognizes the challenge Marx posed when he saw communism as both impossible, but having to remain possible all the same if the state (and capitalism) is to be challenged. As Badiou put it in *Theory of the Subject*, 'those who imagine that anything whatsoever of Marxism can subsist if one pretends to do without the impossible revolution are just good for the absolving talent quest of academia.'[104]

5

Ideology and Insurrection: 'Saint Badiou,' Postanarchism, and Servitude

Having made a case for a selective reading of Marx as an alternative to the poststructuralist anarchist critique of reductionism and essentialism, and using Badiou's materialist dialectic and his treatment of the proletariat to draw comparisons between elements of Marxian theory and postanarchism, I will now consider the role of ideology in postanarchism and Badiou's works, and how this relates to Marxian theory. Here the question of collective action becomes important, as do the factors which otherwise inhibit it.

For Badiou, it is not that the functioning of ideology is hidden from view for those who care to look, but that the proletariat or anyone else whose subjectivity the bourgeoisie considers a threat is not represented within the dominant system of ideas, or at least not to the extent that it presents a threat. Badiou has developed a theory of ideology without a notion of false consciousness as false ideas, but rather false representation of ideas as facts by the bourgeoisie, in a post-Althusserian innovation that attempts, as he put it in *Of Ideology*, to understand ideology as a process, as indeed Marx did.[1] Ideology is not immediately intelligible for Badiou, but for those who care to look, ideology can be seen for what it is. This does not mean that ideology is easily critiqued, and an event and collective political action does much to help this endeavour. This may mean that an effective challenge to ideology is rare, but for both Badiou and Newman, we cannot simply think or talk our way out of ideology as Habermas might imagine. To challenge ideology, or what we might call the dictatorship of the bourgeoisie or bourgeois democracy, it remains vital to challenge presentation through collective political action because ideology is so closely linked with the power of the state, including the 'democratic' structures and practices it uses to legitimize itself.

Postanarchism can find common cause with Badiou here in proposing a theory of ideology which relies neither on Althusserian false consciousness, nor the remnants of the human nature found in classical and even more recent anarchism. While Badiou's theory shares some traits with postanarchist thought on ideology, his theory of presentation seeks to explain how people come to obey, without reference to the unconscious (an ontological rather than phenomenological approach). The proletariat may be seen as likely subjects, but Badiou steers clear of placing hope in the 'general intellect' or in new groups such as the cognitive worker, which some theorists, including Antonio Negri, have placed their hope in.[2]

In Badiou's materialist approach, the state and states are challenged after the event and through whichever subjects declare fidelity to it—it is as if there is no such thing as a communist (or, for that matter, an anarchist) until the event. Yet ideology abhors a vacuum, and if subjects do not leave a trace of the event on presentation, capitalist values will leave their mark instead. Badiou (and postanarchism) may be seen to overlook the importance of political economy and the concept of value in their critiques of capitalism (a charge we will see Slavoj Žižek make against Badiou), but the priority afforded to extra-parliamentary political action by both remains perhaps the most effective means to challenge capitalism. There remains, however, a challenge in how to take on ideology at its own game. Confidence in an approximate truth may be a necessity, post-event, even if it means an element of 'impurity' tarnishes the event as those defending its consequences resort to tactics (or even strategies) resembling ideology. Positive post-event tactics aside, what unites Badiou and Newman is a negative or subtractive approach to ideology, pointing out its lack and illegitimacy.

5.1 In Defence of the Concept of Ideology

In the first chapter I maintained, in agreement with Ellen Meiksins Wood, that in critiquing an essentialist notion of the proletariat, post-Marxists have actually marginalized the proletariat, despite the analytical evidence that it continues to exist and the fact that it continues to make its presence known through various protests across the globe, even if those involved do not all call themselves the 'proletariat.' Indeed, those influenced by poststructuralist thought sometimes seem to not only have dismissed the proletariat, but also the concept of ideology. The latter phenomenon, as Newman notes, is down to a mistrust of those who claim to know the true interests of humanity outside of the obfuscating effects of ideology, or the notion in Marx that in capitalist societies the people 'do not know it, but they are doing it.' However, by contrast, Newman retains a certain notion of ideology.[3]

This is important, for if we bypass ideology we bypass a key concept for understanding why people obey, and why they revolt. It is for this reason that Newman's work will be the focus of this chapter where postanarchist theory is concerned.

It is fitting, then, that in comparing the approaches of postanarchism and of Badiou towards ideology, we remind ourselves of that old rivalry between Marx and Engels, and 'Saint Max' Stirner. Indeed, Badiou reminded us of this rivalry himself in 1975 when he parodied these adversaries in referring to 'saint Gilles, saint Félix, [and] saint Jean-François [Lyotard]' in *Théorie de la Contradiction*.[4] Stirner is an important thinker for Newman, and having been written off by Marx and Engels as 'Saint Max' for his supposed idealism and neglect of political economy and the material basis of social relations, Žižek almost makes the same critique of 'saint Badiou' (as he might call him), arguing that Badiou dismisses political economy as a separate sphere of positive social relations which cannot possibly become the site of an event.[5]

So, we find again that postanarchism and Badiou have more in common than we thought (including, sometimes incorrectly, in the eyes of their peers), and in comparing the two we revive aspects of Marxian thought, especially the proletariat and the materialist dialectic. While I have described Badiou's system as operational and neutral and drawn parallels with postanarchist thought insofar as all Ones and states are processes and temporary in nature, his approach to ideology also shares some common ground with that taken by Newman, and helps reinvigorate both anarchist and Marxian approaches to ideology while raising important questions.

5.2 Badiou, Postanarchism and Capitalism

5.2.1 Beyond Althusserian Interpellation

While it would be needlessly provocative to refer continuously to 'saint Badiou,' the charge has nevertheless been made that Badiou is not interested in political economy. However, if Badiou does not care for political economy, it is not in the sense that he imagines the economy has no impact on presentation and ideology. I would argue that this perception arises due to the lack of effort Badiou expends on describing the role of capitalist *value* and its impact on ideology, even though he is not reticent in his critique of capitalism. For the most part, Badiou gives us a theory of presentation and the subject through which we can think for ourselves about how the subject might relate to the state and capitalism. The problem is that the latter disperses power and presentation more widely than does the state, understood in the traditional sense. Of course, there are other kinds of state for Badiou, or states within states, as we saw in chapter 3, but capital often seems to disregard the regime of presentation. This, however, is an acknowledgement that capitalism cannot simply be challenged through the state or the regime of presentation, but that does not mean that capital does not appear in a world (or state) and cannot be challenged by a subject. Capital usually uses the state to further its cause where convenient, and this is something of which both Badiou and Newman are aware. In Badiou's 1976 essay *Of Ideology* he explicitly links ideology to the regime of presentation that he would set out much more systematically in *Being and Event* and *Logics of Worlds*. Badiou sets himself apart from the notion of false consciousness we find in much of Marxian theory, as well as Althusser's dialectical materialism. He considered that 'every layer of gloss on ideology as 'imaginary representation,' every discourse aiming to tie Marxism to the theory of the unconscious by way of ideological phantasmatics... or the theory of the subject, ends up stubbornly obfuscating the question.' Referring to Marx and Engels's *The German Ideology*, Badiou takes a thinly veiled swipe at Althusser when he calls for an end to the theory of ideology as 'imaginary representation and interpellation of individuals as subjects.' The idea that the dominant ideas are the expression of the dominant material relationships is interpreted by Badiou as the *reflection* of a class's practices of domination, for it '*expresses* those "material relationships"; it is not a specific *function*, operating in the element of the unconscious.' Exploiters use philosophy to legitimize their class interests behind the veil of universality. However, ideology can only be understood by 'including in this comprehension the movement by which it appears in its historical division, and which is the insurrectionary movement of the ideological struggle.' There exists, in practice, that which cannot be represented in the 'dominant ideology,' or that which is '*irrepresentable*' (such as the proletariat), so in this sense ideology is intelligible as representation.[6]

So rather than rely on any psychoanalytic theory to explain ideology, Badiou's approach is almost purely ontological, without the consideration given to consciousness or language which we would find in a phenomenological approach. Change is only feasible (or even desirable) when conditions are suitable and there is an event. While Badiou came

IDEOLOGY & INSURRECTION   113

to be influenced heavily by Lacan and his use of the concept of the real, there is no reliance on psychoanalysis to explain why individuals obey.

However, just as psychoanalysis shaped Althusser's theory of ideology, Badiou's post-Althusserian thought was still heavily influenced by Lacan, or at least by a certain reading of Lacan. Althusser's take on psychoanalysis, in his essay *Freud and Lacan*, reminds us of the way in which Althusser returned to Marx to develop the mature Marx, without the humanism that came before the epistemological break of *The German Ideology*. Just as Marx was to use Hegelian concepts at times, Althusser argued that Freud was forced to develop his discovery using existing concepts. Making his case in Kantian terms, Althusser argued that Freud had to use imported concepts, with 'no legal inheritance behind him,' except for philosophical concepts such as consciousness and unconsciousness. In developing his new science, Freud produced his own concepts, but under the protection of existing ones 'from within the horizons of the ideological world in which these concepts swam.'[7] Lacan, then, seems to be to Freud what Althusser was to Marx. For Althusser, Lacan does not return to Freud because his original works are pure, but because there is much impurity in the development of this science. The aim of Lacan was to return to the mature Freud to distinguish the science of psychoanalysis from those youthful concepts in Freud that muddy the waters.[8]

This was, perhaps, Althusser's way of saying that Freud had failed to see the connection between consciousness and ideology, given that he does not take a materialist approach. For Warren Montag, all of Althusser's work on Freud and Lacan had an 'overwhelmingly negative objective' through which his misgivings on the concept of the unconscious would show. Nevertheless, Lacan, Montag argues, 'seemed to suggest [for Althusser] ways of refusing ideologies of consciousness and subjectivity without denying the objective existence of the phenomena to which they referred.' Instead of simply arguing that the object analysed through psychoanalysis could be explained through its underlying materiality, as Marxian critiques might, Althusser aimed to 'theorize the materiality of what was once thought to be the domain of subjectivity and interiority.'[9]

The subject is a constitutive part of ideology for Althusser, determined in the last instance by the economy (or rather, 'determinant instances,' as discussed in the first chapter). This is succinctly explained in *On the Reproduction of Capitalism* with reference to his concepts of interpellation and hailing. For Althusser, '*all ideology hails or interpellates concrete individuals as concrete subjects*, through the functioning of the category of the subject' [italics in the original].¹⁰ Althusser distinguishes between individuals and subjects through what he calls a commonplace example of hailing, which is that of the police officer hailing 'Hey, you there!' It is when the individual turns around that he becomes a subject, realizing it is he who is being addressed, but the subject remains within ideology. Indeed, Althusser is keen to stress that those of us who think we are outside of ideology are still within it. Ideology is quite modest—'Ideology never says "I am ideological".'¹¹

I discussed Badiou's development from Sartrean to Althusserian to post-Althusserian positions in the second chapter. The obvious difference between Althusser and Badiou when it comes to ideology is that, for Badiou at least, the subject *can* escape ideology. Individuals live under a regime of presentation or ideology, but the subject is partly freed from this, at least in the sense that they declare fidelity to an event that would otherwise have been excluded from the regime of presentation. We have seen how the event leaves a trace in the field of knowledge, or the regime of presentation, and the subject at least declares fidelity to this event even if he or she might not exist to a high degree in the sphere of political representation or the state. Something resembling an advance on Althusser's definition of 'situation' continues in Badiou's work. Althusser's situation is 'a formation of the ideological,' in which experience is informed by structure. As if to put psychoanalysis in its place, Althusser states in *The Humanist Controversy*:

> When someone 'tells the story of his life,' describes his feelings in a 'situation he has experienced,' recounts a dream, and so on, his discourse is informed by ideological discourse, by the 'I' who speaks in the first person and by the subject before whom he speaks, the Judge is the authenticity of his discourse, his analysis, his sincerity, and so forth.¹²

Althusser thereby dispenses with consciousness, and 'literally objectifies' representation, as Montag puts it.¹³ Yet even though Althusser makes the case for ideology over consciousness, all of his work is devoted in this way to a consideration of why it is people obey. Badiou's materialist dialectic has an outside to ideology, to an extent, but this is discerned by observing regimes of presentation and contradictions within these, as we have seen. Events are not in the hands of individuals or subjects (there is no hero of the event), but Badiou leaves it to the subject to manage their relation to the event. The *sans papiers* will have a place within presentation for Badiou, being included but not fully belonging, but their legal position in society does not make them subjects in the way this would for Althusser. While Badiou is no psychoanalyst, he considered Lacan a contemporary who saw the necessity of saving the category of the subject, while also renouncing the subject as the centre of all experience. He was an antihumanist, without discarding the category of subject. Having left Sartre behind, Badiou recalls that 'in the 1960s and 1970s, Lacan allowed me to align myself with the theoretical anti-humanism of the period while remaining faithful to my Sartrean youth and to the notion of the subject.'[14]

5.2.2 Badiou and the Problem of Capitalist Presentation

While Žižek argues that Badiou is dismissive of political economy, this is not really the case, even when it comes to ideology as an expression of the economy. Furthermore, although capitalist presentation comes with its own set of problems for Badiou (as does capitalist power for Newman), this does not mean that Badiou's communism is defeated by capitalism. It may mean, however, that Badiou's theory of fidelity to an event may eventually need to rely on a presentation that itself may be called ideology, but that would be an acknowledgement of ideology as the logic of appearance, or as the way things are. It does not mean the event to which fidelity is declared did not disrupt the regime of presentation and ideology. The event lives on through such fidelity, even if ideology is otherwise all-pervasive.

Badiou argues that 'number' dominates all manner of fields, including the economy and ideology. It also dominates the political through opinion polls and polling booths, 'science' and cultural representations. The ideology of 'modern parliamentary democracies,' he argues, is not 'humanism, law, or the subject,' but 'number, the countable, countability,' with citizens 'expected to be cognisant of foreign trade figures, of the flexibility of the exchange rate, of fluctuations in stock prices.' These figures, Badiou argues, 'are presented as the real to which other figures refer: governmental figures, votes and opinion polls.' This is how ideology appears to Badiou writing in 1990's *Number and Numbers*, maintaining the position he took in 1976's *Of Ideology*. Badiou distinguishes between 'Number' and 'number,' with Number having access to pure multiplicity and being. It is not constructed, nor is it merely an operation, although that may follow later. Number is 'not itself an operational concept, it is a particular figure of the pure multiple, which can be thought in a structural and immanent fashion.'[15] While there may be a truth of Number, or Number may designate something as being, number has no such role, and is merely an operation that does not think Number. In short, Number is mathematical in the sense that

Badiou understands this (and which we have seen in earlier chapters), while number is not.

Perhaps the best way to compare Number and number is with reference to the simplicity of capitalist value, in which we find number but no deeper consideration of what this means for being. It is non-eventual. As Badiou explains, under our present situation, which is that of the law of capital, capital ensures the count-for-one for everything that is presented in the situation. However, the reign of number under capital is an 'unthought slavery of numericality itself,' even proscribing any thought of Number. It 'cannot make any claim to truth: neither to a truth of Number, nor to a truth which would underlie that which Number designates as form of being.'[16] In other words, we are told to accept capitalist values, without being able to think what these values mean on an ontological level.

As we know from *Being and Event*, which was discussed in chapter 3, for being, the event is not. We see this reiterated with reference to Number. A truth can depend on neither being, nor capital. It does not signal itself through Number, although 'the event is not non-being, however much it exceeds the resources of situation-being.' Instead, Badiou describes the event as 'of the order of trans-being: at once 'held' within the principle of being (an event, like everything else that is, is a multiple) and in rupture with this principle (the event does not fall under the law of the count of the situation, so that, not being counted, it does not consist).'[17] As we saw in chapter 3, self-belonging is prohibited by the axiom of foundation, so the event is not recognized ontologically, except that by declaring that an event belongs to a situation, the situation is forced to acknowledge its own void and the non-being of an existence. Deciding that an event belongs to a situation is a wager, given its undecidability. So the event is not signalled through Number because the event is trans-being (or does not exist for being), but nor is it signalled through capital and number, because that would mean it is part of the contemporary situation, and already present. Summing up, Badiou writes:

> To think Number, as we have tried to do, restores us, either through mathematics, which is the history of eternity, or through some faithful and restrained scrutiny of what is happening, to a supernumerary hazard from which a truth originates, always heterogeneous to Capital, and therefore to the slavery of the numerical.[18]

Badiou does, therefore, consider political economy in the sense that he considers capitalist numericality and value, and as presentation or ideology: it can be questioned and critiqued. We can at least think beyond ideology in a way that Badiou thought Althusser had made impossible. To challenge ideology effectively nevertheless requires an event and collective political action, leaving a trace of the event in the field of presentation, or ideology, or knowledge. Žižek's claim that Badiou treats capital as a site of positive relations where no event can take place does not mean that Badiou dismisses the role of political economy.

I have maintained that Badiou's system is a neutral one insofar as it is concerned with operations of the One and multiplicity, yet suited, like postanarchism, to critiquing power when it is dispersed, as it is under capitalism. For Badiou, capitalism follows certain laws and logics (and the state imposes its own laws onto capitalism for various reasons and to varying degrees, and vice versa), and it usually has less regard to the sanctity that humans may place on certain relations. Badiou's discussion of capital in his *Manifesto for Philosophy* draws on its un-binding of relationships. In his discussion on nihilism, which he describes as the 'rupture of the traditional figure of the bond, un-binding as a form of being of all that pretends to be of the bond,' Badiou argues that our time 'indubitably sustains itself with a kind of generalized atomism because no symbolic sanction of the bond is capable of resisting the abstract potency of Capital,' drawing comparison with *The Communist Manifesto* and the passage on how the 'bourgeoisie ... has pitilessly torn asunder the motley feudal bonds that unite man to his 'natural superiors,' and has left remaining no other bonds between man and man than naked self-interest, callous "cash payments".'[19]

Alberto Toscano has written that capital is, for Badiou, not the 'irruption' of the multiple as such, since while capital destroys bonds, it reproduces figures of the bond, supplying it with materials for surplus. In other words, territorialization of production, of exploitable sources of surplus value, are necessary for capital to accumulate. Capital, Toscano argues, is 'a pure operation and not a truth procedure'; a singularity with no regard for singularity as such (drawing on Badiou here). Its ontological status is not the same as that of the state, in Badiou's sense of the state, being the relationship of a parasite (capital) to the host (the state). Rather than capital 'itself' representing something or someone, it destroys bonds in order to create surplus value and couples with representations that enable it to produce an excess, an excess of representation. However, capital is not technically, Toscano writes, an 'excrescence' (represented but not presented), since although it breaks bonds and counts in a way that the representations of the state cannot compete with, it disregards the 'stable figure or symbol of the count.' Capital here is not an event for Toscano, concerned as it is with representation rather than presentation. If the state and capital are not isomorphic, with comparable structures that can be mapped across to each other, we should be able to assess how a counter- or extra-state politics differs from anti-capitalist politics from the point of view of the political subject of an event, concluding that the singularity (which is not really a singularity for Badiou) of capital, or the 'anti-singular (or indifferent) singularity of Capital,' should be countered by diverting politics away from a demand for representation and towards the idea that there is no pre-existing subject that 'anticipates the invention of egalitarian political modes that might be capable of forcing the dysfunction of the transcendental rule of surplus value.'[20] In other words, capitalist (and other) values are challenged through new subjects loyal to an event, and not through business as usual and representation by the state or states. Representation may come, but the evental presentation comes first.

The role of representation remains an area of contention in Badiou's work. For example, Toscano notes how after *Of Ideology* there is a move from antagonism between the proletariat and the state, towards subtraction. With 1985's *Can Politics Be Thought?*, there is a break with 'the very idea of a dialectical transitivity between the politics of non-domination and the system of representation,' so that the 'very place of the Two in political subjectivity' is 'no longer to be configured as destructive antagonism but rather as a discontinuous and event-bound subtraction.'[21] Instead of an ongoing antagonism between the unrepresented and the order of representation, we have already seen how Badiou's event has since evolved into one of subtraction. The event is not the continuous struggle between the unrepresented and representation, but rather the (exceptional) effective subtraction and separation that brings the unrepresentable to the attention of the regime of presentation, with a wager to name this undecidable by those pledging fidelity to the event. What is interesting is that Toscano has more recently noted the problem of representation remains in Badiou's thought, asking whether for Badiou's idea of communism there is a need for ideology or representation to mobilize those loyal to the consequences of an event. If the consequences of an event are to survive, are we not 'consequently obliged to erect a kind of fiction of consistency?'[22]

We see how Badiou has moved from the position in *Of Ideology* whereby the dominant ideology includes an 'irrepresentable' practice,[23] to one where ideology is challenged from the outplace, to an inexistent in the regime of presentation that emerges through the event. It is a challenge to ideology by a truth, or that which is not ideological and did not belong to a situation, even if it was included in the count. However, if we are considering what happens after the event with those who are loyal to its consequences, they perhaps need to rely on ideology and their own representation as things develop, despite having their origins in a truth. I would argue that there is no need to worry about this too much when it comes to philosophy, which has done its job in identifying a truth. Political strategy can then be left to those claiming fidelity to the consequences of the event.

Badiou has hinted at the danger in doing this, however, given that defending the purity of an event may be fraught with difficulties and descend into a violent ideological struggle. In discussing his movement from destruction to subtraction between *Theory of the Subject* and *Being and Event*, as we saw in the last chapter, Badiou has described the passion for the real that was present last century. The obsession with isolating the identity of the real, or differentiating between the real and the semblance of the real, had led to purging within the Communist party in the Soviet Union. As he puts it, 'The passion for the real is also, of necessity, suspicion. Nothing can attest that the real is the real, nothing but the system of fictions wherein it plays the role of the real.' Unlike the destructive approach that seeks to purify the real, the subtractive one understands that the gap itself is real.[24] Like Claude Lefort's 'empty place of power' that Newman develops, the important point is to recognize this empty place where power and identity is partially fixed, with no one able to fill this place absolutely.

5.2.3 Postanarchist Ideology and Ontology

The destruction Badiou sees in the passion for the real, and the importance instead of acknowledging that the gap in presentation is real and cannot be closed, reminds us that there is no absolute commencement for Badiou. There is never a permanent one, and the left should not aim at such an absolute state.[25] Although I maintain that the ontological aspect of Badiou's theory is neutral because it 'simply' concerns itself with operations of the One, and he does not predict an end to capitalism or a withering away of the state (or the withering away of the law and commodity exchange, as Althusser put it),[26] the ontological impossibility of the absolute end of all states hints at an acceptance of a dictatorship of the bourgeoisie.

While there will always be other Ones to contend with, and all of these are temporary, it is the bourgeoisie that currently makes a place rather than a subject. Badiou does not say whether or not capital and the bourgeoisie are here to stay, but there will always be dominant Ones or states against which the communist Idea and the subject will attempt to preserve the consequences of an event. If they do not, again, ideology (the regime of presentation that the bourgeoisie dominates) abhors a vacuum.

From what we have seen in chapter 3, there are some similarities between Deleuze and Guattari's analysis of capitalist deterritorialization/reterritorialization, and Badiou's understanding of capitalism. Of course they are presented in different ways, but capitalism is to be treated not as pure multiple or a force that simply unbinds. It does unbind relations, but it also latches onto representations which serve its cause and help it to create surplus value. It deterritorializes so that commodity fetishism, for example, takes precedence over other values, while using the state to regulate flows of capital through an act of reterritorialization. Newman draws our attention to this, reminding us at the same time of how Deleuze and Guattari are not just interested in the state in the traditional sense, but the function of the 'abstract machine.'[27] We can see here how capital would seek to territorialize any gap, bending representation towards its own interests.

Yet the ontological approach taken by Newman shows how capitalist territorialization, or any other kind of domination, rests on weak (or rather no) foundations. Newman draws on Reiner Schürmann's reading of Heidegger and his privileging of action over thinking or metaphysics. Schürmann argues that Heidegger recognizes the lack of foundations, or a beginning or *archē*, in an oblique way in his works, but nevertheless does this consistently from *Being and Time* onwards, and 'makes action deprived of archē the condition of the thought which deconstructs the archē,' thereby making action prime over any *archē* or foundation.[28] Newman is influenced by the notion of ontological 'an-archy,' and acting without foundation, noting that for Schürmann, this is what makes it impossible to sustain the idea of domination: anarchy is precisely what destabilizes any idea of a natural inequality between people that forms the justification for political or economic oppression.'[29] This view builds on the approach taken by a number of writers in the last century. Indeed, Jason Harman has noted the rise of ontological '*anarché*' in the twentieth century, with theorists of radical democracy such as Cornelius Castoriadis and Claude Lefort, as well as Miguel Abensour and Jacques Rancière, making a case for an anarchic ontology and a cosmos without order.[30]

So anarchist and postanarchist thought has drawn on ontology for a long time, but while Badiou's approach is mostly ontological, Newman also draws on psychoanalysis where Badiou seeks to avoid this approach. We know that Lacan influenced both Newman and Badiou, but Newman's retention of the concept of ideology is more explicitly linked to Lacan. Using a different notion of truth to that which Badiou uses, Newman says that a Lacanian approach to ideology might be that 'ideology does not operate through distortion or deception but through truth itself, and yet this does not make it any less ideological.' This truth amounts to objectively 'true' facts that conceal a deeper underlying truth. For psychoanalytic theory it is the place of enunciation where the unconscious psyche of the subject is spoken rather than distinguishing between truth and falsehood. So ideology does not conceal the real interests of subjects, but it does conceal the position of power that articulates the objective 'truth.' Ideology does not conceal this objective truth, but it does, through the Lacanian concept of fantasy, make us think that the symbolic order of signifiers and representations that passes for 'reality' is full and whole. The subject cannot bear to think that his or her identity is lacking, just as the symbolic that constitutes it is lacking. Fantasy masks the trauma of this lack with an illusory fullness.[31]

As Newman has noted,[32] Žižek sees one way to challenge ideology as being simply to do what is allowed, playing ideology at its own game. This is more subversive than transgression, revealing what is possible if one follows the law, ideology or capitalism to the letter.[33] As far as post-evental politics is concerned, perhaps some of the practices of ideology will need to be adopted in order to challenge ideology and preserve the consequences of an event. For Badiou, ideology is the way things appear, masking the interests of those in the outplace (or in his later work, those who are included in the count but do not belong) but barely concealing the fact that representation is in the interests of the bourgeoisie. Acting as ideology does to defend the consequences of an event could mean defending a notion of the One that is itself seen as a whole. This may land participants in an ethical quandary, concerned that they may be defending a model of absolute power. However, we know that all Ones are temporary, and that the empty place of power cannot be filled absolutely—so, regardless of the ideology that fills the place of power, it will always be destined to collapse. What happens before then is up to the subject(s). Defending an event with actual demands may turn out to be more effective, even if their coherence relies on a fantasy that there is no longer a void on the edge of the situation.

If ideology is to be understood as the way things appear and a regime of representation to be interrupted, the notion of fantasy and the real should remind us that representation and ideology always has a void (or masks a void), so our own ideological constructs should not be enforced through destruction of that which fails to live up to this ideology, but through an insistence that subtraction takes precedence over the destruction of that which does not accord with the purity of the event, and that no form of domination has an ontological claim to dominate another. In this way we bring Newman's and Badiou's way of challenging ideology together, with a minimal ethics to guard against terror. It is important to note that Badiou does not, however, advocate so explicitly playing the game of ideology if we remember that for him the subject forces the consequences of the event by taking a decision to force a statement upon a situation, despite that statement not being verifiable by knowledge (or ideology) and belonging to the indiscernible.[34] While it is possible that playing ideology at its own game is 'impure' by Badiou's standards, such an attempt, difficult as it is without tarnishing what remains eventual of the event, is one possible strategy of politics that cannot be overlooked.

5.3 Voluntary Servitude

5.3.1 Liberal Democracy and Postanarchism

Describing how ideology works is one thing, but explaining why people go along with it is another. We have already seen fantasy, and the avoidance of trauma, as one explanation. For Newman, the success of liberalism (by its own standards) is explained in part by its ideological operation. The dominance of the state as guardian of the 'free' individual and market exchanges is not a new notion, reminding us of Hobbes and the theory of 'possessive individualism,' to use CB MacPherson's model.[35] Liberal ideology, which makes us think the state is protecting the rule of law, civil liberties and rule by consent, no longer holds true for Newman, with liberal states appearing more like the authoritarian regimes through the state of exception.[36] I would argue that it is widely acknowledged that the state claims legitimacy, and power is hoarded by the state, through the clumsy tool of the ballot box. There is, however, a state of exception that is increasingly seen as being fairly uncontroversial in liberal democracies. Newman, drawing on anarchist theory, as well as Walter Benjamin's 'Critique of Violence,' points out that this state of exception is not really exceptional, but is a permanent feature of sovereignty.[37]

In this light, the safeguards offered by liberal democratic 'human rights' are questioned. With reference to Giorgio Agamben, Newman and John Lechte see human rights as defining a field of subjectivity which, at the same time includes the form of exclusion, tied as they are to the sovereign order. Human rights situate the individual within the politico-legal order which includes the possibility of the state of exception. Any discussion of human rights must consequently bear this critique in mind.[38] With Badiou, we find a general distrust of the liberal obsession with human rights, in keeping with his theory of the subject. In *Ethics*, he describes 'Law,' which includes human rights, as that which is always already there, and not open to unexplored possibilities of '*our* situation' (italics in original) or some variable elsewhere.[39]

Through Stirner, Newman extends his analysis of the individual's ontological relationship with the state under liberalism. Stirner sees equality of rights as being, in practice, a reduction of the individual to an abstract generality, ignoring the differences between us as individuals. In this sense, the individual (or a group) is reduced to a subject whose primary relation is to the state rather than to other individuals or groups. In any pluralistic society, there will be a level of sameness that the state would rather exclude (such as the *sans papiers* Badiou campaigns for, or the proletariat), as well as any new, post-eventual sameness. In contrast to pre-eventual sameness that Badiou usually associates with particularism and the 'right to be different,' he argues that the truth is indifferent to difference and that the truth convokes its own sameness.[40]

While Stirner opposes state-imposed sameness, Badiou supports the sameness that the state refuses to accept. For both these thinkers, however, we must acknowledge that which the state would rather not acknowledge, and which does not figure on its ontological horizon. As Stirner writes, 'As a universal principle, in the "human society" which the humane liberal promises, nothing "special" which one or another has is to find recognition, nothing which bears the character of "private" is to have value.'[41] The universal as espoused by Badiou and Newman is a recognition of the universal significance of a singular event, as we have seen, rather than an attempt to impose universal values on society. In a liberal democracy, the values of the state and the individual-for-the-state trump those of singular events.

5.3.2 *Voluntary Servitude in La Boëtie, Landauer and Abensour*

With Badiou's more ontological approach, what is lacking is an explanation of *why* the individual obeys. In doing this, perhaps Badiou avoids opening himself up to the kind of criticism that may be levelled at psychoanalytical accounts of human behaviour. Newman insists that we need to challenge the way in which the individual is enthralled to the state. While we see that this is an approach common amongst the anarchists Newman refers to, it is also common to many Marxian theorists—albeit lacking in Badiou. Badiou explains how ideology and representation works, not why the individual obeys. He does, however, show us how the subject may challenge ideology and representation after an event, even if he does not explicitly advocate challenging ideology by playing its own (potentially destructive) game. Perhaps the 'voluntary inservitude' that Newman espouses avoids playing ideology at its own game, but this alone does not seem enough to keep the consequences of an event alive in a positive way.

The question for us here is the degree to which we can see things as they 'really' are, how far this can be challenged and by whom (remembering that Badiou's understanding of ideology is not one of false consciousness from which it is impossible to escape in the Althusserian sense, and that Newman does not rely on the concept of false consciousness at all). Newman draws on Étienne La Boëtie to look for one explanation of why it is we obey, even when it does not seem in our interests to do so—for example, why we obey tyrants who dominate and oppress us. La Boëtie offers us a series of possible explanations. One is custom or habit: 'in the beginning men submit under constraint and by force; but those who come after them obey without regret and perform willingly what their predecessors had done because they had to.' Servitude is explained by a 'habituation to subjection.'[42]

What Newman takes from the notion of voluntary servitude is that power must be challenged on a number of levels, as we would expect. However, the problem voluntary servitude presents is whether there is an anarchist subject at all—that is, a subject naturally predisposed to rebel. Given the internalization of authoritarian structures within the psyche, Newman argues that the state needs to be overcome as an *idea* first (including the way in which people identify with 'self-defined roles of citizenship'), before it can be overthrown as an external structure. In the words of Landauer, whom Newman invokes in many places:

> The state is a social relationship; a certain way of people relating to one

another. It can be destroyed by creating new social relationships...we are the state! And we will be the state as long as we are nothing different; as long as we have not yet created the institutions necessary for a true community and a true society of human beings.[43]

This is also similar to Stirner's notion of the insurrection—as opposed to the revolution—which proposes the individual's self-liberation from fixed ideas: 'The Revolution aimed at new *arrangements*; insurrection leads us no longer to *let* ourselves be arranged.' The insurgent does not aim for new institutions to be founded, but 'strives to become constitutionless' through 'a rising of individuals.' While this might appear to be an entirely individualistic enterprise, Newman sees in Stirner the possibility of a collective politics, referring to his 'union of egoists' (whereby individuals unite voluntarily, rather than flee from one imposed society based around the family and so on to another form of society in the form of the state, which exists without our cooperation).[44]

This focus on dispersed power, rather than just the state as a single entity, is something that Badiou's theory is well suited to, as we have considered through his focus on states (as operations), even if a state may sit under another state. What Badiou offers postanarchism is the capacity to recognize an event, such that the subject can be galvanized to support it. The anarchist approach may favour a perpetual struggle against the state and power, and we have seen how Badiou agrees with this and practices it through his activism, but this requires collective action at a time when it is likely to be most effective. Badiou has argued against 'micro-revolutions,' stating in *Theory of the Subject* that 'No individual has the power to exceed the era and its constraints, except by the mediation of the parts, and, let's say it, of parties,' and we have seen how this position has developed (especially on the role of parties) over the years.[45] As to the question whether an anarchist subject is possible, I would argue that it is as possible as a communist subject is for Badiou. The subject is not always already there, but emerges through an event.

Similar to the way in which Badiou views the phrase 'communist state' as an oxymoron, Miguel Abensour sees the 'democratic state' as a contradiction in terms as democracy is a struggle against the state: 'Democracy is anti-statist or else it is not.' The administration of things replacing the government of men was not the point, for Marx; rather, the key point, according to Abensour, was that the advent of democracy involves the disappearance of the state, or a rising up against the state. As with the performative sense of the proletariat and communism I have discussed, Abensour identifies, between Marx's 1843 work the *Critique of Hegel's Philosophy of Right* and his 1871 address following the

Paris Commune, a movement from a thought of process to a thought of conflict. Abensour uses the term 'insurgent democracy' to describe what democracy is—an action and not a political regime, and an action not confined to an event, but action that continues through time. His notion of insurgent democracy also does not simply dismiss institutions, but favours institutions where the social is instituted and the institution is directed at non-domination, reinventing itself over time. It is selective towards which institutions it supports, because 'it tends, like any political movement, toward enduring through time, [so] it distinguishes between institutions that promote the people's political action and those that do not, with non-domination serving as the criterion.'[46]

Insurgent democracy is also collective action, not of individuals, as with the radical-liberal project, but by the community of citizens against the state. Drawing on La Boëtie, Abensour describes this as the 'all Ones' against the 'all One' that would otherwise deny plurality. Noting that Marx, in the 1844 *Manuscripts*, views human servitude as servitude to production, when it comes to the 1871 Commune he revives the figure of democracy, and in the 1843 *Critique* he also demonstrates that the tragedy of culture does not only appear in the field of economy, but in the political as well. This is Marx's Machiavellian moment, according to Abensour, in the sense that insurgency keeps true democracy alive.

5.3.3 Badiou, Liberal Democracy and Voluntary Servitude

We have seen how Badiou's theory has been placed in the materialist dialectical tradition. We have also seen how Badiou describes ideology as the way that things appear, and in liberal democracies this appears through, for example, the reign of number through opinion polls and polling booths, and through the insistence that only certain types of subjects and cultures will be counted and represented. Badiou uses the name 'materialist dialectic' to describe 'the ideological atmosphere in which my philosophical undertaking conveys its more extreme tension.'[47] He opposes this materialist dialectic to what he calls 'democratic materialism,' which recognizes only bodies. The 'human animal' is granted human rights, and every particularism (which we know Badiou is critical of in philosophy and associates with postmodernism) is recognized and protected by law. However, democratic materialism has a 'global halting point for its multiform tolerance.' Any language that does not recognize 'the universal juridical and normative equality of languages' does not benefit from this equality and is seen as totalitarian. This reminds us of the state of exception, but where there is no tolerance in the logic of democratic materialism (that is, the way things appear in a liberal democracy) is for that which does not comply with its logic. Badiou summarises the democratic materialist credos as *'There are only bodies and languages, except that there are truths'* [italics in original]. Democracies tend to establish dualities, such as democracies against totalitarianism in the Cold War, or democracies against terrorism today. The dialectic is the third term that marks the gap in the duality, with truth registering itself in a world, disrupting its logic.[48]

This explains logically (that is, in the regime of appearance) the difficulties encountered in challenging representation, but it does not explain why people obey. There are, nevertheless, some resemblances between anarchist thought on servitude and Badiou's work. The terms 'all One' and 'all Ones' in La Boëtie's work remind us of Badiou's reference to Ones on more than just a superficial level. Overcoming servitude, or the 'all One,' or challenging the One or the space, requires a political collective. However, there is no single revolutionary event, and the insurgent politics invoked in different senses by Stirner, Landauer and Abensour is not aimed at abolishing all institutions. As we saw in the last chapter, there might be singular events for Badiou, but they are not absolute commencements of a new regime. Instead, the collective as subject declares fidelity to an event to keep its consequences alive, and through this the event leaves a trace in the whole, just as the clinamen, as a vanishing term and unlocatable movement that is unintelligible in the space, leaves a trace that is not comprehendible in the place, but carries force nevertheless.[49] In other words, the consequences of an event and the trace they leave on the state may not be officially acknowledged, but the trace is nevertheless there. I noted the similarities and differences between Badiou's theory and the return to seriality post-event in Sartre's *Critique of Dialectical Reason* in the last chapter, but an earlier theory of revolution and its relation to the whole or totality is found in Landauer's *Revolution*.

Landauer's use of the term 'topia' to describe authoritative stability offers a much simpler explanation of social change than Sartre's theory of seriality, and he also hints at something similar to inert matter (albeit without labour's inscription in produced matter) when explaining how the past is manifested in everything we do, where everything that happens is the past itself. There is also another concept of past, of which we are conscious, and which only changes when there is revolution. As Landauer summarises his pre-emption of Sartre and Badiou, 'For many reasons, utopia never turns into actual (material) reality, and revolution gets stuck in its transitional role: it marks merely the space between two topias.' However, 'utopia always reappears, no matter how often it dissolves and disappears in what it has produced. Revolution is always alive, even during the times of relatively stable topias.' Furthermore, while revolution is 'underground,' it 'creates a complex unity of memories, emotions, and desires,' and 'This unity will then turn into a revolution that is not merely a boundary (or a spate of time) but a principle transcending all eras (topias).'[50]

It appears that revolution is generic and universal for Landauer. It is also worth noting the nuanced way in which Landauer describes collective action not with reference to the 'community' or 'whole,' which usually manifest themselves in the form of the 'state' or the 'people,' nor with reference to the 'proletariat' for that matter. Instead, in *The Socialist Way* he refers to 'the few' who lead revolt against the state, while clarifying what is meant by this 'individualism' against those who charge Landauer with vanguardism. Landauer is opposed to a simple understanding of masses and individuals, complaining that individualists have failed to understand the relation between themselves, the masses and social circumstances, while what Landauer strives for is to overcome the opposition between communism and individualism, hinting at something like a generic event that 'the few,' as subjects, lead. As Landauer puts it, '*Through separation to community*' [italics in original].[51]

Whatever the similarities might be between Landauer, Sartre and Badiou, what Badiou does not consider is voluntary servitude. He acknowledges that individuals can be misguided by ideology and number, but not locked into ideology and false consciousness in a way Althusser maintained. There are advantages to utilising the theories of Stirner, Deleuze and Lacan, but Badiou's reluctance to draw on theories relating to consciousness (including Lacan's notion of fantasy) perhaps stems from a suspicion of theories relating to human nature. Perhaps it is Badiou's concern with scientific credibility that means the easiest path is to not engage at length with theories of consciousness on the level of consciousness, going one step further than Althusser, who at least critiqued Freud's work while refusing to engage on the same level.

While Badiou does not consider the consciousness of individuals and identifies subjects ontologically, leaving them to identify with an event, there is a fleeting resemblance to Heidegger's description of *Dasein*, where our ontological relation to others is not immediately apparent. As Heidegger put it, 'That which is ontically closest and well known, is ontologically the farthest and not known at all; and its ontological signification is constantly overlooked.'⁵² Graham Harman has made some interesting observations in comparing Badiou's *Theory of the Subject* to Heidegger's thought. I have already said how Badiou avoids dealing with consciousness as a psychoanalyst would, and Harman notes how Badiou's subject is depersonalized, in a similar way to how Heidegger's *Sein* is. The subject in *Theory of the Subject* is 'mentioned only in connection with the proletariat (even though each proletariat is historical and local), and in *Theory of the Subject* the 'proletariat' often verges on functioning as a name for being as such, not for a particular assembly of downtrodden humans.'⁵³ Harman also argues that Badiou and Heidegger follow the same assumption that individuality and relationality are always a pair, with algebra concerned with individuals and the rules that govern their relation to one another. For Heidegger, Harman argues, we only escape this pair 'by appeal to an ominous being that rumbles like a quasi-articulate lump, forever withdrawn from all access,' while Badiou counters relational individuals 'with a rather shapeless outplace.' In Badiou's more recent work, with his use of topology in *Logics of Worlds*, he departs from Heidegger through enacting 'the rather non-Heideggerian programme of partially entangled horizontal collectives, for which change comes not by drawing on a vast indeterminate surplus, but by triggering chain reactions from one local neighbourhood to another,'⁵⁴ reminding us of a post-Marxist hegemonic project, but one which develops around an event rather than already established particularisms.

While Badiou does not consider the being of equipment as Heidegger does, this comparison strengthens the case that Badiou's subject is understood ontologically, not psychologically. In *Being and Event* we see Badiou comparing the subject in Descartes and Lacan, for whom the subject must be 'maintained in the pure void of its subtraction if one wishes to save truth. Only such a subject allows itself to be sutured within the logical, wholly transmissible, form of science.'⁵⁵ The subject is identifiable within networks of experience, with Descartes's cogito encountering objects that throw doubt on knowledge, and Lacan's subject encountering language. Descartes's subject, as Hallward writes, provides for its own ontological foundation ('I think, therefore I am'), a 'self-grounding *activity* of thought' which explains why Badiou claims to be a Cartesian.⁵⁶ The subject is not seen as substance or consciousness for Badiou (and Descartes and Lacan), but ontologically, grounding itself on itself, but within a situation or world. As Badiou puts it, 'to identify a cause of the subject, one would have to return, not so much to truth, which is rather its stuff, nor to the infinity whose finitude it is, but rather to the event.'[57] The subject declares fidelity to the indiscernible that is the truth.

So while servitude is not discussed by Badiou on the face of his work, the subject is presented in an ontological manner, in situations and worlds where representation is ideology, plain to see but rarely unstable enough to lead to an event. It is clear that Badiou is adamant that an event should not go to waste, but this also hinges on the subject having the confidence to force statements of the subject-language after an event (as Badiou would put it),[58] so the question of the subject's consciousness is not entirely avoided.

5.4 Overcoming Ideology

When a subject declares fidelity to an event and the indiscernible that is the truth, they are neither conscious nor unconscious of the true, according to Badiou. Fidelity involves a wager. Badiou uses the term 'confidence' to name the process through which 'the subject believes that there is a truth, and this belief occurs in the form of a knowledge.' The operator of fidelity can only make finite enquiries to establish connections (and disconnections) linking multiples of the situation and the event, so any discernment is an 'approximate truth.' The operator of fidelity has confidence in the 'what-is-to-come' under the name of the truth.[59]

We have seen the dangers involved in differentiating between the real and semblance of the real, but we have also sensed a reticence on the part of Badiou to play ideology at its own game, unlike Žižek, whose notion of 'overidentification' involves following the commands of the ideological message to the letter as a form of resistance. Žižek notes that Badiou's identification of the passion for the real as purification in the twentieth century, and his call for a subtractive politics, creates a problem. With further reference to Lacan, Žižek discerns in Badiou's description of the passion for the real and subtractive politics a Lacanian triad—'the Real attained through violent purification, the Imaginary of the minimal difference, the Symbolic of the pure formal matrix.' The problem, as far as Žižek is concerned, is that Badiou remains stuck in the matrix of his ontology. There is a gap between being and event (the event is not, for being), so Badiou remains within a dualism and an oppositional stance, according to Žižek, 'advocating the impossible goal of pure presence without the state of representation.' The dilemma is what to do with power once you have it, and the purification that the statist passion for the real involved is not a solution for Badiou, as we have seen; neither is 'democracy,' given that it, too, involves purification against that which is non-democratic.[60]

However, in my view, given the subject is only able to be an operator of fidelity to an approximate truth, the dilemma the subject faces is of deciding to move on from simply following a politics of subtraction and opposition, towards constructing demands as an act of confidence to keep the consequences of an event alive. Strictly speaking, defending the purity of an event is guess work anyway, as is the defence of any kind of political purity. We have already seen how all Ones are temporary, inevitable operations that come to an inevitable end, and in this sense Badiou's system can be quite indifferent to the politics that emerges from an event. Even if a Leninist politics were to emerge, we know that it would be temporary (although there would be other strategic considerations about whether it is the right choice).

Constructing positive demands is something that anarchists often seem less reluctant to do, even if they do sometimes seem disparate and oppositional. Newman writes that the central challenge of radical politics today 'is to propose forms of transnational organization that are non-authoritarian, and which invent new modes of non-representative or direct democratic politics.' Newman sees this in terms of a 'post-identity' politics, with grass-roots mobilizations, and mass protests as well as 'creative forms of civil disobedience and non-violent confrontation, but also the occupation of spaces and other forms of subversion—rather than formal political representation.'[61]

I have argued that class politics is still very much a part of these movements, and the Occupy movement demonstrated this. It may not be easy for social scientists or the commentariat to categorize movements as 'proletariat,' and to an extent this does not matter. I have argued that we can still identify, analytically, what would traditionally be called the proletariat, but at the same time I have endorsed a performative understanding of the proletariat (traced through Marx) which means revolutions or events are often led by those oppressed under capitalism (something that either most of us have in common analytically, or at least most people feel they have in common when mobilising against neoliberalism, whatever our other identities). Most recently, the term '99 per cent' was favoured by many involved in Occupy, with their concerns converging with those which traditionally were those of the proletariat, such as workers' rights and employment, even if many did identify as middle class (that is, labourers who have more to lose than just their chains, as Marcuse put it).[62]

What I think is lacking in Badiou's thought and postanarchism in general is the confidence to oppose ideology with solid values that confront capitalist values, due to the risk that such an approach is deemed ideological. Yet, as I have shown in my discussion of the theory of the event, values change, and direct action can be seen as a legitimate means to challenge value, ideology and the dictatorship of the bourgeoisie. As we will see in the next chapter, contingency may be the only absolute there is. For Badiou, all Ones are temporary operations, while for Newman anarchism is the horizon of politics. The weak philosophical foundations on which the state and capitalist ideology stand should give us confidence that the event itself, and insurrection in postanarchist theory, are the very means through which ideology and political economy can most effectively be critiqued, even if there remains uncertainty over what tactical or strategic (or even hegemonic) approach to take afterwards. I maintain, however, that there are tactical post-event options available, to which, I argue, Badiou and postanarchism have led us, and which I will develop in the next chapter. Complemented with more recent theories on contingency, we can not only provide options for post-event tactics, but also further develop the work of Marx.

6

Post-Evental Politics: The Self-Pricing of the Proletariat

While it may be impossible to overcome bourgeois ideology, it *has* to be possible to oppose bourgeois value forms with alternatives. This final chapter therefore focuses on what might happen after an event.[1] We know that both Badiou and Newman avoid a prescriptive politics, but that one of Badiou's aims is to preserve the consequences of political events. I have argued that this demand—fidelity to an event—should be taken at face value, which means preserving the truth that was presented by an event, and not adding to it various non-evental demands, as appeared to happen in the Occupy movement. In most of Badiou's works this means a class-led event against capitalist exploitation. Badiou is quite flexible as to what this class, the proletariat, looks like. He argues that we should go beyond a pure nothingness whereby the proletariat identifies itself as the last class in history before all classes cease to exist, in favour of a genericity built on differences united around a singular and universal event.[2] But given that Badiou largely avoids prescriptive post-event strategies, how might we tie the approximate truth Badiou sees in the event to actual modes of politics that are loyal to the event?

My answer is that we should turn to Badiou's former student, Quentin Meillassoux, and his 'speculative materialism,' which is associated with the wider 'object-oriented ontology' school of thought, and not Ernst Bloch's speculative work which earned him outsider status in Western Marxism and the dismissal by Jürgen Habermas as a speculative materialist.[3] Whatever the merits of Bloch's speculative materialism and the dismissal in Marxian circles (and by Marx and Engels) of speculative thought, I turn to Meillassoux's speculative materialism to develop Badiou's theory of the event, as well as Elie Ayache's work in applying Meillassoux's thought to the derivatives market in order to question the belief that the pricing of derivatives follows the logic of probability, rather than pricing being a contingent act. In other words, pricing in the derivatives market is whatever participants say it is, and the only thing that is absolute is contingency. Even though this is not the usual way in which most wages are determined, there are parallels that can be drawn with the labour market after an event has made subjects alive to capitalist exploitation, enabling labourers to make wage demands against the capitalist construct that is the 'going rate.' Those on the side of 'the markets' claim to have the final word on pricing, but this can be opposed with alternative value forms emerging from the political event. This opens up a political tactic that avoids being prescriptive, while also not being inimical to Marx's thought (as we shall see), nor that of postanarchism.

6.1 Why speculative materialism?

As I have stated throughout this work, contingency has the philosophical upper hand, as Badiou and many postanarchists demonstrate (whether epistemologically or ontologically), as well as being the position taken in object-oriented ontology and speculative materialism. While object-oriented ontology has been criticized by Peter Wolfendale[4] for propping up the very thing it wishes to critique (that is, neo-Kantian philosophy, to simplify matters for now, or correlationism, as Meillassoux calls it),[5] the works of Meillassoux, Graham Harman and others provide not only a convincing defence of contingency, but also a refutation of finitude through a revival of the notion of the absolute in the form of contingency. Indeed, contingency is the only absolute according to this philosophy. This offers new tools with which to critique capitalist values. My argument in this project has progressed through an argument that Marx widens our understanding of power through the critique of the economy and the role of values, making the case that this form of power is indifferent to all identities and is most likely to be challenged by the singular and universal event and a collective agent, i.e. class. Situations characterized by a proletarian presence remain important for Badiou as potential eventless, and the importance of the proletariat is also acknowledged by Newman. The role of value in our lives is fertile ground for an event, and the problem of value and value form, including commodity fetishism, so long an issue for Marxian theory, should be taken up by postanarchists.

Speculative materialism may create more questions than it answers when attempting to view issues important to critical theory through its prism, but this is no reason to ignore it, no matter how convenient that would be. Kojin Karatani utilizes Kant to challenge capitalist value, but a non-Kantian approach is possible as well. If speculative materialism tells us that the thing-in-itself is hidden as the result of correlationism itself (initially at least), and any number of things may reveal themselves given that nothing can be ruled out (this is the absolute of contingency), we cannot simply defend existing values against contingent demands on the grounds that they are extant values. William E. Connolly critiques apparently self-organizing processes (such as the neoliberal trust in the free market) and systems such as Kant's that disregard pluralism through the selectiveness of the assumptions on which they are built in an attempt to provide us with an entirely 'rational' system.[6] It follows, I argue, that we cannot simply trust free-market determination of value forms, which can become ideological and violent in the law-preserving and mythic sense that I will come to.

Speculative materialism does not directly link events to the critique of capitalist values, but does give primacy to contingency over thinking what the thing-in-itself may be through a restrictive metaphysics, as this limit placed on thought is the product of correlationism (that we can only know things as they are for us through their secondary qualities, not their primary qualities). In the language of Marx, it is a case of confusing value form and commodity fetishism with the thing-in-itself of something, or the closest we may get to this using the correlate of 'the market' (that we can only know value as it appears in the market for us). Marxian theory may be seen as a critical theory at odds with object-oriented ontology, but the latter still strengthens the case for the contingency of the event, even if the Badiouan event is only 'for us,' or the proletariat understood in the performative sense. It may not be possible to know the thing-in-itself of value, but there are grounds for challenging the value forms capitalism produces (or excuses) by the correlate of the market with values and prices determined by subjects to an event.

6.2 Correlationism

Before looking at the relevance of speculative materialism in more detail, a key term, 'correlationism,' needs to be explained. There are certainly things we do not know, and this much speculative materialism has in common with what Meillassoux calls correlationism. A correlationist like Kant would say, however, that we can only know posited phenomena and not the thing-in-itself. The phenomena we study cannot be known to be the thing-in-itself, as we use subjective forms to understand it (our categories and concepts of space and time). So for Kant, science demonstrates that we do not know the thing-in-itself, although Meillassoux argues that he is open to the possibility that the world in-itself is exactly as it is for us, except that correlationism says this is impossible to know.[7] Meillassoux's speculative materialism precisely challenges this claim.

Meillassoux begins with a succinct example of correlationism by comparing primary and secondary qualities—when you burn your finger on a candle, you do not touch a pain that is present in the flame (what might be its primary quality), but sense the way your nerves respond to the flame (a secondary quality). This example can be extended by the correlationist to all of our encounters with entities, with the distinction between the 'in-itself' and the 'for-us' at the heart of what Meillassoux calls the 'correlationist circle.' The correlationist relies on the 'capacity-to-be-other' of everything, especially other than things are for us, except that they will not admit that this prohibition on knowing anything other than it is *for us* is, in fact, an absolute. They remain steadfastly opposed to such a concept as the absolute while believing that we cannot 'absolutely' know anything.[8] The correlationist, without realizing, relies on the absolute of contingency. However, it is not the correlation, but the 'facticity' of the correlation that reveals this.

Meillassoux derives the term facticity from what he calls 'strong correlationism.' 'Weak' correlationism is associated with Kant, who as we know maintains that the thing-in-itself is thinkable, but that we cannot have any knowledge of it. Strong correlationism, on the other hand, is associated more with Heidegger, and maintains that it is also illegitimate to claim that we can think the thing-in-itself. While Kant argues that we cannot know whether there is a God powerful enough to make a contradiction true, strong correlationists deny the possibility that we can attempt to refute the existence of a God that can render a contradiction true (Meillassoux refers to Descartes here). With strong correlationism, the correlation is not just the best we can hope for given the (Kantian) circumstances, but unwittingly becomes absolute through its attempt to de-absolutize and make the in-itself unthinkable. If the correlation is absolute and we cannot think the in-itself, Meillassoux writes that 'it seems the wisest course is simply to abolish any such notion of the in-itself.' The absolute becomes unthinkable, and what we are left with is facticity, or the facticity of the correlation itself. Facticity is the 'structural invariants' that strong correlationists would say govern the world—they may differ from one correlation to another, but they are used to describe the world rather than deducing (as Hegel would) anything absolute, since we cannot, according to this view, ground these in necessity. As Meillassoux puts it, 'if contingency consists in not knowing that worldly things could be otherwise, facticity just consists in not knowing why the correlational structure has to be thus.' Facticity does not describe an objective reality, but instead faces the 'limits of objectivity.' Facticity does away with the Leibnizian principle of sufficient reason, with there being no way to prove something as true, and no principle of non-contradiction. However, it is because we cannot think these things that strong correlationism leads us towards the absolute of contingency, with Meillassoux summing up strong correlationism in the thesis that 'it is unthinkable that the unthinkable be impossible,' since 'I cannot provide a rational ground for the absolute impossibility of a contradictory reality, or for the nothingness of all things, even if the meaning of these terms remains indeterminate.'[9]

6.3 Badiou, Metaphysics, and the Critique of Value

While I argue that Badiou cannot be called a true Kantian (but perhaps a metaphysician without metaphysics), Meillassoux argues that Badiou does not get around correlationism. Instead, Badiou's and Žižek's materialism, along with the projects of Freud, Derrida and Lacan, are a 'misfired correlationism.' It is, according to Meillassoux, 'always for a subject that there is an undecidable event or a failure of signification,' and the subject is a speculative one, 'assured a priori, and according to a properly absolute Knowing, for which things always turn out badly in its world of representations.'[10]

Still, Meillassoux acknowledges that Badiou's work is crucial in freeing us from calculatory reason through his interpretation of Cantorian mathematics, enabling us to conceive the detotalization of being-qua-being.[11] Because Badiou goes some way towards avoiding the pitfalls of correlationism, with the event not being presented in the situation and being undecidable, he privileges the subject as the only means of making an intervention and a wager that backs the event. Meillassoux's approach is to rely instead on the facticity (which I will come back to) of the correlate rather than a subject.[12]

However, as Ayache has pointed out, events happen outside the domain of philosophy for Badiou, and yet they condition its discourse. When Meillassoux refers to the 'Hume-event,' the 'Kant-event' and the 'Galileo-event,' Ayache argues that he is implicitly acknowledging that his philosophy is conditioned by the 'Badiou-event,' and that 'Meillassoux, as subject, is presently making the decision to embrace serious contingency, or the event, and obtaining, as a derivative consequence, the un-totalization of possibilities.' Ayache (with a background in trading derivatives) draws on Meillassoux, along with Badiou and Deleuze, to critique probability theories in finance, arguing that the market is the medium of contingency, not possibility. Ayache is opposed to theories of possibility and probability, and in relation to the market argues that 'To bet is not to expect; it is a material, almost corporeal, commitment, which doesn't even involve thought.' It is the act of writing that matters for Ayache, and Meillassoux's theory appeals to him for its absolute contingency that retains necessity (the necessity of contingency).[13] Badiou's influence can also be seen in Ayache's discussion on the rolling of a die. The transition from the probable to the real (when the die actually lands as a six, for example) gives probability its meaning, but this meaning is mythical and 'really concerns an ultimate and global event with no relation or correspondence to the local throw.'[14] This is not the Badiouan event, opposed as he is to absolute commencement and the dawn of false universality opposed to the aleatory event. Probability theory, including that at work in the market, limits possibility and ignores contingency, as we shall see.

We saw in the last chapter that while Badiou has been said to neglect questions of political economy, and certainly does not critique value in the same way Marx and a number of Marxian theorists would, he nevertheless broadly considers value under capital, and links this to ideology. In Badiou's view, capital assigns everything a value in terms of numericality, but not in terms of what he calls 'Number,' which is akin to the ontological approach and a deeper understanding of being.[15] We accept capitalist values, but these are parasitic on other representations and states, rather than representing themselves, as Alberto Toscano explains.[16] Others defend values under capital, but it lacks any deeper ontological defence, tying itself to the free circulation of commodities, or simply what we, or more often the bourgeoisie, want to believe.

The advent of speculative materialism and object-oriented ontology complements the theory of the event, and can make it especially relevant for a critique of political economy (that is, the state and capitalist values). Given that speculative materialism targets the neo-Kantian approach, or correlationism (as we shall see), we should briefly deal with the charge that Badiou has Kantian tendencies. This is Žižek's view, since what was once hidden (or excluded) in Badiou's theory appears through the event and is inscribed in the (symbolic) order of ideology.[17] It is as if Badiou had already anticipated this charge in *Metaphysics and the Critique of Metaphysics,* arguing that there are things that are exposed to the thinkable, but that these things are linked to ideas, and to link these ideas to thought 'it suffices to decide upon the appropriate axioms,' calling such an approach a 'metaphysics without metaphysics.'[18] Badiou accounts for the way things appear in a world or situation, but what is not Kantian is the event itself, and the fact of contingency is key for Badiou.

Badiou provides a bridge between critical theory and speculative materialism. Levi R. Bryant summarises critical theory as 'any theory that contests the naturalness of categories pertaining to human identities and social relations, revealing how they are socially constructed, contingent, and historical.' Against the claim that capitalism and the market are the natural form of exchange, Marx would say that this argument is reified through commodity fetishism. What unites the speculative realists or object-oriented ontologists against critical theory is, according to Bryant, a defence of 'some variant of realism or materialism,' and 'a critique of correlationism.' Instead of just critiquing discourses and their essentialist claims, Bryant sees speculative realism as offering a political opportunity arising from 'the ability of these orientations to reveal unexpected sites of political concern, unexpected ways in which power functions through non-signifying agencies, and through opening new and creative ways of responding to destructive and oppressive forms of power.'[19]

Although Badiou has repeatedly referred to the political potential of the proletariat and the factory as a likely event-site,[20] the event remains aleatory and removed from any probability theory. The event could leave a lasting impact on institutions or state apparatuses, but for Badiou the naming that is undertaken following the event is, for the state and situation, illegal and unpresentable, just as the event itself is for ontology. That is why the subject's intervention is a wager, and why they need to actively preserve and further the consequences of an event that remains indiscernible for the state.[21] As I argued in the last chapter, defending the consequences of an event might require the subject to take on ideology with their own ideological construct, and as Balibar has commented, Badiou stresses how vital naming is in revolutionary politics, along with the cult of personality.[22] But even if that approach is taken and is at all Kantian (and if we know the event only as it exists for us), at least Badiou does not exclude the possibility of something which does not presently exist becoming thinkable.

6.4 Value, the Event and Class

We have seen how the proletariat features prominently in Badiou's work, and how their workplace is a likely evental-site (and I have taken a wide interpretation of what the proletariat is, drawing on Erik Olin Wright as well as observations around the Occupy movement and the '99 per cent'). Although we have no control over the event (when it occurs, and where), we can still make observations over who is included in the count of any state without belonging, and who might therefore benefit from the unpredictable and indiscernible event—a practical example of Badiou's metaphysics without a metaphysics, understanding things as they appear to us while being open to contingency. After an event, decisions need to be made by those defending its consequences, and this is where philosophy, in working with truths rather than creating them, can help. For Badiou, as well as Meillassoux, events and contingency are there whether we like it or not. We cannot predict them, but a philosophical undertaking to defend them and their consequences is still required. Otherwise, why would these two figures bother producing works, except for the materialist imperative and it being one way to earn an interesting living? The event may challenge capitalist ideology and values, emerging in response to it, but if there is no philosophical case for defending the consequences of an event, such as self-pricing for the proletariat, for example, there is little hope for those making such a wager. Marxian theories of value, along with Badiou's theory of the event, provide such philosophical support.

6.5 The Marxian Theory of Value

In considering the event as an event against the prevailing values within the state, we can also consider the relevance of Marx's critique of value and its effect in exposing the weak foundations of the state's defence of capitalist values. And this Marxian critique of value is, in return, also complemented by theories of contingency, including speculative materialism.

6.5.1 The Problem

Marx gives us a clear analysis of how wages are determined, and that is through the amount of labour time required to produce a commodity and to ensure enough subsistence for the worker. However, it would be wrong to say that this is all there is to say on the determination of wages under capitalism, as if there is a fixed formula for calculating wages that the exploiter or the market will not, and cannot, depart from. Of course, Marx's analysis is based on his labour theory of value, but as I explained earlier, there are complicating factors in determining price, such as tastes and commodity fetishism, even if these are not necessary to establish a labour theory of value and the social relations of production specific to capitalism. Furthermore, there are real world factors that can determine the price of labour (wages), for example, but this does not undermine the labour theory of value.[23]

Indeed, as Elena Louisa Lange writes, the continued failure to distinguish between value and value form is seen as the original sin of conventional political economy. Value as socially necessary labour (that is, Marx's labour theory of value) should be distinguished from the value *forms* of money, wage, price, and so on. The latter presents itself as 'value in itself,' revealing the fetishism that supports it. Only value *form* has its basis in exchange, and not value, which is determined by socially necessary labour.[24] Ayache, in his non-Marxian and also nonclassical approach, also distinguishes between value and price in the market, and it is the latter which he links to contingent claims, as I will for the value form of wages expressed as prices.[25] This is why I refer to the self-pricing of the proletariat rather than self-valorization.

Marx distinguished between 'real wages' that express the price of labour as a commodity in relation to the price of other commodities and the labour time taken to produce them, and 'relative wages' that express the price of labour in a newly created value in relation to the share that falls to capital.[26] However, real wages can fluctuate. As Michael Lebowitz argues, Marx refers in *Capital* to a 'necessary' quantity of subsistence for the worker which partly determines the value of labour-power, but that does not mean that real wages remain constant. Marx wrote of a changing level of necessity (rising necessity) as capitalism developed, and Lebowitz also argues that Marx's point about necessary subsistence was simply a methodologically 'sound' working assumption for *Capital*, which may have been addressed fully had Marx's 'missing' volume on wages appeared. Indeed, writes Lebowitz:

> Nothing could be further from Marx than the belief in a fixed set of necessaries.... From his earliest days, Marx rejected a concept of 'Abstract Man' and stressed the emergence of new human needs with the development of society.[27]

For the purpose of this work, however, I am more concerned with the mystification of value under capitalism, and aspects of the Marxian theory of value provide a firm basis for understanding this problem—that is, how to challenge a claim that a value is the closest possible to a 'true' value, given that the correlate of 'the market' is absolute if we cannot know the thing-in-itself of a thing or a value. Challenging values—whether it is through the self-valorization of the proletariat that Negri saw in the *Grundrisse*,[28] or through questioning the value of commodities—needs to be on a firm footing to withstand those who defend the market as if it is something we have no control over.

Marx sought to explain how value is created, and this is evident in both the production and the consumption stage. My premise is that establishing the value and price of something, or defending it, is vulnerable to contingency, and to demands that something be valued or priced differently. The key point is not that we will never know the thing-in-itself of value, but rather that value form and price is the act of humans writing the price of something (drawing on Ayache, as we will see), whether through complex means or through relatively simple means, such as the rare event that a political collective demands new values or the writing of a price. It is us humans who write value form and price, even if we might pretend the situation is natural or part of a free-market rational process. Events can therefore surprise us and reveal to us values that we did not know were there.

6.5.2 The Mystery of Value

In Marx's *Capital*, we see the commodity described as what appears to be an extremely obvious and trivial thing at first sight, but 'its analysis brings out that it is a very strange thing, abounding in metaphysical subtleties and theological niceties.' This mysterious quality is not contained in the commodity's use value, but the form of the commodity itself, as the embodiment of labour power and social relations, the mystery of the commodity-form consisting 'therefore simply in the fact that the commodity reflects the social characteristics of men's own labour as objective characteristics of the products of labour themselves.' Our knowledge of the commodity evades the real relation we have with the commodity, and Marx draws on the 'misty realm of religion' to make an analogy, where 'the products of the human brain appear as autonomous figures endowed with a life of their own, which enter into relations both with each other and with the human race. So it is in the world of commodities with the products of men's hands.' Marx calls this the 'fetishism which attaches itself to the products of labour as soon as they are produced as commodities, and is therefore inseparable from the production of commodities.'[29]

The value that is imposed on commodities and labour power, through human processes, becomes, through the complexities involved in determining value and because of the fetish, something that is not easily grasped. Those who sell their labour power do not equate the products of their labour with each other as the objects of the human labour they all have in common, as homogeneous human labour, but rather they equate their products with each other as exchange values that equate their different kinds of labour as human labour, without always being immediately aware of it: 'Value, therefore, does not have its description branded on its forehead; it rather transforms every product of labour into a social hieroglyphic.'[30] Value relies on faith and a notion of universality. As Marx says, 'as paper, the monetary existence of commodities has a purely social existence. It is faith that brings salvation. Faith in money value as the immanent spirit of commodities, faith in the mode of production and its predestined disposition, faith in the individual agents of production as mere personifications of self-valorizing capital.'[31]

We can therefore think about what something is worth, including within what we might think of as the categorical imperative of the market (limiting us by claiming we cannot think the thing-in-itself of value by an alternative logic), but this is no straightforward process.

Moishe Postone views the world of commodities in a secular manner, different to the misty realm of religion in terms of the effect it has on (false) consciousness, but nevertheless as a complex world. Commodities are objects that can be grasped mathematically and measured, but they still retain a secularized power to confuse. More importantly for Postone, commodities and values need to be understood and analysed together with the production process, and not in isolation. (The mode of production, social relations and values that exist are, for Postone, all linked to capitalism, and need to be understood in this historical context.)[32] There have been attempts, however, to isolate exchange as the problem, or at least something that can be addressed on its own. Postone takes issue with Alfred Sohn-Rethel's approach on this point, since Sohn-Rethel does not see abstract labour as the issue, but instead the means of exchange. Sohn-Rethel 'evaluates positively the mode of social synthesis purportedly effected by labor in industrial production as noncapitalist and opposes it to the mode of societalization effected by exchange, which he assesses negatively.'[33]

Sohn-Rethel's argument that 'None of the activities of production and consumption, on which the life of every individual depends, could take place in the social system of the division of labour without the intervention of commodity exchange,' with 'the synthesis of commodity-producing societies ... to be found in commodity exchange,' is not intended to be a Kantian synthesis. Kantian synthesis is an a priori one, attributed to a 'transcendental spontaneity,' and thereby making a fetish out of his own explanation of synthesis, according to Sohn-Rethel, who instead locates this synthesis in the fetish of the commodity, which 'impels solipsism between its participants'; the participants of exchange accept their reliance on each other and mutual interests in this process. Sohn-Rethel therefore goes on to argue that false consciousness is not faulty consciousness, but is rather 'logically correct, inherently incorrigible consciousness' that understands the process of synthesis, even if it can be faulty against the standards of social existence.[34] The synthesis of commodity exchange is prior to any judgements we make. As Žižek puts it, Sohn-Rethel's conclusion is that the categorical imperative is present already in the act of commodity exchange, so thought cannot arrive at pure abstraction before this abstraction gets to work in the market.[35]

Žižek introduced Lacan's notion of fantasy to the analysis of the commodity, following Sohn-Rethel's assertion that individuals act as if a commodity is not submitted to physical and material exchanges, to a natural cycle of generation and corruption (damage) in the act of exchange, even though they know this is not the case. In other words, as Žižek illustrates the point, money (as a commodity) suffers wear and tear through time as a material object, but its effectiveness (social effectivity) in the market is not diminished through this wear and tear, since we act as if it has an immutable power not diminished through this process. This is what Žižek calls the sublime (rather than empirical) material of money, involving the individual in the 'real abstraction' that has nothing to do with 'reality,' although it does not mean that participants are 'blind' to what they are doing. Instead, according to Žižek's reading of Sohn-Rethel, individuals proceed during the act of exchange as 'practical solipsists,' misrecognizing the act of exchange which is 'real abstraction,' a 'form of socialization of private production through the medium of the market,' a misrecognition that is essential for effecting an act of exchange. We come to witness a 'non-knowledge' of the participants in this process, which is essential to ensure they do not know too much, so much that this knowledge would reveal the functioning of social reality and cause it to dissolve itself. For Žižek, this is fundamental to understanding 'ideology,' which is not simply false consciousness, but a reality that is itself 'ideological.' This is the symptom that Marx invented, a consistent structure that relies on non-knowledge: 'the subject can 'enjoy his symptom' only in so far as its logic escapes him—the measure of the success of its interpretation is precisely its dissolution.' The effectiveness of social relations rely on individuals not knowing what they are doing, Žižek encapsulating his understanding of ideology as 'not the "false consciousness" of a (social) being but this being itself in so far as it is supported by "false consciousness".'[36]

Bourgeois rights and duties are inconsistent as an ideology, in Žižek's view; every 'ideological Universal' is '"false" in so far as it necessarily includes a specific case which breaks its unity, lays open its falsity.'[37] Two examples that Žižek provides is the false freedom of the worker to freely sell their labour on the market ('this freedom is the very opposite of effective freedom: by selling his labour 'freely,' the worker loses his freedom—the real content of this free act of sale is the worker's enslavement to capital'), and equivalent exchange which, unlike the artisan act of exchange where there is no exploitation in principle (a simplification on Žižek's part), the act of exchange under capitalism contains a negation, internal to its equivalent exchange, which is the creation of surplus value above the value of the labour force. This much we know, along with Marx's description of the commodity fetish where social relations are disguised as relations between things, which Žižek calls the 'hysteria of conversion' proper to capitalism.'[38]

For Žižek, there may be a practical solipsism that the individual takes part in, but this does not imply a choice in everyday life. Individuals know that money is an expression of social relations and not in any way 'magical,' that there are relations between people behind relations between things, according to Žižek. Yet individuals act as if money is the 'immediate embodiment of wealth as such,' being 'fetishists in practice, not in theory,' who misrecognize that in the act of commodity exchange 'they are guided by the fetishistic illusion.' So people know the real of the situation, but they do not act as if this is the case. The 'illusion' that structures our real situation is overlooked, and this 'unconscious illusion is what may be called the ideological fantasy,' following a particular kind of freedom (to sell one's labour on the market), knowing that it is a form of exploitation. Commodities and the relationship of things, rather than social relations, do the believing for them, as we saw with Marx's understanding of myths and saints created in the human mind appearing to be autonomous, relieving believers of the burden of believing. Žižek follows Lacan here, with belief being radically exterior. The fantasy represses the fact that authority is without truth, is false, seeing it instead as necessary.[39]

Although Badiou is influenced by Lacan, he does not apply his concept of fantasy in this way, and nor does he discuss consciousness at length. We are nevertheless reminded of Badiou's views on numericality under capital, which describes the way value appears under capital (much like ideology is the way that things appear) if not its effect on consciousness.

There have been other attempts to challenge value through a Kantian reading of Marxian value theory. Kojin Karatani posits value transcendentally in a Kantian sense, and focuses on the link between surplus value and circulation where 'industrial capital earns surplus value not only by making workers work, but also by making them buy back—in totality—what they produce.' Karatani locates the creation of surplus value not just in the exploitation of the production process, but in the differences between value systems when goods are consumed, criticising those who see the relationship between the capitalist and the worker as a modern equivalent of the relationship between feudal lord and serf. This idea originates, Karatani explains, in the Ricardian socialists who saw in Ricardo's theory the rate of profit being equal to the exploitation of surplus labour.[40] The consumption of goods is just as much tied to exploitation, the commodity fetish being a key aspect of Marx's *Capital*, which Karatani seeks to counter with an alternative deliberative means of valuation.

Karatani draws on Kant's *Critique of Pure Reason*, along with his earlier work *Dreams of a Visionary*, to explain the antinomy between values. As Karatani explains the 'pronounced parallax' in Kant's work, both the subjective and objective viewpoint is an optical delusion, so it follows that 'if the history of philosophy is nothing but the history of such reflections, then the history of philosophy is itself nothing but optical delusion.' The pronounced parallax emerges in the form of antinomy where the optical delusion that is the thesis and antithesis is exposed. Karatani proceeds by arguing that Marx stresses the priority of circulation in *Capital* and describes an antinomy in which surplus value cannot, in itself, be attained in the production process, and cannot, in itself, be attained in the circulation process either. The antinomy, for Karatani, can be undone 'only by proposing that the surplus value (for industrial capital) comes from the difference of value systems in the circulation process,' that is, the different exchange values contained in wages and prices, and so on, through which surplus value is made, 'and yet that the difference is created by technological innovation in the production process.... Capital has to discover and create the difference incessantly.'[41]

This leads Karatani to the ultimate antinomy in *Capital*: 'money should exist; money should not exist.' Karatani notes that Marx said nothing about a notion of money that could satisfy these conflicting conditions.[42] Throughout Karatani's 'transcritique' he posits the point at which goods are consumed and money is circulated as the opportunity to challenge capital's production of surplus value, the point at which workers can place their own value on goods should this become possible. To this end, Karatani points, as a solution to the antinomy, to the Local Exchange Trading System (LETS) which enables participants to exchange goods with others where the sum total of gains and losses is zero for all involved.[43] Karatani does not explain how individuals are to decide what equal exchange means in a way that takes us beyond fetishism or the influence of the market as is.

Whether deception, fantasy or simply apathy are the reasons for us accepting the value of commodities (including what we are paid for our labour, given that money is a commodity), a philosophical retort that people can believe in is necessary, and it need not follow Kant or draw on theories of consciousness. The Marxian critique of value can be complemented by the speculative materialist critique, exposing even further the weak foundations on which the law-preserving violence of the state rests, as we will see.

6.6 Speculative Materialism

6.6.1 'Factiality'

I briefly outlined Meillassoux's use of the term 'correlationism' above. Meillassoux goes beyond strong correlationism to deduce the absolute of contingency. The strong model of correlationism absolutizes facticity, even though it aims to de-absolutize. As Meillassoux says, 'facticity will be revealed to be a knowledge of the absolute because we are going to put back into the thing itself what we mistakenly took to be an incapacity in thought':

> In other words, instead of construing the absence of reason inherent in everything as a limit that thought encounters in its search for the ultimate reason, we must understand that this absence of reason is, and can only be the ultimate property of the entity. We must convert facticity into the real property whereby everything and every world is without reason, and is thereby capable of actually becoming otherwise without reason.[44]

Meillassoux introduces the term 'factiality' to describe the essence of facticity, or rather the speculative essence, because the facticity of things is not actually fact. Factiality is the 'non-facticity of facticity,' giving us the principle of factiality as 'the non-factual essence of fact as such,' but also its necessity: 'To be is necessarily to be a fact, but to be a fact is not just to be anything whatsoever.' Factiality is speculation, just as facts are.[45]

There may be many possibilities open to us if contingency is a necessary absolute. One proof from the past that Meillassoux uses is what he calls the 'ancestral' and the 'arche-fossil,' the former being any reality anterior to humans (such as the formation of stars), and the latter being the materials indicating such an ancestral event. The correlationist account and the arche-fossil cannot both be true at the same time, and the correlationist, in light of a scientific discovery of something independent of human thought, usually acts in a manner not consistent with correlationism—they refuse to say that the recently discovered event could never have happened in the way we describe it. Or the correlationist will seek to defend their position, and Meillassoux gives us some possible refutations, but what the arche-fossil should encourage us to do is 'to get out of ourselves, to grasp the in-itself,' against the last two centuries of modern [western] philosophy.' We end up with the 'principle of unreason,' whereby 'there is no reason for anything to be or to remain the way it is; everything must, without reason, be able not to be and/or be able to be other than it is.'[46]

The non-factual essence of facticity reminds us of the anti-essentialist approach taken by postanarchism; but speculative materialism also deepens the analysis of states as temporary formations that we find in Badiou's work and postanarchist theory. The critique of power can no longer be limited by the dogmatic argument that there are certain things we cannot know, such as the true value of something. It is not that speculative materialism reveals to us the in-itself of value, but it does point towards the factiality of value and the possibility that value can be something other, there being no philosophical reason why something cannot change.

Meillassoux does not bring Marx into his philosophy in any significant way, although he does question the approach taken by Marx (and Freud) in their attempt to resist those who oppose their realist approach. Both point towards class interests or libido as the motivation for their adversaries, what Meillassoux calls a 'theory of suspicion,' which can amount to refuting the argument of a mathematician on the grounds that he or she is sickly or suffering a frustrated libido. Instead, realism should retain a certain rationalism. Meillassoux does not want to engage with correlationists simply by refuting them once and for all through an axiom outside of the correlation, but through a refutation of the correlationist circle, as we have seen. It contains its own refutation.[47] This is not to say that Meillassoux disagrees with Marxian theory in its entirely, but it might suggest that the critique Marx was looking for was already within the value form of the commodity—the impossibility of the unthinkable in-itself of value being unthinkable. We have seen already the neo-Kantian critique of value under capital. Now we can challenge it through factiality and the necessity of contingency.

6.6.2 Speculative Materialism in the Derivatives Market

Although it may be nothing new to see theorists turning away from Marx, we have seen theorists such as Suhail Malik study the 2008 financial crisis not through Marxian theory, but through the derivatives market in particular, arguing that this is where the most sophisticated analytical tools are to be found.[48] Ayache also uses the derivatives market in which he works as the source for his theory of contingency in the markets, and is interesting to us for the use he makes of Meillassoux and Badiou (while Marx does not figure in his works). Just as Meillassoux finds within correlationism the source of a contingency with which he refutes it, Ayache finds within the markets the means to develop a theory of contingency with which to critique probability theories. Money is, for example, seen by Ayache as a better count of randomness than any chronological count of randomness associated with probability, and he casts aside the notion that time is money.[49]

While derivatives are contracts that are indexed to an 'underlying' value (of stocks or interest rates, for example) from which they derives their value, they can be traded in their own right, betting on the future price of the underlying, thereby offering 'insurance' for those who want to invest in state bonds (as with credit default swaps) or commodities (as with the futures market). Leaving aside the critique of derivatives and the impact their use may or may not have on, say, macro-economic stability and the price of wheat, Ayache's argument is that derivatives are always possible as an act of exchange, or writing, based on the knowledge we have now, and not the ability to predict the future (drawing on Badiou here in making the point that invention and creation are incalculable). Ayache argues against models of probability used in this process, and especially the Black-Scholes-Merton model that Nassim Nicholas Taleb critiques. This model helps traders to estimate the price of trading options for buying or selling derivatives, but Ayache sees it as a model that is used to fill in the 'blanks,' regardless of what the 'real' underlying is.[50] There is no need to focus on Taleb's book

150   THE PROLETARIAT RELOADED

here, except to say that his reference to the 'black swan' in finance is drawn from Hume's problem that no matter how many white swans we observe, we cannot infer that all swans are white. If one black swan is eventually observed, any conclusion that all swans are white based on previous observation is refuted. This analogy can have calamitous effects on traders if they ignore the probability of the black swan one day making an appearance.[51]

While Ayache draws on philosophy, Taleb is unfortunately disparaging of the philosophical works he struggles to understand, arguing that works commensurate to Derrida can be produced using Monte Carlo generators, piecing together random words to create texts convincing enough to be published, as with the Alan Sokal hoax. Taleb also criticizes Hegel (whom Taleb condescendingly calls a 'philosopher') by quoting the discredited Karl Popper on the subject of Hegel.[52] The Hegel scholar Charles Taylor long ago compared Popper's views on certain philosophers to 'the political opinions of a great performer or writer [who is] ... often listened to with an attention and respect that their intrinsic worth hardly commands.'[53] And on Hegel specifically, Walter Kaufmann famously highlighted the flaws in Popper's work, missing sections of Hegel's work, which led to glaring factual errors, and arguing that Popper relied on Scribner's *Hegel Selections*, 'a little anthology for students that contains not a single complete work.'[54] Taleb's attempt to marginalize the role of philosophers in understanding the markets perpetuates this myth, and should embarrass the author.

Fortunately, there is no such marginalization of philosophy in Ayache's work. If Meillassoux advances a philosophy that is confident in engaging with science, Ayache puts Badiou, Deleuze and especially Meillassoux's philosophy to work on the financial markets, proving philosophy's contemporary relevance.

Derivatives, which Ayache calls the 'natural offspring of the market' and 'the stuff the market is made of' are written and recorded as a value in order to trade on a future date, but it is the act of writing that creates their price in an instant. The trading process is not the reiteration of values already decided upon. Despite the pricing model, contingency exceeds this. The market is a writing process that cannot be reduced to a stochastic, probabilistic process—it is a medium of contingency that cannot be reduced to possibility. Probability may decide on possible outcomes, but Ayache distinguishes between possibility, as being defined by a fixed context, and contingency as the capacity for changing the context, drawing on (the fictional) Pierre Menard's work. Ayache is clear here that he is not just thinking of the derivatives market (even if that is the ground on which he develops his theory), but also the wider markets.[55]

When we trade in the market, Ayache argues that it is because we do not know something and cannot predict something, rather than us actually knowing. Otherwise, there would be little reason to trade for profit if we already knew the value of everything. With basic assets such as stocks, commodities and currencies, the neoclassical view is that value is strongly influenced by supply and demand, but with derivatives one 'steps into the market to exchange those derivatives' and to 'change the values one has just computed,' seeking the liquidity of the trading floor.[56] The derivatives market makes this part of the trading process more obvious than it is with basic assets.

Ayache argues that the common conception of the market seeks to exclude its inhabitants from its ontological foundations in one of two possible ways. In one sense it operates without regard to the individual as such, but as a system, while in another it could be seen as a process for generating data which is independent of individuals and which they try, but apparently fail, to discover from the outside. However, the market is a material thing, and needs an ontological foundation that includes a material element, which Ayache sees as the body of the inhabitant. It is the individual who writes the price of something to be traded, writing at the surface of the market and not at some depth that involves probability or submission to the history of the markets. Ayache calls this 'metaphysically new kind of process' the 'writing process' or the 'pricing process,' which is the process of the 'differentiation of the virtual,' drawing on Deleuze here and the realization of that which is real but not actual.[57] In other words, traders write the price, which is essentially real even if it is not actual, with contingency traversing price. Given that this takes place at the surface, we see contingency in action rather than an acceptance that there is some in-itself lurking beneath, which we can do our best to access through probability models but never quite know.

Ayache, then, compares his view of the market to Meillassoux's factiality, writing that while it appears that the market conditions contingency, he also argues that the market is not a being, and acts, rather, as the medium of contingency. Factial speculation is carried out within the marketplace. Because Meillassoux has a notion of speculative thought that is necessary but not the thought of a necessary being, Ayache argues that this stands at the extreme opposite of metaphysics, and in Ayache's work manifests itself as the pricing or writing process. Instead of belonging to the realm of trading and risk exposure, speculation is instead associated with philosophy and contingency. Philosophy ceases to be passive and associated with 'depth,' and instead, in traversing the correlationist circle and metaphysics, becomes active, concerned with the contingent claim and the pricing process (of the surface). Philosophy becomes concerned with the future, albeit 'not the metaphysical or chronological future, of course, but the future of thought or of the market. The future (as in speculation) as opposed to the past (as in debt).'[58]

Ayache seems to depart slightly from Meillassoux insofar as he sees him as relieving himself not only from the past, but also the future, because he is concerned only with speculation (what he calls 'Meillassoux's pass'). Ayache, on the other hand, wants to apply his theory to the market, and is concerned with the implication of speculative materialism for thought, instead of only refuting correlationism. Ayache maintains that he believes in absolute contingency, but retains a belief that 'physics will not change'; in other words, that the market and trading will remain. As Ayache puts it, 'I only retain from factial speculation the suspension of the whole outlook regarding future world changes.' Ayache talks of the future being there and necessary, which he thinks may be an assumption too far for Meillassoux, but assures himself that Meillassoux hints at such a future, which Ayache maintains is not 'chronological' but contingent and 'the future of thought itself, the exact opposite of the passivity of philosophical credit' which draws on the past as correlationism does. Ayache compares Meillassoux's pass to Badiou's impasse or event, the un-totalization of possibilities (or of the mathematical field in Badiou's work), which does not prevent something you might think possible from happening, but simply means that it will not be an event if it does happen. I would say this is a stringent interpretation of the event, but the point is that the event is unexpected. While Ayache concerns himself with the future, it is an unexpected one. He sees the important shift in discourse as being one from a change in the laws of nature that does or does not occur due to totalization or un-totalization of possible worlds and possible future repercussions, to

> a change that can happen and can only happen (in the sense of the degree of happening, which is enough) due to the gravity of a happening that could never be assumed by the presentable idea of totalization of possibilities (it doesn't matter whether it is itself a success or a failure) and can, therefore, only be assumed by the future.

Ayache argues that he can leave aside any question about the laws of nature changing, as this change is for the future and has not happened yet. This should not, therefore, prevent us from applying factiality to the market. As with Badiou's event, Ayache argues, it remains mathematical even after the event.[59] It seems that the market remains the market even if we apply the factiality argument to the trading process. It is still a valid argument, even if the market may cease to exist one day.

Pricing or writing contingent claims should, Ayache argues, be our only other way of thinking, and the way in which the relation between being and thought be settled. This can only happen in the material and non-metaphysical mode of writing. As with correlationism and its own critique being already present within it, 'Meillassoux has ipso facto established himself in the space of writing, where the un-totalization of possibilities was always already given and metaphysics already surpassed.'[60] Price is seen as the 'immanent translation of the contingent claim,' as opposed to a transcendent claim as a value which requires the category of possibility:

> Price is the ethical obligation of the future. It is the 'value' binding the future, that is to say, the 'value' of the contingent claim. The contingent claim admits of no bound (and no binding) other than the market (the market is the future made partner of the exchange). This is an immanent binding, which depends on no transcendent principle of valuation.[61]

The market, for Ayache, can no longer defend its position as a generator of data, or of prices over time, but an 'atemporal medium that is conductive of contingent claims and then transmits them as prices.'[62] Similarly to Badiou's view of history as non-linear—the claim that history does not exist, but just historicizations in which subjects have a hand[63]—the market as the writing process is the process of history. It is not one guided by possibilities, but by contingency, and it is in this way that it is written—through contingent claims.[64]

6.6.3 The Post-Evental Pricing Process: A Democracy of 'Self-Pricing'

On a philosophical level, there is no reason why the pricing process cannot be applied to the labour market. The pricing process, at least, cannot be ruled out in favour of relying only on the self-valorization of capital and associated value forms (relying on the correlation of the market), including for 'basic' assets and commodities such as labour, where there is a significant amount of supply and demand at work (although supply and demand does not alone determine wages even for conventional economists).⁶⁵ There will be other reasons, such as affordability, for ruling out contingent claims on wages (this argument is regularly made whenever unions demand better pay, except when de facto unions for the highly paid, such as the Institute of Directors, defend pay levels at the top end), but they do not work on a philosophical level if we follow the speculative materialist approach. Indeed, the pricing process can be found in the labour market, although it is not as prevalent as Ayache would say it is in the derivatives market. Instead, it is more likely to be found in the better paid sections of the labour market where a price is named before employment is accepted. Such near-self-pricing is not found in most of the labour market, but the pricing process has as much legitimacy here, philosophically speaking. However, to move towards self-pricing and the contingent claim of the writing or pricing process, there needs to be an event, which, if we agree with Badiou, would be collective political action.

I maintain that self-pricing sits on firmer ground than the self-valorization of the proletariat, although it is easy to see how Marx's analysis can be used as a basis for the latter. Marx's theory of surplus value, as is well known, concerns unpaid labour time: 'The value contained in a commodity is equal to the labour time taken in making it, and this consists of both paid and unpaid labour.' This follows the general formula for capital developed by Marx, M-C-M', i.e. money capital converted into commodities to extract a greater sum of money capital. The capitalist interacts with the worker as the 'mere owner of labour-power,' and this labour power is objectified in the commodity, part of which the capitalist has paid for, and part of which costs the capitalist nothing, despite costing the worker labour. This is where, for Marx, the capitalist's profit is derived, from that value for which the capitalist did not pay, the commodity value over its cost price (the total sum of labour contained in the commodity).⁶⁶ In *Capital*, the sale of labour power 'always takes place for definite periods of time.' An external measurement of time, it would seem, is required in order for labour time and surplus value to be measured: 'The sum of the necessary labour and the surplus labour, i.e. the sum of the periods of time during which the worker respectively replaces the value of his labour-power and produces the surplus value, constitutes the absolute extent of his labour time, i.e. the working day.'⁶⁷

The problem of time and value as an external element has been addressed by Antonio Negri, but his approach does not pave the way (to the extent that Badiou's approach does) for an active politics whereby contingency is more easily grasped by workers. In *Marx beyond Marx*,

Negri sees in the *Grundrisse* a communism that is synonymous with liberty, a liberated subjectivity that is a working class negation of the power of capital, a communist revolution involving the emergence of the social individual creating a wealth of alternatives.[68] Negri traces this liberation from exploitation back to the production process and the theory of wages and time in the *Grundrisse*. Marx describes, in the *Grundrisse*, the creation by capital of disposable time ('not-labour' time) for society's members in order to reduce (necessary) labour time to a minimum, giving capital more disposable time that it can eat into in order to create surplus labour—capital tends to attempt to create disposable labour, but only for its own benefit (i.e. the exploitation of surplus labour to create surplus value). As Marx put it, capital's 'tendency [is] always, on the one side, to create disposable time, on the other, to convert it into surplus labour.' If too much disposable time is created by capital, Marx explains, there is surplus production as a result of the increased availability of surplus labour at first. However, this surplus of production then interrupts necessary labour as no surplus labour can be realized by capital, since there is no demand for it—a contradiction resulting in the impossibility of the appropriation of alien labour by capital and the need for the workers to appropriate their own surplus labour. Once they have done this, 'on one side, necessary labour time will be measured by the needs of the social individual, and, on the other, the development of the power of social production will grow so rapidly that, even though production is now calculated for the wealth of all, disposable time will grow for all.' Disposable time, rather than labour time, becomes the measure of wealth, 'existing in and because of the antithesis to surplus labour time; or, the positing of an individual's entire time, and his degradation therefore to mere worker, subsumption under labour.'[69]

For Negri, the displacement is complete here: social capital corresponds with the collective worker, the social individual of the communist revolution. The law of surplus value is reversed so that the refusal to work becomes the worker's prerogative—social subsumption leads to the social individual and communism as a negation and reappropriation of surplus labour, where the worker can control necessary labour to the point that surplus labour is destroyed. Working class power is the 'negation of the power of capital,' since surplus labour is no longer uniform as it is usually under capital but, under the refigured shape of capital, 'the wage as it developed became self-valorization and reappropriation of surplus labour.' This puts an end to 'all rules useful for development' so that there is no more capitalist rationality but instead a liberating subjectivity.[70] There is no longer an outside value with which to measure exploitation, as value is subordinated to social time—antagonism is now immanent.

In the *Constitution of Time*, Negri sees Marx's philosophical impasse as the reliance on an external element (use value) to explain the internal element that is productive power, and the real subsumption that Negri elaborates in *Marx beyond Marx* provides what he sees as a way out of this aporia. The real subsumption of the social whole by capital, the appearance of collective social labour, and the impossibility of an external measure of labour time, opens the way to go beyond Marx and theorize the subjectivity of the revolutionary worker. For Negri, this subsumption is productive, for 'now we know that time cannot be presented as measure, but must rather be presented as the global phenomenological fabric, as base, substance and flow of production in its enemy.' Real subsumption does not equal indifference, but rather reveals the real relations of individuals, class and force, maximising plurality and dynamism, and opening up antagonism precisely because action cannot be reduced to an average value or unified time. When capitalism has destroyed time as measure, 'capital constructs time as collective substance.... This substance is a multiplicity of antagonistic subjects.'[71] This understanding of time as substance, of antagonism and social labour, provides the background to Negri's theory of the multitude. Already, however, we see the optimism that is also evident in *Empire* and *Multitude*, the belief in the possibility of a revolution without a theory of the event comparable to Badiou's theory.

Negri's theory of time and wages is therefore potentially a waiting game that assumes capitalism will take a certain path. Capitalism may well take this path, but to bank on this leaves us in the unrealistic realms of possibility (that is, the prediction of possible outcomes). Badiou's event, on the other hand, discards possibility/probability. He may look towards the factory or the proletariat as potential event-sites while excluding capital as an event-site, but Meillassoux, especially in Ayache's reading of him, shows that any attempt to predetermine sites for an event is incompatible with Badiou's own theory of the event. The event cannot be predicted, and furthermore, the truth of the event is an approximate truth for the subject. The collective political action of the event involves an intervention and a wager, a process of naming similar to the process of writing or pricing, and this is the tactical approach that continues the work of Marx through the self-pricing of labour.

6.7 Countering Accelerationism

Any pricing process that is led by the demands of a political collective (through a mass movement or a union, for example) is difficult when not linked to an event; but when the situation is right for an event to emerge, the prevailing conditions for those claiming fidelity to the event are much more favourable when seeking to write contingent claims, as Ayache would call them. One way to challenge the capitalist power that prevails through its value system is through the event (and many events at that, rather that the absolute commencement of an eternal utopia). However, recently, the accelerationist approach has gained ground.

It is worth countering aspects of this here, for it seems to be taking us back to a vanguardist approach where power can be challenged from behind the desk of those who rely on their cognitive labour to make a living. However, it is also true that if those declaring fidelity to an event are to benefit from being able to make the philosophical case for contingent claims, the case that recent accelerationist authors have made for a tech-savvy collective cannot be dismissed.

Following a line of thinkers that includes Jean-François Lyotard and Nick Land, Alex Williams and Nick Srnicek advocate, in their *#Accelerate: Manifesto for an Accelerationist Politics,* an accelerationism that is a 'navigation' and 'experimental process of discovery within a universal space of possibility.' They argue that the left should embrace technology not as techno-utopians who seek to overcome social conflict, but that the development of technology should be accelerated in order to win social conflicts, with the left taking advantage of every technological and scientific advance. The accelerationist left should become literate in the fields of 'social network analysis, agent-based modelling, big data analytics, and non-equilibrium economic models.' Direct action is looked upon as insufficient, and, rather than the 'fetishization of openness, horizontality, and inclusion' which they see as ineffective, Williams and Srnicek advocate 'Secrecy, verticality, and exclusion' as viable political strategies. Direct action does not appear to be completely ruled out, however, with the two advocating the reconstitution of proletarian power through various 'partial proletarian identities' often 'embodied in post-Fordist forms of precarious labour' (fortunately they do not adopt the term 'precariat').[72]

While the use of technology and the drawing together of proletarian identities is not something one would expect Badiou to disagree with, there is a risk here that the proletariat is dismissed, against recent evidence that the proletariat is alive and (un)well (even if they, along with fellow travellers, call themselves the 99 per cent and do not appear to work in factories). This dismissal is present in Negri and his analysis of #Accelerate, where he argues that with 'all due respect to those who still comically believe that revolutionary possibilities must be linked to the revival of the working class of the twentieth century,' we are actually dealing with a class 'endowed with a higher power.' This is the class of cognitive labour—'This is the class to liberate, this is the class that has to free itself.'[73] Negri is selecting a subject here rather than letting subjects choose themselves; whereas the definition of the proletariat I have used throughout this work still holds and is flexible enough to incorporate the cognitariat (as Franco Berardi refers to cognitive labour, or the office worker who feels the need to give up their surplus labour more freely in today's flexible workplace).[74]

It may be the case that #Accelerate does not advocate doing anything but encouraging the acceleration of capitalism and inequality, but this criticism has been directed at earlier writers associated with accelerationism. As Benjamin Noys has noted, where Deleuze and Guattari saw hope in capitalist deterritorialization (even if it does seek to reterritorialize as well), Lyotard saw masochistic joy (or what Lacan would call *jouissance*) in the faces of the striking English workers he observed and the financial burden they were suffering, departing from the usual narrative of the left that workers suffer alienation through their predicament. Noys also argues against attempts to see Marx as an accelerationist, since, while he wrote of ever greater capitalist development bringing an end to itself, he also welcomed direct action and the shorter working day.[75] Marx wrote of automation, but labour is still exploited to supplement automation. Most people continue to sell their labour to make a living. So, for Noys, we should guard against the idea that increased automation has or will improve life for those who sell their labour. Many workers find themselves working longer days as they take their office home with them in the evening (or their home *is* their office). Accelerationists, Noys argues, try to engage with the problem of labour by 'reintegrating labor into the machine,' but he sees this as a symptom of our present predicament rather than a solution.[76]

One theoretical reason given for the move towards non-eventual political action, against the understanding of the event Badiou puts forward whereby the political collective defends the consequences of the event, is the fragment on machines and the general intellect found in Marx's *Grundrisse*. We have seen how this passage influenced Negri decades ago, and is included in Robin Mackay and Armen Avanessian's *Accelerationist Reader* alongside Williams' and Srnicek's work.

It should be remembered that the *Grundrisse* is a collection of notebooks, and not Marx's more considered view on capitalism that would appear later. The fact that machines were thought of by Marx as 'organs of the human brain, created by the human hand; the power of knowledge, objectified'[77] does not mean that knowledge can be relied on to challenge the power of capital. Collective political action is still required, accompanied by knowledge.

If there is a limit to the materialist dialectic, Raya Dunayevskaya wrote, this occurs when we treat it as an applied science. Dunayevskaya took issue with those who put their faith in the fragment on machines in the 1970s, and the 'emphasis in the *Grundrisse* on machinery as providing the material basis for the dissolution of capital as the workers stand alongside of production as their "regulator".' Even in the *Grundrisse*, Marx 'at no time looked at the expanding material forces as if they were the condition, the activity, the purpose of the liberation,' but he did, nevertheless, break with 'the entire structure of the work,' and even, in the move to *Capital*, 'with the very concept of theory.'[78] Noting the challenge the role of machines posed for Marx in his correspondence with Engels, he arrived at a position in *Capital* where, far from the worker as appendage to machines, simply becoming an automaton and toiling at its speed, the resistance of workers was observed to have increased. This is a different position to that in the *Grundrisse*, where workers seem to be subsumed. Workers continue to have an antagonistic relationship with the production process. Automation does not overcome the materialist dialectic or show us its limitations because workers become one with capital and can choose, if they wish, to apply their intellect in other ways. The *Grundrisse*, for Dunayevskaya, instead shows us both the limitations and the indispensability of the dialectic—it is not an applied science, but one that 'has to be recreated as it spontaneously emerges from the developing Subject.' The analysis in the *Grundrisse*, taken without that which we see in *Capital*, is not concrete enough.[79] In other words, it does not develop from the action of political collectives or events, as it should.

So while the speculative materialist approach is not the traditional way in which Marxian theorists have critiqued capitalist values, direct action is a key component of Marxist politics, and the absolute of contingency is another string to the bow of anarchism and communism. It gives legitimacy to the democratic event, which philosophers should work with as it emerges spontaneously.

6.8 Violence

We have seen how the state, in both postanarchist theory and Badiou's theory, is contingent and temporary, with the onus on the state to prove its own legitimacy. We have also seen how speculative materialism gives us a theory of contingency which can be developed to dispute the assumption that values determined by the market are the truest values we can hope for, and that such values can be challenged with alternative pricing. The same philosophy can also be used to challenge the assumption that the state is as good as it gets, complementing the anarchist and communist views that the end of the state is the horizon of politics. The role of political collectives in evental politics has been maintained throughout, especially given the fact that the proletariat remains a significant potential force whose exploitation can be observed, but which, theoretically, we leave entirely to events on the ground for subjects to decide whether they feel part of this collective. Subjects also only grasp at approximate truths through a wager to intervene, the truth of the event remaining indiscernible.

Given this, the question of violence, both by subjects and against subjects, should be addressed. Newman has noted a fetishization of the revolutionary terror and authoritarian politics in Badiou's work—especially in his veneration of figures like Robespierre, Saint-Just, Lenin and Mao.[80] Badiou does refer to violent events on a regular basis, although there are also a number of occasions in which he disavows terror, without resolving the problem of the event potentially conjuring up its own forms of violence. Badiou has written that *'what experience shows is that, over the long term, neither antagonistic action, based on the military or police model, directed against enemies, nor Terror within your own camp can resolve the problems created by your own political existence'* [italics in original].[81] For Badiou, a 'communist-type' politics (drawing on his theory of the subject and event) is determined not by external economic or legal constraints, but under a shared Idea. Badiou draws on Mao (an enduring trait in his works) in arguing that 'the key to a victorious treatment of antagonisms lies in the correct handling of contradictions among the people—which also happens to be the real definition of democracy.' Terror uses state coercion to deal with threats to those defending the consequences of an event, but Badiou does not think it will succeed. Furthermore, he distances the communist idea from terror, arguing that it cannot be the consequence of the communist Idea.[82] Although the question of violence is a complex one, and Badiou maintains that violence can never be ruled out, he maintains that the constant use of violence transforms subjectivity, weakening the signification of revolutions, using the Bolshevik Revolution and the ensuing civil war as an example.[83]

A key question that emerges here is whether preserving the consequences of an event itself becomes an act of what Walter Benjamin would call 'law-preserving violence,' as opposed to the 'divine violence' we might generally associate with an event itself.[84] The question of violence is relevant whenever we discuss values, whether they be the values and value forms the state wishes to defend, or values that emerge with an event. I have demonstrated that the event and the challenge to state values is on firm philosophical ground, and this could be supported by a negative notion of freedom from violence: in short, the freedom to challenge values that are imposed on us, without being beaten up, arrested and incarcerated by the state. The theoretical approach I take towards challenging capitalist values may therefore also be a means to guard against post-eventual politics becoming another form of law-preserving violence, which is something I will now turn to.

Most theoretical discussions on violence draw on Benjamin's 'Critique of Violence,' and it is with reference to this that we see a problem emerge *if* a non-tactical approach is taken post-event. Žižek compares Badiou's revolutionary event to Benjamin's 'divine violence.' Mythic and law-preserving violence is compared by Žižek to the order of being as it appears in Badiou's thought, and divine violence to the order of the event, there being 'no 'objective' criteria enabling us to identify an act of violence as divine.'[85] While mythic violence is law-making, and described by Benjamin as being the mere manifestation of the gods, divine violence is law-destroying. The former sets boundaries and is bloody, and the latter destroys them while being bloodless. Benjamin draws on Georges Sorel's distinction between the *political* general strike, which does nothing to challenge the power of the state, and the *proletarian* general strike, which transcends state power altogether and affirms the autonomy of workers. The first of these is considered violent in its interruption of work and mere 'external modification of labor conditions,' while the proletarian general strike is non-violent and anarchistic. This is a sort of symbolic and 'ethical' violence—it invokes the name of Justice—outside the law; it is pure and immediate and 'the highest manifestation of unalloyed violence by man.' However, as we have seen with Žižek's comparison to Badiou's event, there is a challenge for us 'to decide when unalloyed violence has been realized in particular cases.'[86]

For Judith Butler, Benjamin describes an anarchism and destruction that should be understood to refer not to another kind of political state or an alternative to positive law, but as a violence that 'constantly recurs as the condition of positive law and as its necessary limit.'[87] This reminds us of Badiou's theory of the event, with the situation including its void or necessary limit, as well as life without the state being the horizon of anarchist and communist politics. But we are nevertheless left with divine violence as something intangible, which we must decide on, just as the subject for Badiou makes a wager to intervene on the side of an indiscernible truth. However, despite the subject only knowing an approximate truth, we nevertheless know when an event has taken place, just as there is nothing in what Benjamin says to suggest that we cannot know when an act of divine violence has occurred. We are less certain when divine violence appears in knowing what to do with it, but we must nevertheless decide.[88]

The issue of (law-making and law-preserving) violence against democratic protest is especially salient given actual police violence used against protesters, whether in relation to Occupy or other protests, as well as what has been called the 'criminalization of protest,' with criminal law used by police forces to charge demonstrators (but often failing in the courts).[89] Furthermore, the attempted criminalization of protest has applied not only to those engaging in what the police deem an illegal act, but those in the vicinity of such acts as the placing of a sticker on a window of a 'luxury' flat, with the joint enterprise principle used to deter protest against wealth inequality.[90]

State violence need not be countered with violence though. Newman speaks of a 'violence against violence' that is present within anarchist discourse, but this is associated with the insurrectionary tactics of postanarchism, and is non-violent insofar as it 'does not turn violence into an instrument for the conquest of power.'[91] The event may be subtractive, and in this sense against the Jacobin-like Terror that Newman sees in some aspects of Badiou's work; but defending the consequences of an event does raise the question of violence, and whether there is a risk (especially if a non-tactical approach is taken, unlike the approach I have set out) that it relies on Benjamin's notion of law-preserving violence, setting boundaries between itself and those it opposes if it is to have lasting success, unlike the bloodless divine violence which is law-destroying.[92] However, we have seen how the subject claiming fidelity to an event is only able to grasp an *approximate* truth of the event, and I have argued for a non-prescriptive post-evental politics that makes demands from a philosophical high ground. Indeed, Badiou has sensibly warned against purging the mere semblance of an event in the name of some pure truth, his subtractive ontology guarding against Stalinist tendencies that any vanguard might have.[93] But does not a commune, or an idea, even if its provenance is an event, need to draw sensible or imagined boundaries to guard the 'peace' which Benjamin has associated with law-preserving violence?[94]

Whether the apparently divine violence of an event leads to law-preserving violence when its consequences are being preserved by its subjects, or the event leaves an indiscernible trace, I maintain that the state (and anyone else) should avoid applying law-preserving and potentially bloody violence after the event. Badiou's subtractive politics reinforces Benjamin's view that law-making violence becomes law-preserving violence; but the *negative* nature of the event (*against* the state, the law, or values within a state) without imposing a *positive* vision (*for* another law, to be preserved within a state) is what puts the event on a better philosophical footing than the state's use of force. Furthermore, this allows for the tactical approach of the self-pricing of labour I have suggested. The event is of a different order to being—while any state is ontologically temporary, subjects loyal to the truth of an event will attempt to keep its consequences alive as long as they can, even though the mass movement disappears through the 'vast stages of the historical splace' while leaving an impression on the whole.[95]

We saw in the previous chapter how subjects defending the consequences of an event may need to construct a discourse to defend their position and to challenge the pervading ideology, even though ideology cannot be universal in the way that the truth of an event is both singular and universal. However, in this chapter I have outlined one form of post-evental politics, which is the critique of value forms under capitalism, without philosophers or anyone else prescribing solutions—as in the marketplace, it is for the subject to determine these as they develop their demands. Furthermore, it is important to hold onto a negative notion of violence, as a freedom from violence. It is philosophically legitimate to make collective contingent claims and for a political collective to demand its own price, without the threat of law-preserving violence.

7

Conclusion

The context for this work is the politics of the last decade, where we saw a spike in collective political action through the Occupy movement and others who saw governments representing the interests of the 1 per cent rather than the 99 per cent. What began as a movement that seemed to endorse the Marxian view of society being broadly divided along class lines often became embroiled in debating the identity politics of pre-existing particularisms rather than what it had the potential to be—a singular and universal class-based event against capitalism. I have argued that this is partly due to class being side lined in post-Marxist and some poststructuralist and anarchist thought.

In the first chapter I therefore defended the Marxian approach and the role of the proletariat in capitalist society. While some anarchists have favoured the pluralist approach to politics, I have shown how postanarchists, and particularly Saul Newman, have developed anarchist theory in a way that is not always inimical to the political goals of Marxists, and I have sought to bridge this divide through the thought of Alain Badiou. While being critical of poststructuralism and anarchism, Badiou has arrived at many of the same positions Newman has, including an ontological approach towards understanding power and the state, and a strong case for the singularity and universality of the political event as opposed to the politics of identity. I demonstrated how all states are temporary and, by extending this analysis through Badiou's former student, Quentin Meillassoux, as well as Elie Ayache, both the capitalist values the state defends, and the force it can use as a means to that end, are vulnerable to contingent demands, with the only absolute being contingency.

7.1 Badiou and Postanarchism—Unwitting Partners

In the second and third chapters, I demonstrated how Badiou shares more with postanarchist thought than he admits. The most obvious common ground between postanarchism and Badiou is to be found in the 'anarchist invariant,' which Newman refers to—the 'desire for life without government that haunts the political imagination.'[1] In a similar vein, communism for Badiou is, I maintain, the stateless horizon of politics, with the state always temporary in its existence.[2] For both Badiou and Newman, I have been clear that the existence of states is an ontological fact, and so is their demise.

I have shown how the advantage of this ontological approach, which I have outlined from both Badiou's and Newman's perspective, is that it seeks to avoid essentialism by not privileging certain groups, instead 'simply' setting out how different groups or objects relate to each other. Newman's 'ontological anarchist' position sees anarchy not as an end goal, but as a point of departure that opens up power and authority to ongoing contestation.[3]

Another important area of commonality between the two approaches is their shared critique of identity politics. While Newman sees proletarian class consciousness as no longer being a basis around which to challenge power, he is also critical of identity politics, which is seen as a potential 'essentialist trap,' as the subject's interests and desires are often constructed by the very modes of power and discursivity they purport to oppose. Here he recalls Foucault's suggestions that we should not discover who we are, but refuse who we are. Coming from what might be seen as the opposite angle, Badiou also arrives at a critique of identity-based politics, seeing this as part of a postmodern worldview, which embraces ethnic, linguistic, sexual and other particularisms, but is particularly harmful when it embraces 'biographical particularity,' and 'the self as that which imagines that it can and must "express itself".'

My argument throughout has been that, like Badiou, I believe identity politics can act as a hindrance to evental politics. The event is rare, so subjects should embrace the newfound sameness of this singular and universal event and focus on defending the consequences of the event that brought them together, and not seek to create a hegemonic project under established, and non-evental, identities. Subjects to a political event that is class-led will have their various identities, but as subjects to an event they will be brought together through the evental politics that unites them.

So as well as critiquing the post-Marxist hegemonic approach (which appeals to already existing identities rather than the new sameness that emerges from an event), I argued that it is a mistake for any radical politics of emancipation today—particularly that which fights against economic inequalities—to ignore the crucial subjectivity that is class (albeit, in evental terms, a performative class which does not have a strong, already established identity in people's minds). This supposed antinomy between class and identity, present at the theoretical and political level, is a needless distraction, and can be overcome only if we consider aspects of Marx and anarchism that are complementary to one another.

7.2 Class—The Unheroic Proletariat and Theories of Action

While I looked at the concept of class in the first chapter, in the fourth chapter I took a closer look at how Badiou refers to the proletariat throughout his works, in order to make a case that we can still call him a Marxist, even if not a conventional one. I have been clear that we should not limit the proletariat to those who work in factories. For Badiou, the proletariat consists of workers who are included in the situation and counted by the state, but do not belong to it, going almost unnoticed in terms of how the state presents itself but still being governed by its laws (an excess of inclusion over belonging).[4] The analytical definition of the proletariat I used in the first chapter draws on Erik Olin Wright's definition of class exploitation, maintaining the Marxian concept of the exploitation of one class by another (of the proletariat by the bourgeoisie), despite attempts over the decades to view the 'middle class' and those in managerial roles as somehow not being working class. Of course, some workers are better off than others, but this work is not devoted to analysing this fact, or in revisiting Marxian explanations for working class conservatism or the notion of labour aristocracy, both of which continue to be discussed in Marxian literature.[5] What I do argue is that the proletariat not only exists in an analytical sense, but also in a performative sense, with workers often identifying as such but made to feel that such self-identification is intellectually bankrupt.

Wright argues that the concept of domination, with managers dominating staff, should not be adopted at the expense of the concept of exploitation. A manager may dominate, but may also be exploited—their interests may be the same as those they manage. However, regardless of what those who dominate might see their interests as being, the concept of exploitation maintains that there are objective interests the exploiter is pursuing through the exploited, such as profit or surplus value.[6]

While this analytical understanding of class is important, I demonstrated in the fourth chapter how it is the performative sense of class that Badiou focuses on, a notion that is also present in Marxian theory as a theory of crisis. By performative, I have described the act of identifying oneself as belonging to a class, as we saw with the Occupy movement, rather than the performativity that Judith Butler and others discuss within discourse theory. It is in a moment of crisis that the nuances of class and identity that people are associated with can become less important as we find significant groups of people identifying themselves as the 99 per cent against the 1 per cent. It is, in other words, an event that forces itself on all of us—the state and philosophers included—and requires that we work with this truth. As Badiou puts it, philosophers work with truths rather than produce them, reminding us of Marx's view that philosophers should not just interpret the world, but change it. The philosopher works with what actually exists (even if what exists is not immediately apparent) in order to interpret the world rather than apply his/her own speculative ideas. Materially and ontologically, the world changes, and as Badiou argues, philosophy should not attempt to paper over the void of a situation, which after all is the function of ideology.

Badiou's references to the proletariat have certainly developed over the years to the extent that hints of essentialism (that the proletariat is a pre-determined subject) are easier to dispel. In *Theory of the Subject* Badiou sees 'the party' as the organ that purifies the working class to isolate them from the whole.[7] However, by the time Badiou gets to *Being and Event*, he is clear that there is no hero of the event, given that, from the point of view of ontology, the event is *not*; but the subject does nevertheless need to defend the consequences of an event that may not be of their own making (something familiar to Marxists). As Badiou puts it, 'Intervention [in making a wager to support the event, despite the undecidability as to its belonging to the situation] generates a discipline: it does not deliver any originality. There is no hero of the event.'[8] This, I have argued, removes any notion of a vanguard and puts the political collective in a position that aligns with the postanarchist approach.

I have also shown how both Badiou's approach, and the postanarchist one, are action oriented. Just as we can say there are no heroes of the event, just those who defend its consequences and who we may therefore call communists, I have said there is no such thing as a ready-made anarchist, but just subjects who become anarchists through their activism. For Badiou, the question of what communism means is one that will never be agreed upon, but it is agreed that it is tied to 'real sequences of emancipatory politics as its essential real condition.'

Indeed, communism must be freed from its predicative usage, having no preconditions other than the event.[9]

Neither postanarchism, nor Badiou and his idea of communism, prescribe any particular end to the event; both are proposing an ontology of contingency. Both are theories of action, with Badiou taking the more Marxian view, arguing that Marxism relies on the 'impossible revolution.'[10] For Marx, I have described how communism seemed impossible after the Paris Commune of 1871, but communism, he argued, had to be something to work towards given the impossibility of continuing under capitalism, even if communism remains impossible.[11] We have also seen how the Paris Commune is seen as a good example of evental politics by both Badiou and Newman, so while an anti-state politics and a politics without a party have been the favoured approach of postanarchists and Badiou, this approach is also not inimical to the Marxian approach.

Furthermore, the Marxist approach to politics is perfectly capable of being an adaptive one. The notion I have used of the Marxist approach being performative is partly borrowed from Étienne Balibar, who sees in Marx a philosophy that works with events, being active and evolving and adapting to every situation and crisis. So I described how Balibar sees Marx's thought as not so much a philosophy, but rather a non-philosophy whereby Marx uses philosophical tools, but at the same time goes beyond philosophy, demonstrating that philosophy is determined by social relations rather than being an autonomous field.[12]

7.3 Ideology and Post-Event Demands—The Self-Pricing of Labour

In the fifth chapter I considered the treatment given to the problem of ideology in both Badiou's and Newman's works, as how we counter ideology is relevant to post-event politics. I considered how the latter draws on Lacan's notion of fantasy, in part, in his critique of ideology, and while Badiou avoids psychoanalytic concepts (although he is influenced by Lacan in other ways), he does share common ground with Newman in his approach to ideology. This is most evident in Badiou's understanding of ideology as simply representing bourgeois ideas, thus avoiding the problematic category of 'false consciousness.' However, this raised some interesting questions as to how to confront ideology, whether to develop a 'construct' after the event, and whether the event ultimately leads to a form of terror. While Badiou does discuss terror and a temptation to differentiate between the real and a semblance of the real, he favours the subtractive approach whereby nothing can prove that what is thought to be the real of an event or revolution is actually the real. Yet this very inability to understand the 'truth' completely *is* real.[13]

So given that the event is subtractive and we view life without the state as the horizon of politics, I discussed in the final chapter something that Marxian theorists have long been considering, which is how to challenge value under a state or capitalism. Kojin Karatani has taken a Kantian approach to this problem, but rather than utilize Kant, I chose to extend the ontological case for contingency with regard to value forms, enabling subjects to make tangible demands against claims that values in the free market are absolute and determined by autonomous economic forces beyond human control.

To do this, I turned to object-oriented ontology and speculative materialism. There have been initial forays into this field within anarchist scholarship, with Matt Bernico drawing on Graham Harman to consider an 'anarchism of things.'[14] However, it is primarily Quentin Meillassoux's focus on 'correlationism' and the way in which Elie Ayache has applied Meillassoux's theory to the derivatives market to understand what 'price' is, that I am particularly interested in.

I then considered what this means for the self-pricing of labour, referring to Marxian thought on commodity fetishism, and more recent ideas for challenging capitalism, such as the approach taken by contemporary accelerationists. I argued that class-led demands for better pay can be supported by an understanding of contingency as absolute, with the Marxist approach of workers realizing one's reification under capital (as Lukács would encourage)[15] strengthened by the realization that market values/value forms are contingent on individuals (sometimes on their own, sometimes collectively) naming their price rather than accepting the going rate or the market value. Just as the question of challenging ideology raised the issue of whether some kind of construct is required, the final chapter also considered how post-event politics could find itself on the terrain of law-preserving violence, but that it need not, with the absolute of contingency bolstering the case *against* the violence of the state as it seeks to enforce its laws and values against the demands of workers who choose to name their price.

7.4 Limitations

Of course, there are limitations with this current work, particularly the applicability of Badiou's articulation of Marxian theory to politics beyond the West (Maoism in China aside). It certainly should be relevant, in my view, given that the event is both singular and universal, but that its universality means it is universal for a situation, and not for all people at all times. It would therefore be interesting to see the theory in this work applied to situations in different contexts, and not because of the flawed argument that Marxian analysis is more relevant to those in developing countries because those in the West have little right to complain. This is an argument used typically to disrupt the logic of protest for all except the most destitute, who are (conveniently, for this school of thought) likely to be no more soon anyway.

Marxian thought, of course, has been influential across the globe and remains relevant, for example in subaltern studies.[16] However, there can be a tendency in the West to focus *only* on the West, and Marxian theorists can tend to overlook the applicability of supposedly universal theory to different situations, or apply it poorly. A fairly recent example is Hardt and Negri's *Empire*, which Perry Anderson argued demonstrated a 'spectacular failure to address the substantive and experiential situations of the settled populations of the nation states of Asia, Africa and Latin America,' despite the book's popularity in postcolonial studies circles.[17] This practice is present in anarchist theory as well, which is especially surprising given the breadth of thinkers who could be considered anarchist. As Süreyyya Evren has written, there are whole histories of anarchism written that assume it is a European idea, or sometimes even a North American one too, with little or no regard to the rest of the world.[18]

Moreover, Cedric Robinson, in the classic work *Black Marxism*, has highlighted how Marxism has overlooked the problems faced by black people in the West. This was often a problem with strategy rather than with the theory, with communist parties distancing themselves from black nationalism, and black people not being recruited to communist parties in the US until 1921. Robinson does illustrate some concerns with Marxism at a theoretical level too, pointing to Richard Wright's concern that Marxism is a petit bourgeois theory aimed at the ruling bourgeoisie, *for* the working classes, rather than *of* the working classes.[19] There are, of course, a number of forces at work in dividing the working class, such as the tactic used by the bourgeoisie to encourage racism among the white working class, against those who might take their jobs.[20] This is, therefore, an area more than appropriate for further inquiry, where race and class intersect not just for those who are the target of racism, but also for those who are privileged by their race and seek to entrench this privilege, but whose interests would be better served in recognizing events that reveal a truth about class.

While Badiou's analysis is focused on class, working *with* a diverse range of events and the factors that give rise to them (not to dilute the truth of an event), rather than deciding what events are possible for established identities, should yield interesting results.

Appendix

— Terminology —

Postanarchism

Where I refer to 'postanarchism,' I am referring primarily to the work of Saul Newman, Todd May and, to a lesser extent, Lewis Call, who draw on aspects of poststructuralist theory in which they identify a certain anarchistic quality. There are other poststructuralist thinkers and more 'traditional' anarchists referred to throughout, but the point is that I refer to writers conducive to the anarchist invariant referred to throughout, which is the desire for life without the state. It is, therefore, a broad ontological view of anarchism that questions the foundations of the state and power. Indeed, as Jason Harman has written of ontological *anarché*, 'Politics, and political regimes, exist precisely because of the absence of *arché* that defines our ontological existence.'[1]

This is in contrast to the position of Michael Schmidt and Lucien van der Walt, who argue that 'Class struggle' anarchism, sometimes called revolutionary or communist anarchism, is not a type of anarchism; in our view, it is the *only* anarchism.'[2] Despite this focus on class, the approach taken by Schmidt and van der Walt does not complement the ontological approach considered here (and whether it usefully complements Marxian discourse on class struggle is a wider discussion that I do not cover in this book). It has also been a divisive approach within anarchist scholarship. Nathan Jun opposes this narrow understanding of anarchism with a wider interpretation of anarchism as a theory that exhibits a commitment to both radical egalitarianism *and* radical antiauthoritarianism (identifying right-wing libertarians and authoritarian Marxists as examples of those who only manage to pursue one or the other). So instead of just identifying anarchists as those tied to actual anarchist movements (as Schmidt and van der Walt do), Jun also draws on writers whose texts can be read 'anarchistically,' including Chinese Taoists and Buddhists, the Greek Cynics and Jewish and Islamic Mystics, among others.[3]

Communism

In accordance with Marx's view of communism as both impossible but also, by necessity, possible, Badiou's own definition may also seem ambiguous, but also quite simple. Communism is that which challenges the state with the creation of new political truths. This is not a communism to be delivered through a new kind of state —the 'workers' state' for instance—but 'the withering away of the State, [which] while undoubtedly a principle that must be apparent in any political action... is also an infinite task, since the creation of new political truths will always shift the dividing line between Statist, hence historical, facts and the eternal consequences of an event.'[4] Communism can be seen as having the end of the state, or the supposition of the state's illegitimacy, as the horizon of its politics. However, calling this 'communism,' or referring to proper nouns such as 'Lenin' or 'Marx,' has little currency for Badiou (despite his frequent references to them), with the usual nouns (e.g. revolution, proletariat) being 'in themselves much less capable of naming a real sequence in the politics of emancipation, and their use is rapidly exposed to an inflation that has no content.' Adjectives are for propaganda, while 'A real politics knows nothing of identities, even the identity—so tenuous, so variable—of "communists".'[5] This is not to say that 'proletariat' should not be the name of a subject, but that such a name, or an alternative name for a similar collective, is to be determined by those defending the consequences of an event.

Badiou's ontology

While Badiou uses set theory and category theory to illustrate his notion of the subject, I do not engage with mathematical theory, and nor do I think it is necessary to engage with Badiou on this level. One thing that attracted me to Badiou at first was his use of science/mathematics to show that all states or Ones are temporary. Whether or not his theory is correct at all times on a mathematical level, however, is not relevant to this book—the validity of a mathematical theory does not automatically mean a theory of the subject (of human behaviour) is also valid. Nevertheless, Badiou's theory is, I maintain, convincing and well argued, although Bruno Bosteels has gone further in explaining the absence of mathematics in his work on Badiou, arguing that once we leave the realm of ontology and logic and consider the implications of Badiou's theory for politics, 'the role of mathematics becomes heuristic at best and analogical at worst.'⁶ Furthermore, we have seen how decidability is crucial for Badiou's theory of the subject. Ultimately, the wager the subject makes is more important than ontology, for which the event is not.

Terminology is explained throughout, and in chapter 3 especially, key terms in *Being and Event* are explained in the course of relating this to postanarchist theory. I will, however, explain very briefly some of the key terms of Badiou's used throughout:

The One

The One can be any state, body or group, although, for Badiou, the One is *not*, and the multiple is the general form of presentation. The One is an *operation* and never absolute or final. The term 'world' describes something similar in Badiou's later *Logics of Worlds*, where he says 'it is of the essence of the world not to be the totality of existence, and to endure the existence of an infinity of other worlds outside of itself.'⁷ The One, unlike being, cannot present itself.⁸ We also see Badiou refer to the 'Two' throughout his career, introducing the dialectical notion of the One dividing into Two in order to set his interpretation of Hegel's dialectic apart from the 'Stalinist' interpretation.⁹ This interpretation also sets Badiou apart from the notion of dialectical synthesis, making his approach more palatable to anarchists.

Multiple and Situation

The multiple is opposed to the primacy of the One, and is the regime of presentation. However, it is still directly relevant to the One, or the process of counting-as-one. A situation (or structured presentation) includes a duality of multiplicities established in the count-as-one—inconsistent multiplicity before the count-as-one, and consistent multiplicity after.¹⁰ Inconsistent multiplicity is pure presentation and forms the basis of ontology and being.

Void

Everything that is presented in a situation is counted, meaning that inconsistency is not presented. In invoking the idea of 'unpresentation in presentation' (that is, inconsistent multiplicity), Badiou arrives at the term 'void' to describe that something on the edge of a situation which is not counted, and whose exclusion is necessary for the operation of the count-as-one, or the One. The Void is not located structurally, within the structure of presentation, although for ontology, everything within a situation must be presented.[11]

Belonging and Inclusion

These two terms are used by Badiou to describe a possible relation between multiples in set theory, but are easily applicable to social relations. In set theory, *'no multiple is capable of forming-a-one out of everything it includes,'* so there will always be an element or a group that is counted by the state, but does not belong—it is merely included, without representation. The void is also included in everything, but nothing belongs to the void, including the void itself.[12]

The Event

While there will always be an excess of inclusion over belonging, after an event the question of belonging emerges in a new way. If a group, such as the proletariat, presents itself during an event where it was previously included in a count-as-one but did not belong in the regime or presentation, where does it belong? Badiou notes that, for ontology, the event is *not*, because self-belonging is prohibited. To acknowledge self-belonging would be to acknowledge a void in the situation. Self-belonging is, for Badiou, constitutive of the event. This is why an intervention is required to decide on the existence of the event, but this wager is 'unpresentable' and ontologically illegitimate, simply because the event is not presented and legitimate within the structure of the count-as-one or the state. The subject therefore has to preserve the consequences of an event that cannot be discerned by the structure.[13] In other words, the event is so radical that the state cannot acknowledge its existence.

The Subject and Approximate Truth

For Badiou, truth is linked to the four generic procedures—love, art, science and politics—but it is only politics that interests us here, and politics is always a collective act. Because the event and truth is indiscernible, it is an approximate truth that the collective subject declares fidelity to. As truth is a subtraction from knowledge, it is also indiscernible, unnameable, and unpresentable. However, Badiou argues that truth can be thought, 'because, in occupying the gaps of available encyclopaedias, [the four generic truth procedures] manifest the common-being, the multiple-essence, of the place in which they proceed.' A subject is manifested locally, and as a finite moment of this manifestation and supported solely by the generic procedure, is able to use his or her experience to think about the truth.[14]

The Singular and the Universal

Singularity has a distinct meaning for Badiou, given it is tied to universality. Badiou opposes the liberal universality of respect for various particularities, or a tautological 'universality of universality' as he sees it, with a singularity that cannot be foreseen by already existing identities. This singularity, or truth, is universal because it is substracted from identitarian predicates, emerging suddenly and having universal relevance beyond established identities.[15] The singular is not represented (by the state, for example), but is instead *presented* and demands attention. The truth that emerges from an event is singular and universal because it is universally indiscernible, unnameable and unpresentable.[16]

The Non-Essentialist and Performative Proletariat

While we will see how Badiou refers frequently to the proletariat as a potential collective subject to the event, we will also see how the proletariat is tied to the singular and universal event in a non-essentialist manner. Indeed, it is probably because the proletariat can do this so convincingly that Badiou talks at length about this collective subject. Rather than selecting the proletariat as an essentialist subject, Badiou's approach is, I maintain, more an ontological observation that the proletariat is the most likely subject in capitalist society. Furthermore, I maintain that the proletariat, for Badiou as well as in Marxian thought more generally, is a performative subject that emerges as a subject in response to actual events, following Balibar's understanding of Marx's proletariat and his non-philosophy referred to above.

Dialectical Materialism

Badiou's materialist dialectic has developed over the years, from something more akin to Althusser's dialectical materialism (when Badiou considered himself an Althusserian), to his more post-Althusserian materialist dialectic that is more compatible with postanarchist thought. However, while Badiou has tended to refer to his 'materialist dialectic' rather than 'dialectical materialism' to distinguish his approach from Althusser's, the terms can be used interchangeably. Badiou opposes his materialist dialectic to 'democratic materialism,' which reifies polling booths and particularisms (as long as they accord with liberal democracy)[17] over real political events and collectives. Badiou seeks to salvage dialectical materialism in order to save philosophy from received opinion.

Bibliography

Abensour, Miguel. *Democracy Against the State: Marx and the Machiavellian Moment*, translated by Max Blechman and Martin Breaugh. Cambridge: Polity Press, 2011.

de Acosta, Alejandro. 'Anarchist Meditations, or: Three Wild Interstices of Anarchism and Philosophy.' *Anarchist Developments in Cultural Studies: 'Post-Anarchism today,'* 1 (2010), 117–138.

Ahmad, Aijaz. *In Theory: Classes, Nations, Literatures*. London: Verso, 2008.

Althusser, Louis. *For Marx*, translated by Ben Brewster. London: Verso, 1977.

———. 'Freud and Lacan.' In *On Ideology*, 140–171. London: Verso, 2008.

———. 'Ideology and Ideological State Apparatuses.' In *On Ideology*, 1–60. London: Verso, 2008.

———. *On the Reproduction of Capitalism: Ideology and Ideological State Apparatuses*, translated by GM Goshgarian. London: Verso, 2014.

———. *Reading Capital*, translated by Ben Brewster. London, Verso, 1970.

———. *The Humanist Controversy and Other Writings*, translated by GM Goshgarian. London: Verso, 2003.

Auten, Gerald and David Splinter, 'Income Inequality in the United States: Using Tax Data to Measure Long-term Trends,' 20 December, 2019. Accessed on 15 September 2020. http://davidsplinter.com/AutenSplinter-Tax_Data_and_Inequality.pdf

Ayache, Elie. 'A Formal Deduction of the Market.' *Collapse VIII* (2014), 959–998

———. *The Blank Swan: The End of Probability*. Chichester: Wiley & Sons, 2010.

Badiou, Alain. *Being and Event*, translated by Oliver Feltham. London: Continuum, 2005.

———. *Can Politics Be Thought*, trans. Bruno Bosteels Durham: Duke University Press, 2018.

———. *Conditions*, translated by Steve Corcoran. London: Continuum, 2008.

———. *Deleuze: The Clamor of Being*, translated by Louise Burchill. Minnesota: The University of Minnesota Press, 2000.

———. *Ethics: An Essay on the Understanding of Evil*, translated by Peter Hallward. London: Verso, 2001.

———. 'The Cultural Revolution: The Last Revolution?' *Positions* 13:3 (2005), 481–514.
———. 'Eight Theses on the Universal.' In *Theoretical Writings*, edited and translated by Ray Brassier and Alberto Toscano, 145–154. London: Continuum, 2006.
———. 'Foucault: Continuity and Discontinuity.' In *The Adventure of French Philosophy*, edited and translated by Bruno Bosteels, 83–100. London: Verso, 2012.
———. 'Fragments of a Public Journal on the American War Against Iraq.' In *Polemics*, translated by Steve Corcoran, 36–61. London: Verso, 2006.
———. 'Infinitesimal Subversion.' In *Concept and Form, Volume One: Key Texts from the Cahiers pour l'Analyse*, edited by Peter Hallward and Knox Peden, 187–208. London: Verso, 2012.
———. *Logics of Worlds: Being and Event II*, translated by Alberto Toscano. London: Continuum, 2009.
———. *Manifesto for Philosophy*, translated by Norman Madarasz. Albany: State University of New York Press, 1999.
———. 'Mark and Lack.' In *Concept and Form, Volume One: Key Texts from the Cahiers pour l'Analyse*, edited by Peter Hallward and Knox Peden, 159–185. London: Verso, 2012.
———. 'Metaphysics and the Critique of Metaphysics.' *Pli* 10 (2000), 174–190.
———. *Metapolitics*, translated by Jason Barker. London: Verso, 2005.
———. *Number and Numbers*, translated by Robin Mackay. Cambridge: Polity, 2008.
———. 'Our contemporary impotence.' *Radical Philosophy* 181 (2013), 43–47.
———. 'Philosophy, Sciences, Mathematics: Interview with Alain Badiou.' *Collapse*, Vol. 1 (2006), 11–26.
———. *Philosophy for Militants*, translated by Bruno Bosteels. London: Verso, 2012.
———. *Pocket Pantheon*, translated by David Macey, London: Verso, 2009
———. *Polemics*, translated by Steve Corcoran. London: Verso, 2006.
———. *Second Manifesto for Philosophy*, translated by Louise Burchill. Cambridge: Polity Press, 2011.
———. *The Adventure of French Philosophy*, edited and translated by Bruno Bosteels. London: Verso, 2012.
———. *The Century*, translated by Alberto Toscano. Cambridge: Polity Press, 2007.
———. 'The Communist Idea and the Question of Terror.' In *The Idea of Communism 2*, edited by Slavoj Žižek, 1–11. London: Verso, 2013.
———. *The Concept of Model*, edited and translated by Zachary Luke Fraser and Tzuchien Tho. Melbourne: Re.press, 2007.

———. 'The Flux and the Party: In the Margins of Anti-Oedipus.' *Polygraph* 15/16 (2004), 75–92.

———. 'The Idea of Communism.' In *The Communist Hypothesis*, translated by David Macey and Steve Corcoran, 229–260. London: Verso, 2010.

———. 'The Idea of Communism.' In *The Idea of Communism*, edited by Costas Douzinas and Slavoj Žižek, 1–14. London: Verso, 2010.

———. *The Meaning of Sarkozy*, translated by David Fernbach. London: Verso, 2008.

———. *The Rational Kernel of the Hegelian Dialectic*, edited and translated Tzuchien Tho. Melbourne: re.press, 2011.

———. *The Rebirth of History*, translated by Gregory Elliot. London: Verso, 2012.

———. *The Subject of Change: Lesson from the European Graduate School*, edited by Duane Rousselle. New York: Atropos Press, 2013.

———. *Théorie de la Contradiction*. 1975. Accessed on 11 January 2017 at http://www.scribd.com/doc/56179831/Alain-Badiou-Theorie-de-la-Contradiction

———. *Theory of the Subject*, translated by Bruno Bosteels. London: Continuum, 2009.

———. 'Third Sketch of a Manifesto of Affirmationist Art.' In *Polemics*, translated by Steve Corcoran, 133–148. London: Verso, 2006.

Badiou, Alain, and François Balmès. *De L'Idéologie*. Paris: François Maspero, 1976.

Badiou, Alain, and Élisabeth Roudinesco. *Jacques Lacan, Past and Present: A Dialogue*, translated by Jason E. Smith. New York: Columbia University Press, 2014.

Badiou, Alain and Simon Critchley. *Democracy and Disappointment: On the Politics of Resistance*, edited by Aaron Levy and Simon Critchley. Philadelphia: DVD, 2007.

Badiou, Alain, Jöel Bellassen, Louis Mossot. 'Hegel in France.' In *The Rational Kernel of the Hegelian Dialectic* by Alain Badiou, edited and translated by Tzuchien Tho. Melbourne: re.press, 2011.

Badiou, Alain, Peter Hallward and Bruno Bosteels. 'Beyond Formalization: An Interview with Alain Badiou Conducted by Peter Hallward and Bruno Bosteels (Paris, July 2, 2002).' In *Badiou and Politics* by Bruno Bosteels, 318–350. Durham: Duke University Press, 2011.

Badiou, Alain and Tzuchien Tho. 'From the 'Red Years' to the Communist Hypothesis: Three Decades of Dividing into Two.' In *The Rational Kernel of the Hegelian Dialectic* by Alain Badiou, edited and translated by Tzuchien Tho, 87–105. Melbourne: re.press, 2011.

Badiou, Alain, and Tzuchien Tho. 'The Concept of Model, Forty Years Later: An Interview with Alain Badiou.' In *The Concept of Model*

by Alain Badiou, edited and translated by Zachary Luke Fraser and Tzuchien Tho, 79–104. Melbourne: Re.press, 2007.
Bakunin, Mikhail. *Statism and Anarchy*, translated and edited by Marshall S Shatz. Cambridge: Cambridge University Press, 1990.
Balibar, Étienne. 'Communism as Commitment, Imagination, and Politics.' In *The Idea of Communism 2*, edited by Slavoj Žižek, 13–36. London: Verso, 2013.
———. *The Philosophy of Marx*, translated by Chris Turner. London: Verso, 2007.
Barrett, Michèle. *Women's Oppression Today: The Marxist/Feminist Encounter*. London: Verso, 2014.
Bastani, Aaron. *Fully Automated Luxury Communism: A Manifesto*. London: Verso, 2019.
Benanav, Aaron. 'Automation and the Future of Work—1.' *New Left Review* 119 (September/October 2019), 5–38.
Benanav, Aaron. 'Automation and the Future of Work—2.' *New Left Review* 120 (November/December 2019), 117–146.
Benjamin, Walter. 'Critique of Violence.' In *Walter Benjamin: Selected Writings—Volume 1, 1913–1926*, edited by Marcus Bullock and Michael W. Jennings, 236–252. Cambridge: Harvard University Press, 2004.
Berardi, Franco. *The Soul at Work: From Alienation to Autonomy*. Los Angeles: Semiotext(e), 2009.
Bernico, Matt. 'Anthropodicy: An Anarchism of Things.' *Anarchist Developments in Cultural Studies* (2015:1), 73–85.
Bey, Hakim. T.A.Z.: *The Temporary Autonomous Zone, Ontological Anarchism, Poetic Terrorism*, 2nd edition. New York: Automedia, 2003.
Black, Bob. *Anarchy after Leftism*. MO: C.A.L. Press Columbia Alternative Library, 1997. Accessed on 30 November 2016: http://theanarchistlibrary.org/library/bob-black-anarchy-after-leftism#toc12.
de La Boëtie, Étienne. *The Politics of Obedience: The Discourse of Voluntary Servitude*, translated by Harry Kurz. Auburn: Ludwig von Mises Institute, 2008.
Bosteels, Bruno. *Badiou and Politics*. Durham: Duke University Press, 2011.
———. *Introduction to Theory of the Subject* by Alain Badiou, xxxi–xxxii. London: Continuum, 2009.
———. 'Post-Maoism: Badiou and Politics.' *Positions* 13:3 (2005), 575–634.
———. *The Actuality of Communism*. London: Verso, 2011.
———. 'The Speculative Left.' *The South Atlantic Quarterly* 104:4, Fall (2005), 751–767.
Bottici, Chiara. 'Black and Red: The Freedom of Equals.' In *The Anarchist Turn*, edited by Jacob Blumenfeld, Chiara Bottici and Simon Critchley, 9–34. London: Pluto Press, 2013.
Brassier, Ray, Iain Hamilton Grant, Graham Harman, Quentin Meillassoux. 'Speculative Realism.' *Collapse III* (2007), 307–450.

Bryant, Levi R. 'Politics and Speculative Realism.' *Speculations: A Journal of Speculative Realism IV* (2013), 15–21.

Butler, Judith. 'Critique, Coercion, and Sacred Life in Benjamin's 'Critique of Violence.' In *Political Theologies: Public Religions in a Post-secular World*, edited by Hent de Vries and Lawrence E. Sullivan, 201–219. New York City: Fordham University Press, 2006.

———. *Bodies that Matter*. New York: Routledge, 1993.

Call, Lewis. 'Buffy the Post-Anarchist Vampire Slayer.' In *Post-anarchism: A Reader*, edited by Duane Rousselle and Süreyyya Evren, 183–194. London: Pluto Press, 2011.

———. *Postmodern Anarchism*. Lanham: Lexington Books, 2002.

Chakrabarty, Dipesh.'Postcoloniality and the Artifice of History: Who Speaks for 'Indian' Pasts?.' In *A Subaltern Studies Reader: 1986–1995*, edited by Ranajit Guha, 263–293. Minneapolis: University of Minnesota Press, 1999.

Chandavarkar, Rajnarayan. '"The Making of the Working Class": E.P. Thompson and Indian History.' In *Mapping Subaltern Studies and the Postcolonial*, edited by Vinayak Chaturvedi, 50–71. London: Verso, 2000.

Choat, Simon. 'Author's Reply to Reviews of Marx Through Post-Structuralism: Lyotard, Derrida, Foucault, Deleuze.' *Global Discourse* [Online], 2:I (2011). Retrieved on 14 January 2017 from http://www.tandfonline.com/doi/pdf/10.1080/23269995.2011.10707898.

Choat, Simon. 'Postanarchism from a Marxist Perspective.' *Anarchist Developments in Cultural Studies* 1 (2010), 51–71.

———. *Marx Through Post-Structuralism: Lyotard, Derrida, Foucault, Deleuze*. London: Continuum, 2010.

Clark, John P. *The Impossible Community: Realizing Communitarian Anarchism*. London: Bloomsbury Publishing, 2013.

Cockshott, W. Paul, and Allin Cottrell. *Towards and New Socialism*. Nottingham: Spokesman, 1993.

Connolly, William E. *The Fragility of Things: Self-organizing Processes, Neoliberal Fantasies, and Democratic Activism*. Durham: Duke University Press, 2013.

Critchley, Simon. *Infinitely Demanding: Ethics of Commitment, Politics of Resistance*. London: Verso, 2008.

Davis, Mike. *Late Victorian Holocausts: El Niño Famines and the Making of the Third World*. London: Verso, 2001.

Dean, Jodi. *Crowds and Party*. London: Verso, 2016.

———. *The Communist Horizon*. London: Verso, 2012.

Deleuze, Gilles. *Difference and Repetition*, translated by Paul Patton. London: Continuum, 2004.

Descartes, René. *Discourse on Method and the Meditations*, translated by F E Sutcliffe. London: Penguin Books, 1968.

Douzinas, Costas. 'Adikia: On Communism and Rights.' In *The Idea of Communism*, edited by Costas Douzinas and Slavoj Žižek, 81–100. London: Verso, 2010.

Draper, Hal. 'The Dictatorship of the Proletariat.' In *Marxism: The Inner Dialogues*, edited by Michael Curtis, 285–296. New Brunswick: Transaction Publishers, 1997.

Draper, Hal. *Karl Marx's Theory of Revolution, Volume III: The 'Dictatorship of the Proletariat.'* New York: Monthly Review Press, 1986.

Dunayevskaya, Raya. *Philosophy and Revolution: From Hegel to Sartre and from Marx to Mao*. Sussex: Harvester Press, 1982.

Egoumenides, Magda. *Philosophical Anarchism and Political Obligation*. London: Bloomsbury, 2014.

El-Enany, Nadine. 'Innocence Charged with Guilt: The Criminalisation of Protest from Peterloo to Millbank.' In *Riot, Unrest and Protest on the Global Stage*, edited by Pritchard, David and Francis Pakes, 72–97. Basingstoke: Palgrave Macmillan, 2014.

Elgot, Jessica and Damien Gayle. 'Lawyers Criticise Decision to Prosecute Housing Protester Over Sticker,' *The Guardian*, 22 October 2015. Accessed 22 October 2015, http://www.theguardian.com/uk-news/2015/oct/22/lawyers-criticise-decision-to-prosecute-housing-protester.

Elson, Diane. *Value: The Representation of Labour in Capitalism*. London: Verso, 2015.

Endnotes No.2. *Misery and the Value Form*. London: 56a Infoshop, 2010. http://endnotes.org.uk/articles/4

Engels, Friedrich. *Anti-Dühring: Herr Eugen Düring's Revolution in Science*, translated by Emile Burns, edited by CP Dutt. New York City: International Publishers, 1972.

———. *Socialism: Utopian and Scientific*. Moscow: Progress Publishers, 1978.

Evren, Süreyyya. 'There Ain't No Black in the Anarchist Flag! Race, Ethnicity and Anarchism.' In *The Bloomsbury Companion to Anarchism*, edited by Ruth Kinna, 299–314. London: Bloomsbury Academic, 2012.

Ferguson, Charles. *Inside Job*. United States: 2010. DVD.

Fine, Ben, and Alfredo Saad-Filho. *Marx's 'Capital.'* London: Pluto Press, 2016.

Finn, Daniel. 'Luso-Anomalies.' *New Left Review* 106 (July/August 2017), 5–32.

Foucault, Michel. 'Nietzsche, Freud, Marx.' In *Aesthetics*, Vol.2, edited by James D. Faubion, 269–278. London: Penguin, 1998.

———. 'Return to History.' In *Aesthetics*, Vol.2, edited by James D. Faubion, 419–432. London: Penguin, 1998.

Franks, Benjamin. 'Post-Anarchism: A Partial Account.' In *Post-anarchism: A Reader*, edited by Duane Rousselle and Süreyyya Evren, 168–180. London: Pluto Press, 2011.

Fraser, Nancy. 'A Triple Movement? Parsing the Politics of Crisis after Polanyi.' *New Left Review* 81 (2013), 119–132.

Freedland, Jonathan. 'No more excuses: Jeremy Corbyn is to blame for this meltdown.' *The Guardian*, 5 May 2017. Accessed on 5 July 2017 at www.theguardian.com/commentisfree/2017/may/05/jeremy-corbyn-blame-meltdown-labour-leader.

Giddens, Anthony. *The Third Way*. Cambridge: Polity Press, 1998.

Giles, Chris, and Ferdinando Giugliano. 'Thomas Piketty's exhaustive inequality data turn out to be flawed.' *Financial Times*, 23 May 2014. Accessed on 15 September 2020 at https://www.ft.com/content/c9ce1a54-e281-11e3-89fd-00144feabdc0?shareType=nongift.

Gordon, Uri. *Anarchy Alive: Anti-Authoritarian Politics from Practice to Theory*. London: Pluto Press, 2008.

Graeber, David. *The Democracy Project: A History, A Crisis, A Movement*. London: Allen Lane, 2013.

Gramsci, Antonio. 'The Revolution Against "Capital".' In *Selections from Political Writings 1910–1920*, translated by John Matthews, edited by Quintin Hoare, 34–37. London: Lawrence and Wishart, 1977.

Habermas, Jürgen. *The Philosophical Discourse of Modernity*, translated by Frederick G. Lawrence. Cambridge: Polity, 1987.

Hallward, Peter. 'Badiou and the Logic of Interruption.' In *Concept and Form, Volume Two: Interviews and Essays on the Cahiers pour l'Analyse*, edited by Hallward, Peter and Knox Peden, 123–145. London: Verso, 2012.

———. 'Order and Event: On Badiou's Logics of Worlds.' *New Left Review* 53 (2008), 97–122.

———. 'Politics and Philosophy: An Interview with Alain Badiou.' In *Ethics: An Essay on the Understanding of Evil* by Alain Badiou, translated by Peter Hallward, 95–144. London: Verso, 2001.

———. *Badiou: A Subject to Truth*. Minneapolis: University of Minnesota Press, 2003.

Hancox, Dan. 'There is no unwinnable seat now'—how Labour revolutionized its doorstep game,' *The Guardian*, 13 June 2017. Accessed on 25 June 2017.

Hardt, Michael and Antonio Negri. *Empire*. Cambridge: Harvard University Press, 2000.

———. *Multitude*. London: Hamish Hamilton, 2005.

Harman, Graham. 'Badiou's Relation to Heidegger in Theory of the Subject.' In *Badiou and Philosophy*, edited by Sean Bowden and Simon Duffy, 225–243. Edinburgh: Edinburgh University Press, 2012.

———. 'Object-Oriented Philosophy.' In *Towards Speculative Realism: Essays and Lectures* by Graham Harman, 93–104. Ropley: Zero Books, 2010.
———. *Quentin Meillassoux: Philosophy in the Making*. Edinburgh: Edinburgh University Press, 2011.
———. *The Quadruple Object*. Alresford: Zero Books, 2011.
Harman, Jason. 'Ontological Anarché: Beyond Arché and Anarché.' *Anarchist Developments in Cultural Studies* (2013.2), 109–120.
Harvey, David. *The Enigma of Capitalism and the Crises of Capitalism*. London: Profile Books, 2011.
Hawking, Stephen, and Leonard Mlodinow. *The Grand Design*. London: Bantam Books, 2010.
Hegel, Friedrich. *Phenomenology of Spirit*, translated by A.V. Miller. Oxford: Oxford University Press, 1977.
———. *Science of Logic*, translated by A.V. Miller. Amherst: Humanity Books, 1969.
Heidegger, Martin. *Being and Time*, translated by John Macquarrie and Edward Robinson. Oxford: Blackwell, 1962.
Hewlett, Nick. 'Politics as Thought? Paradoxes of Alain Badiou's Theory of Politics.' *Contemporary Political Theory* 5 (2006), 371–404.
———. *Badiou, Balibar, Rancière: Re-thinking Emancipation*. London: Continuum, 2007.
Hirst, Paul. *Associative Democracy: New Forms of Economic and Social Governance*. Cambridge: Polity Press, 1994.
Horton, John. *Political Obligation*. Basingstoke: Palgrave Macmillan, 2010.
Jameson, Fredric. *Archaeologies of the Future: The Desire Called Utopia and Other Science Fictions*. London: Verso, 2005.
———. Foreword to *Critique of Dialectical Reason: Volume Two*, by Jean-Paul Sartre, ix–xxiii. London: Verso, 2006.
Johnson, Gaye Theresa, and Alex Lubin, ed. *Futures of Black Radicalism*. London: Verso, 2017.
Jun, Nathan. 'Rethinking the Anarchist Canon: History, Philosophy, and Interpretation.' *Anarchist Developments in Cultural Studies* (2013.1), 82–116.
Kant, Immanuel. *Critique of Pure Reason*, edited by Vasilis Politis. London: Everyman, 1993.
Karatani, Kojin. *Transcritique: On Kant and Marx*, translated by Sabu Kohso. Cambridge: The MIT Press, 2003.
Kaufmann, Walter. *From Shakespeare to Existentialism: Studies in Poetry, Religion, and Philosophy*. Boston: Beacon Press, 1959.
Kliman, Andrew. *Reclaiming Marx's 'Capital': A Refutation of the Myth of Inconsistency*. Lanham: Lexington Books, 2007.

Koch, Andrew M. 'Post-Structuralism and the Epistemological Basis of Anarchism.' In *Post-anarchism: A Reader*, edited by Duane Rousselle and Süreyyya Evren, 23–40. London: Pluto Press, 2011.

Kouvelakis, Stathis. 'The Crises of Marxism and the Transformation of Capitalism.' In *The Critical Companion to Contemporary Marxism*, edited by Jacques Bidet and Stathis Kouvelakis, 23–38. Chicago: Haymarket Books, 2009.

Lacan, Jacques. *The Seminars of Jacques Lacan, Book II: the Ego in Freud's Theory and in the Technique of Psychoanalysis*, edited by Jacques-Alain Miller. Cambridge: University of Cambridge, 1988.

Laclau, Ernesto, and Chantal Mouffe. *Hegemony and Socialist Strategy: Towards a Radical Democratic Politics*. London: Verso, 2001.

———. 'Post-Marxism without Apologies.' *New Left Review* I/166 (1987), 79–106.

Landauer, Gustav. 'Revolution.' *Revolution and Other Writings: A Political Reader*, translated and edited by Gabriel Kuhn, 110–187. Oakland: PM Press, 2010.

———. 'The Socialist Way.' *Revolution and Other Writings: A Political Reader*, translated and edited by Gabriel Kuhn, 191–195. Oakland: PM Press, 2010.

———. 'Weak Statesmen, Weaker People!' *Revolution and Other Writings: A Political Reader*, translated and edited by Gabriel Kuhn, 213–214. Oakland: PM Press, 2010.

Lange, Elena Louisa. 'Money versus Value?: Reconsidering the 'Monetary Approach' of the 'post'-Uno School, Benetti/Cartelier, and the Neue Marx-Lektüre.' *Historical Materialism* 28.1 (2020), 51–84.

Lartice, Jonathan. "The Return of the Proletariat: Badiou's Dialectical Materialism as an Unintentional Bridge Between Marx and Postanarchism." PhD diss. University of London, 2017.

Laruelle, François. *Anti-Badiou: On the Introduction of Maoism into Philosophy*, translated by Robin Mackay. London: Bloomsbury Academic, 2013.

———. *Introduction to Non-Marxism*, translated by Anthony Paul Smith. Minneapolis: Univocal Publishing, 2015.

———. *Philosophies of Difference: A Critical Introduction to Non-philosophy*, translated by Rocco Gangle. London: Continuum, 2010.

Lazarus, Neil and Rashmi Varma. 'Marxism and Postcolonial Studies.' In *The Critical Companion to Contemporary Marxism*, edited by Jacques Bidet and Stathis Kouvelakis, 309–331. Chicago: Haymarket Books, 2009.

Lebowitz, Michael A. *Beyond Capital: Marx's Political Economy of the Working Class*. Basingstoke: Macmillan, 1992.

Lechte, John, and Saul Newman. 'Agamben, Arendt and human rights: Bearing witness to the human.' *European Journal of Social Theory* 15 (2012), 522–536.

Lefebvre, Henri. *Critique of Everyday Life: Volume 1*, translated by John Moore. London: Verso, 2008.

———. *Critique of Everyday Life: Volume 2*, translated by John Moore. London: Verso, 2008.

Lenin, Vladimir. *'Left Wing' Communism: an infantile disorder*. London: Bookmarks, 1993.

———. *The State and Revolution*, translated by Robert Service. London: Penguin, 1992.

———. *What is to be Done?*, translated by Joe Fineberg and George Hanna. London: Penguin, 1989.

Lukács, Georg. *History and class consciousness*, translated by Rodney Livingstone. London: The Merlin Press Ltd., 1971.

———. *The Ontology of Social Being 2: Marx*, translated by David Fernbach. London: The Merlin Press, 1978.

Luke Fraser, Zachary. Introduction to *The Concept of Model* by Alain Badiou, edited and translated by Zachary Luke Fraser and Tzuchien Tho, xiii–ixv. Melbourne: Re.press, 2007.

MacPherson, CB. *The Political Theory of Possessive Individualism: Hobbes to Locke*. Oxford: Oxford University Press, 1964.

Malik, Suhail. 'The Ontology of Finance: Price, Power, and the Arkhéderivative.' *Collapse VIII* (2014), 629–811.

Marcuse, Herbert. *Counterrevolution and Revolt*. London: Allen Lane The Penguin Press, 1972.

Marx, Karl. *A Contribution to the Critique of Political Economy*, edited by Maurice Dobb. New York City: International Publishers, 1999.

———. *Capital: Volume 1*, translated by Ben Fowkes. London: Penguin, 1990.

———. *Capital: Volume 3*, translated by David Fernbach. London: Penguin, 1991.

———. 'Conspectus of Bakunin's Statism and Anarchy.' In *Karl Marx, The First International and After*, edited by David Fernbach, 333–338. London: Verso, 2010.

Marx, Karl. 'Critique of the Gotha Programme.' In *Karl Marx, The First International and After*, edited by David Fernbach, 339–359. London:Verso, 2010.

———. *Grundrisse*, translated by Martin Nicolaus. London: Penguin, 1973.

———. 'Political Indifferentism.' In *Karl Marx, The First International and After*, edited David Fernbach, 327–332. London:Verso, 2010.

———. 'The Civil War in France: Address of the General Council.' In *Karl Marx, The First International and After*, edited by David Fernbach, 187–268. London: Verso, 2010.

———. 'Theses on Feuerbach.' In *The German Ideology*, 572–574. New York: Prometheus Books, 1998.
———. *1844 Economic and Philosophic Manuscripts*, translated by Martin Milligan. Amherst: Prometheus Books, 1988.
———. 'Value, Price and Profit.' In Karl Marx, *Wage Labour and Capital/Value, Price and Profit*, 49–62. New York: International Publishers Co., 1976.
———. 'Wage Labour and Capital.' In Karl Marx, *Wage Labour and Capital/Value, Price and Profit*, 15–48. New York: International Publishers Co., 1976.
Marx, Karl, and Friedrich Engels. *The Communist Manifesto*. London: Penguin, 1985.
———. *The German Ideology*. Amherst: Prometheus Books, 1998.
Marx, Karl and Joseph Weydemeyer. 'Marx to Joseph Weydemeyer, 5 March 1852.' In *Collected Works, Volume 39* by Karl Marx and Friedrich Engels, 62–65. London: Lawrence and Wishart, 1983.
May, Todd. 'Badiou and Deleuze on the One and the Many.' In *Think Again: Alain Badiou and the Future of Philosophy*, edited by Peter Hallward, 67–76. London: Continuum, 2004.
———. *The Political Philosophy of Poststructuralist Anarchism*. Pennsylvania: Pennsylvania University Press, 1994.
Mayer-Schönberger, Viktor, and Thomas Ramge. *Reinventing Capitalism in the Age of Big Data*. London: John Murray, 2019.
Mazzalini, Jon, 'The Value of Nothing and the Price of Labour.' *Pli* 30 (2019), 72–97.
Meiksins Wood, Ellen. *The Retreat From Class: A New 'True' Socialism*. London: Verso, 1998.
Meillassoux, Quentin. *After Finitude: An Essay on the Necessity of Contingency*, translated by Ray Brassier. London: Continuum, 2008.
Moir, Cat. 'In Defence of Speculative Materialism.' *Historical Materialism*, 27.2 (2019), 123–155.
Montag, Warren. *Althusser and His Contemporaries: Philosophy's Perpetual War*. Durham and London: Duke University Press, 2013.
———. 'Spectres of Althusser.' *Historical Materialism* 19.3 (2011), 147–156.
Mouffe, Chantal. *The Democratic Paradox*. London: Verso, 2000.
———. *The Return of the Political*. London: Verso, 1993.
Negri, Antonio. 'Some Reflections on the #Accelerate Manifesto,' In *#Accelerate: The Accelerationist Reader,* edited by Robin Mackay and Armen Avanessian, 365–378. Falmouth: Urbanomic Media Ltd, 2014.
———. 'The Constitution of Time.' In *Time for Revolution*, translated by Matteo Mandarini, 21–130. London: Continuum, 2003.
———. *Insurgencies*, translated by Maurizia Boscagli. Minneapolis: University of Minnesota Press, 1999.

———. *Marx Beyond Marx*, translated by Harry Cleaver, Michael Ryan and Maurizio Viano. London: Pluto Press, 1991.
Newman, Saul. 'Anarchism and Law: towards a postanarchist ethics of disobedience.' *Griffith Law Review*, 21 (2012), 308.
———. *From Bakunin to Lacan: Anti-Authoritarianism and the Dislocation of Power*. Lanham: Lexington Books, 2001.
———. *Postanarchism*. Cambridge: Polity Press, 2015.
———. *Power and Politics in Poststructuralist Thought*. Abingdon: Routledge, 2005.
———. 'Review of 'Marx Through Post-Structuralism: Lyotard, Derrida, Foucault, Deleuze' by Simon Choat.' *Global Discourse* [Online], 2:I (2011). Retrieved on 14 January 2017 from http://www.tandfonline.com/doi/abs/10.1080/23269995.2011.10707896
———. 'The Place of Power in Political Discourse.' *International Political Science Review* 25:2 (2004), 139–157.
———. *The Politics of Postanarchism*. Edinburgh: Edinburgh University Press, 2010.
———. *Unstable Universalities: Poststructuralism and Radical Politics*. Manchester: Manchester University Press, 2007.
———. 'Voluntary Servitude Reconsidered: Radical Politics and the Problem of Self Domination.' In *Anarchist Developments in Cultural Studies* 1 (2009), 31–49.
Noys, Benjamin. *Malign Velocities: Accelerationism and Capitalism*. Alresford: Zero Books, 2014
———. 'Through a glass darkly: Alain Badiou's critique of anarchism.' *Anarchist Studies* 16.2 (2008), 107–120.
Okishio, Nobuo. 'Technical Changes and the Rate of Profit.' *Kobe University Economic Review*, 7 (1961), 85–99.
Olin Wright, Erik. *Class Counts: Comparative Studies in Class Analysis*. Cambridge: Cambridge University Press, 1997.
———. 'Understanding Class: Towards an Integrated Analytical Approach.' *New Left Review* 60 Nov/Dec (2009), 101–116.
———. 'What is middle about the middle class?.' In *Analytical Marxism*, edited by John Roemer, 114–140. Cambridge: Cambridge University Press, 1986.
Parker, George, Chris Giles and Josephine Cumbo. 'Savid Javid risks Tory ire with Budget tax raid on top earners.' *The Financial Times*, 7 February 2020. Accessed on 15 September 2020 at www.ft.com/content/09e535b8-4902-11ea-aeb3-955839e06441.
Piketty, Thomas. *Capital in the Twenty-First Century*, translated by Arthur Goldhammer. Cambridge: Harvard University Press, 2014.
Pistor, Katharina. *The Code of Capital: How the Law Creates Wealth and Inequality*. Princeton: Princeton University Press, 2019.

Polanyi, Karl. *The Great Transformation: The Political and Economic Origins of Our Time*. Boston: Beacon Press, 2001.

Post, Charles. 'Exploring Working-Class Consciousness: A Critique of the Theory of the Labour-Aristocracy.' *Historical Materialism* 18 (2010), 3–38.

Postone, Moishe. *Time, Labor, and Social Domination: A Reinterpretation of Marx's Critical Theory*. Cambridge: Cambridge University Press, 1993.

Power, Nina. 'The Truth of Humanity: The Collective Political Subject in Sartre and Badiou.' *Pli* 20 (2009), 1–27.

Rahman, Mujtaba (@Mij_Europe). 'Our revised, short term #Brexit probabilities.' 18 July 2019. Accessed on 15 September 2020 at https://twitter.com/Mij_Europe/status/1151771425818185728?s=20

Rancière, Jacques. *Althusser's Lesson,* translated by Emiliano Battista. London: Continuum, 2011.

———. *The Philosopher and His Poor*, translated by John Drury, Corinne Oster and Andrew Parker. Durham: Duke University Press, 2004.

Rawnsley, Andrew. 'How do the Tories seriously imagine they can get a majority by 2015?' *The Guardian*, 8 July 2012. Accessed on 5 July 2017 at www.theguardian.com/politics/2012/jul/08/andrew-rawnsley-can-cameron-increase-vote-share.

Robinson, Cedric J. *Black Marxism: The Making of the Black Radical Tradition*. North Carolina: University of North Carolina Press, 2000.

Roediger, David R. *The Wages of Whiteness*. London: Verso, 1991.

Roffe, Jon. *Badiou's Deleuze*. Durham: Acumen Publishing Limited, 2012.

Rousselle, Duane. *After Post-Anarchism*. Berkeley: Repartee, 2012.

———. 'Georges Bataille's post-anarchism.' *Journal of Political Ideologies* 17(3) (October 2012), 235–257.

Sartre, Jean-Paul. 'France: Masses, Spontaneity, Party.' In *Between Existentialism and Marxism*, translated by John Matthews, 118–140. London:Verso, 2008.

———. *Being and Nothingness*, translated by Hazel E Barnes. London: Routledge, 2003.

———. *Critique of Dialectical Reason, Volume One*, translated by Alan Sheridan-Smith. London: Verso, 2004.

———. *Critique of Dialectical Reason: Volume Two*, translated Quintin Hoare. London: Verso, 2006.

———. *Search for a Method*, translated by Hazel E. Barnes. New York: Vintage Books, 1968.

———. *The Transcendence of the Ego*, translated by Andrew Brown. Abingdon: Routledge, 2004.

Schmidt, Michael and Lucien van der Walt. *Black Flame: The Revolutionary Class Politics of Anarchism and Syndicalism*. Oakland: AK Press, 2009.

Schürmann, Reiner. *Heidegger: On Being and Acting—From Principle to Anarchy*, translated by Christine-Marie Gros. Bloomington: Indiana University Press, 1990.
Shiying, Zhang. 'The Rational Kernel of Hegel's Philosophy.' In *The Rational Kernel of the Hegelian Dialectic* by Alain Badiou, edited and translated by Tzuchien Tho, 2147. Melbourne: re.press, 2011.
Simmons, A. John. *Justification and Legitimacy: Essays on Rights and Obligations*. Cambridge: Cambridge University Press, 2001.
Smith, Brian A. 'Badiou and Sartre: Freedom, from Imagination to Chance.' In *Badiou and Philosophy*, edited by Sean Bowden and Simon Duffy, 203–223. Edinburgh, Edinburgh University Press, 2012.
Sohn-Rethel, Alfred. *Intellectual and Manual Labour: A Critique of Epistemology*, translated by Martin Sohn-Rethel. London: Macmillan, 1978.
Sotiris, Panagiotis. 'Beyond Simple Fidelity to the Event: The Limits of Alain Badiou's Ontology.' *Historical Materialism* 19.2 (2011), 35–59.
Spivak, Gayatri Chakravorty. 'The New Subaltern: A Silent Interview.' In *Mapping Subaltern Studies and the Postcolonial*, edited by Vinayak Chaturvedi, 324–340. London: Verso, 2000.
Srnicek, Nick. 'Capitalism and the Non-Philosophical Subject.' In *The Speculative Turn: Continental Materialism and Realism*, edited by Levi Bryant, Graham Harman & Nick Srnicek, 164–181. Melbourne: re.press, 2011.
Stiglitz, Joseph E. *The Price of Inequality*. London: Penguin, 2013.
Stirner, Max. *The Ego and Its Own*, edited by David Leoplold. Cambridge: Cambridge University Press, 1995.
Taleb, Nassim Nicholas. *Fooled by Randomness: The Hidden Role of Chance in Life and in the Markets*. London: Penguin, 2004.
Taylor, Charles. *Philosophical Arguments*. Cambridge: Harvard University Press, 1995.
The Invisible Committee/Tiqqun, *The Coming Insurrection*. Los Angeles: Semiotext(e), 2009.
———, *This Is Not a Program*, translated by Joshua David Jordan. Los Angeles: Semiotext(e), 2011.
Tho, Tzuchien. 'One Divides into Two? Dividing the Conditions.' In *The Rational Kernel of the Hegelian Dialectic* by Alain Badiou, edited and translated by Tzuchien Tho, xi–xxvi. Melbourne: re.press, 2011.
Toscano, Alberto. 'Can Violence Be Thought? Notes on Badiou and the Possibility of (Marxist) Politics.' *Identities: Journal for Politics, Gender, and Culture* 5:1 (2006), 9–39.
———. 'Communism as Separation.' In *Think Again: Alain Badiou and the Future of Philosophy*, edited by Peter Hallward, 138–149. London: Continuum, 2004.

———. 'From the State to the World? Badiou and Anti-Capitalism,' *Communication & Cognition* Vol. 37, Nr. 3 & 4 (2004), 199–224.
———. 'Marxism Expatriated: Alain Badiou's Turn.' In *The Critical Companion to Contemporary Marxism*, edited by Jacques Bidet and Stathis Kouvelakis, 529–548. Chicago: Haymarket Books, 2005.
———. 'Politics in Pre-Political Times.' *Politics and Culture*, September (2004). Accessed on 11 January 2017 at 1836: http://politicsandculture.org/2014/09/01/politics-in-pre-political-times-by-alberto-toscano/
Tronti, Mario. *Workers and Capital*. London: Verso, 2019.
Webber, Jeffery R. 'Resurrection of the Dead, Exaltation of the New Struggles: Marxism, Class Conflict, and Social Movement.' *Historical Materialism* 27.1 (2019), 5–54.
Wells, Anthony. 'Final eve-of-election polls,' *UK Polling Report*, 7 June 2017: http://ukpollingreport.co.uk/blog/archives/9909. Accessed on 25 June 2017.
Williams, Alex, and Nick Srnicek. '#Accelerate: Manifesto for an Accelerationist Politics.' In *#Accelerate: The Accelerationist Reader*, edited by Robin Mackay and Armen Avanessian, 349–362. Falmouth: Urbanomic Media Ltd, 2014.
Wolfendale, Peter. *Object-Oriented Philosophy: The Noumenon's New Clothes*. Falmouth: Urbanomic Media Ltd., 2014.
Wolff, Michael. *Fire and Fury: Inside the Trump White House*. London: Little, Brown, 2018.
Žižek, Slavoj. 'Class Struggle or Postmodernism? Yes, please!' In *Contingency, Hegemony, Universality,* edited by Butler, Judith, Ernesto Laclau and Slavoj Žižek, 90–135. London: Verso, 2000.
———. 'From Purification to Subtraction: Badiou and the Real.' In *Think Again: Alain Badiou and the Future of Philosophy*, edited by Peter Hallward, 165–181. London: Continuum, 2000.
———. *Living in the End Times*. London: Verso, 2011.
———. *The Fragile Absolute, Or Why is the Christian Legacy Worth Fighting For?* London: Verso, 2000.
———. *The Sublime Object of Ideology*. London: Verso, 2008.
———. *The Ticklish Subject*. London: Verso, 2008.
———. 'Who is responsible for the US shutdown?' *The Guardian*, 11 October, 2013, accessed 3 March, 2014, http://www.theguardian.com/commentisfree/2013/oct/11/who-responsible-us-shutdown-2008-meltdown-slavoj-zizek
———. *Violence*. London: Profile Books Ltd., 2009.

Notes

Introduction

1. See, for example, *Inside Job*. United States: Charles Ferguson, 2010. DVD.
2. Anthony Giddens, *The Third Way* (Cambridge: Polity Press, 1998), 122. The term 'human capital' has been used since Adam Smith up to the present day by politicians of high rank. See George Parker, Chris Giles and Josephine Cumbo, 'Savid Javid Risks Tory Ire with Budget Tax Raid on Top Earners,' *The Financial Times*, 7 February 2020, www.ft.com/content/09e535b8-4902-11ea-aeb3-955839e06441.
3. Mario Tronti, *Workers and Capital* (London: Verso, 2019), 12.
4. Daniel Finn, 'Luso-Anomalies,' *New Left Review* 106 (July/August 2017), 5–32.
5. Alain Badiou, *Number and Numbers*, trans Robin Mackay (Cambridge: Polity Press, 2008), 213
6. Alain Badiou, *The Meaning of Sarkozy*, trans. David Fernbach (London: Verso, 2008), 12.
7. See, for example, Jonathan Freedland, 'No more excuses: Jeremy Corbyn is to blame for this meltdown,' *The Guardian*, 5 May 2017. Accessed 5 July 2017 at www.theguardian.com/commentisfree/2017/may/05/jeremy-corbyn-blame-meltdown-labour-leader. Or on the precedents being against the Conservatives winning in 2015, see Andrew Rawnsley, 'How Do the Tories Seriously Imagine They Can Get a Majority by 2015?' *The Guardian*, 8 July 2012. Accessed on 5 July 2017 at www.theguardian.com/politics/2012/jul/08/andrew-rawnsley-can-cameron-increase-vote-share.
8. See predictions made by the Eurasia Group which get significant attention in the mainstream media. Mujtaba Rahman (@Mij_Europe), 'Our Revised, Short Term #Brexit Probabilities,' 18 July 2019, https://twitter.com/Mij_Europe/status/1151771425818185728?s=20.
9. Thomas Piketty, *Capital in the Twenty-First Century*, trans. Arthur Goldhammer (Cambridge: Harvard University Press, 2014), 571, and 271ff.
10. Chris Giles and Ferdinando Giugliano, 'Thomas Piketty's Exhaustive Inequality Data Turn Out to Be Flawed,' *Financial Times*, 23 May, 2014, https://www.ft.com/content/c9ce1a54-e281-11e3-89fd-00144feabdc0?shareType=nongift. Piketty's earlier work from 2003 has

also been disputed recently by US Government officials for being based on households filing single tax returns and overlooking an increase in divorce rates among the less well-off and the possibility of more than one tax return per household, although this critique does not consider Piketty's more substantial work from 2013. See Gerald Auten and David Splinter, 'Income Inequality in the United States: Using Tax Data to Measure Long-term Trends,' 20 December 2019, http://davidsplinter.com/AutenSplinter-Tax_Data_and_Inequality.pdf.

11. Michael Wolff, *Fire and Fury: Inside the Trump White House* (London: Little, Brown, 2018), 237.

12. Franco Berardi, *The Soul at Work: From Alienation to Autonomy* (Los Angeles: Semiotext(e), 2009), 77–8.

13. Antonio Negri, 'Some Reflections on the #Accelerate Manifesto,' in *#Accelerate: The Accelerationist Reader*, eds. Robin Mackay and Armen Avanessian (Falmouth: Urbanomic Media Ltd, 2014), 367–8.

14. Aaron Bastani, *Fully Automated Luxury Communism: A Manifesto* (London: Verso, 2019), 194–6. For a commentary on Bastani's and other theories of automation, see Aaron Benanav, 'Automation and the Future of Work—1,' *New Left Review* 119 (September/October 2019), 5–38; and Aaron Benanav, 'Automation and the Future of Work—2,' *New Left Review* 120 (November/December 2019), 117–146.

15. Ben Fine and Alfredo Saad-Filho, *Marx's 'Capital'* (London: Pluto Press, 2016), 19–20.

16. Piketty, *Capital in the Twenty-First Century*, 332, 308.

17. Katharina Pistor, *The Code of Capital: How the Law Creates Wealth and Inequality* (Princeton: Princeton University Press, 2019), 47.

18. W. Paul Cockshott and Allin Cottrell, *Towards and New Socialism* (Nottingham: Spokesman, 1993), 48.

19. Viktor Mayer-Schönberger and Thomas Ramge, *Reinventing Capitalism in the Age of Big Data* (London: John Murray, 2019).

20. Evgeny Morozov, 'Digital Socialism? The Calculation Debate in the Age of Big Data,' *New Left Review* 116/117 (March/June 2019), 33–67.

21. Alain Badiou, 'Third Sketch of a Manifesto of Affirmationist Art,' in *Polemics*, trans. Steve Corcoran (London: Verso, 2006), 134.

22. Key works include Lewis Call, *Postmodern Anarchism* (Lanham: Lexington Books, 2002); Todd May, *The Political Philosophy of Poststructuralist Anarchism (*Pennsylvania: Pennsylvania University Press, 1994); and Saul Newman, *The Politics of Postanarchism* (Edinburgh: Edinburgh University Press, 2010).

23. May, *The Political Philosophy of Poststructuralist Anarchism*, 18.

24. Alain Badiou, 'The Idea of Communism,' in *The Communist Hypothesis*, trans David Macey and Steve Corcoran (London: Verso, 2010), 240.

25. Alain Badiou, 'The Cultural Revolution: The Last Revolution?'

Positions 13:3 (2005), 507.

26. Chiara Bottici, 'Black and Red: The Freedom of Equals,' in *The Anarchist Turn*, eds. Jacob Blumenfeld, Chiara Bottici and Simon Critchley (London: Pluto Press, 2013), 12, 20–1, 23.

27. Jodi Dean, *The Communist Horizon* (London: Verso, 2012), 200–201, 219–20, 69.

28. On the motivations behind Black Lives Matter, including racial capitalism, see Gaye Theresa Johnson and Alex Lubin, 'Introduction,' in *Futures of Black Radicalism*, ed. Gaye Theresa Johnson and Alex Lubin (London: Verso, 2017*)*, 9–18.

29. Alain Badiou, *Being and Event*, trans. by Oliver Feltham (London: Continuum, 2005), 85. As Badiou puts it, 'no multiple is capable of forming-a-one out of everything it includes.'

30. Jeffery R. Webber, 'Resurrection of the Dead, Exaltation of the New Struggles: Marxism, Class Conflict, and Social Movement,' *Historical Materialism* 27.1 (2019), 11.

31. Quentin Meillassoux, *After Finitude: An Essay on the Necessity of Contingency* (London: Continuum, 2008).

32. For a record of the Goldsmiths conference, Speculative Realism, of 27 April 2007, see Ray Brassier, Iain Hamilton Grant, Graham Harman, Quentin Meillassoux, 'Speculative Realism,' *Collapse* III (2007), 307–450.

33. Saul Newman, *Unstable Universalities: Poststructuralism and Radical Politics* (Manchester: Manchester University Press, 2007), 34–5.

34. See Nick Hewlett, *Badiou, Balibar, Rancière: Re-thinking Emancipation* (London: Continuum, 2007), 62–3.

35. Alain Badiou, *The Subject of Change: Lesson from the European Graduate School*, ed. Duane Rousselle (New York: Atropos Press, 2013), 66.

36. Alain Badiou, François Balmès, *De L'Idéologie* (Paris: François Maspero, 1976), 34–35.

37. Kojin Karatani, *Transcritique: On Kant and Marx*, trans. Sabu Kohso (Cambridge: The MIT Press, 2003),

38. Elie Ayache, *The Blank Swan: The End of Probability* (Chichester: Wiley & Sons, 2010).

Chapter 1

1. May, *The Political Philosophy of Poststructuralist Anarchism*, 18.
2. Dean, *The Communist Horizon*, 200–201, 219–20.
3. Jodi Dean, *Crowds and Party* (London: Verso, 2016), 69, 150.
4. David Graeber, *The Democracy Project: A History, A Crisis, A Movement* (London: Allen Lane, 2013), 38–40, 58.
5. May, *The Political Philosophy of Poststructuralist Anarchism*, 18.
6. Levi R. Bryant, 'Politics and Speculative Realism,' *Speculations: A Journal of Speculative Realism* IV (2013), 18.

7. Judith Butler, *Bodies that Matter* (New York: Routledge, 1993), 224–5.
8. A selection of various communiques from protests at the time is available here www.opendemocracy.net/freeform-tags/occupy-communiques. Also see Hardt and Negri, *Declaration*, https://antonionegriinenglish.files.wordpress.com/2012/05/93152857-hardt-negri-declaration-2012.pdf, accessed 10 January 2017.
9. Dean, *The Communist Horizon*, 200–1, 219–220.
10. Saul Newman, *From Bakunin to Lacan: Anti-Authoritarianism and the Dislocation of Power* (Lanham: Lexington Books, 2001), 55–74 and 137–156.
11. For example, see Alain Badiou, *Deleuze: The Clamour of Being*, trans. Louise Burchill (Minneapolis: University of Minnesota Press, 2000), and Alain Badiou, 'Fragments of a Public Journal on the American War Against Iraq,' in Alain Badiou, *Polemics*, trans. Steve Corcoran (London: Verso, 2006), 44–5.
12. Newman, *Unstable Universalities*, 11.
13. Bruno Bosteels, *Badiou and Politics* (Durham: Duke University Press, 2011), 13, 77.
14. Newman, *The Politics of Postanarchism*, 153.
15. Jon Roffe, *Badiou's Deleuze* (Durham: Acumen Publishing Limited, 2012), 60.
16. Simon Choat, *Marx Through Post-Structuralism: Lyotard, Derrida, Foucault, Deleuze* (London: Continuum, 2010),174, 126, 128, 130.
17. Karl Marx and Friedrich Engels, *The German Ideology* (Amherst: Prometheus Books, 1998), 481–568.
18. Ellen Meiksins Wood, *The Retreat From Class: A New 'True' Socialism* (London: Verso, 1998), 1–2, 5–6, 10.
19. Chantal Mouffe, *The Democratic Paradox* (London: Verso, 2000), 21.
20. Fredric Jameson, *Archaeologies of the Future: The Desire Called Utopia and Other Science Fictions* (London: Verso, 2005), 243.
21. Ernesto Laclau & Chantal Mouffe, *Hegemony and Socialist Strategy: Towards a Radical Democratic Politics* (London: Verso, 2001), 3–4.
22. Laclau & Mouffe, *Hegemony and Socialist Strategy*, 69.
23. Laclau & Mouffe, *Hegemony and Socialist Strategy*, 69.
24. Laclau & Mouffe, *Hegemony and Socialist Strategy*, 108, 134, 170, 192.
25. See Chantal Mouffe, *The Return of the Political* (London: Verso, 1993), 98–100, and Paul Hirst, *Associative Democracy: New Forms of Economic and Social Governance* (Cambridge: Polity Press, 1994). Hirst, *Associative Democracy*, 44–74.
26. Slavoj Žižek 'Class Struggle or Postmodernism? Yes, please!' in *Contingency, Hegemony, Universality*, eds. Judith Butler, Ernesto Laclau and

Slavoj Žižek (London: Verso, 2000), 95, 99, 96.
27. Laclau & Mouffe, *Hegemony and Socialist Strategy*, 97–99, 104–5.
28. Laclau & Mouffe, *Hegemony and Socialist Strategy*, 104–5, 107–108.
29. Dean, *The Communist Horizon*, 220.
30. Ernesto Laclau & Chantal Mouffe, 'Post-Marxism without Apologies,' *New Left Review* I/166 (1987), 88.
31. Jacques Rancière, *Althusser's Lesson,* trans. Emiliano Battista (London: Continuum, 2011), 27.
32. Vladimir Lenin, *'Left Wing' Communism: an infantile disorder* (London: Bookmarks, 1993), 52, 70, 42.
33. Karl Marx, 'Political Indifferentism,' in Karl Marx, *The First International and After*, ed. David Fernbach (London: Verso, 2010), 327–32.
34. Antonio Gramsci, 'The Revolution Against "Capital",' in *Selections from Political Writings 1910–1920*, trans. John Matthews, ed. Quintin Hoare (London: Lawrence and Wishart, 1977), 34.
35. Louis Althusser, *Reading Capital* (London, Verso, 1970), 120, 141.
36. Louis Althusser, *For Marx (*London: Verso, 1977), 111.
37. Althusser, *For Marx*, 162, 166–8.
38. Althusser, *For Marx*, 170. See also Louis Althusser, 'Ideology and Ideological State Apparatuses,' in *On Ideology* (London: Verso, 2008), 8.
39. Alain Badiou, *Metapolitics* (London: Verso, 2005), 60–1.
40. Bosteels, *Badiou and Politics*, 77.
41. Warren Montag, 'Spectres of Althusser,' *Historical Materialism* 19.3 (2011), 153.
42. Althusser, *For Marx*, 113.
43. Montag, 'Spectres of Althusser,' 154.
44. Georg Lukács, *History and Class Consciousness,* trans. Rodney Livingstone (London: The Merlin Press Ltd., 1971), 70.
45. Choat, *Marx Through Post-Structuralism*, 17, 18, 20 and 21.
46. Althusser, *For Marx*, 35.
47. Choat, *Marx Through Post-Structuralism*, 30–1.
48. Newman, *From Bakunin to Lacan*, 14–15.
49. Jürgen Habermas, *The Philosophical Discourse of Modernity*, trans. Frederick G. Lawrence (Cambridge: Polity, 1987), 7.
50. Newman, *From Bakunin to Lacan*, 32.
51. Saul Newman, 'The Place of Power in Political Discourse,' in *International Political Science Review* 25:2 (2004), 151.
52. Laclau, in Butler et al, *Contingency, Hegemony, Universality*, 45, 53.
53. Newman, *The Politics of Postanarchism*, 92.
54. May, *The Political Philosophy of Poststructuralist Anarchism*, 4–7.
55. May, *The Political Philosophy of Poststructuralist Anarchism*, 7–8.
56. May, *The Political Philosophy of Poststructuralist Anarchism*, 10,

18n3, 40–1.
57. May, *The Political Philosophy of Poststructuralist Anarchism*, 10, 18n3, 40–1.
58. Nobuo Okishio, 'Technical Changes and the Rate of Profit,' *Kobe University Economic Review*, 7 (1961), 85–99. See Andrew Kliman, *Reclaiming Marx's 'Capital': A Refutation of the Myth of Inconsistency* (Lanham: Lexington Books, 2007).
59. May, *The Political Philosophy of Poststructuralist Anarchism*, 44, 12–13, 68.
60. Newman, *From Bakunin to Lacan*, 34, 76.
61. Newman, 'The Place of Power in Political Discourse,' 143, 148, 145–6.
62. Jacques Lacan, in *The Seminars of Jacques Lacan, Book II: the Ego in Freud's Theory and in the Technique of Psychoanalysis*, ed. Jacques-Alain Miller (Cambridge: University of Cambridge, 1988), 192, 313.
63. Newman, 'The Place of Power in Political Discourse,' 146, and Newman, *From Bakunin to Lacan*, 10.
64. Newman, 'The Place of Power in Political Discourse,' 150.
65. Newman, *The Politics of Postanarchism*, 2.
66. Michel Foucault, 'Nietzsche, Freud, Marx,' in *Aesthetics, Vol.2*, ed. James D. Faubion (London: Penguin, 1998), 276, and Michel Foucault, 'Return to History,' in *Aesthetics, Vol.2*, 423.
67. Choat, *Marx Through Post-Structuralism*, 6, 130, 21.
68. Simon Choat, 'Postanarchism from a Marxist Perspective,' *Anarchist Developments in Cultural Studies* 1 (2010), 61–5.
69. Tiqqun, *This Is Not a Program*, trans. Joshua David Jordan (Los Angeles: Semiotext(e), 2011), 12.
70. The Invisible Committee, *The Coming Insurrection* (Los Angeles: Semiotext(e), 2009), 45 and 67.
71. Erik Olin Wright, 'What is middle about the middle class?' *Analytical Marxism*, ed. John Roemer (Cambridge: Cambridge University Press, 1986), 115–17.
72. Erik Olin Wright, *Class Counts: Comparative Studies in Class Analysis* (Cambridge: Cambridge University Press, 1997), 10.
73. Erik Olin Wright, 'Understanding Class: Towards an Integrated Analytical Approach,' *New Left Review* 60, Nov/Dec (2009), 101, 109, 107.
74. Wright, 'Understanding Class,' 107, 103.
75. Michael Hardt and Antonio Negri, *Empire* (Cambridge: Harvard University Press, 2000), 52–3, 61.
76. Antonio Negri, *Marx Beyond Marx*, trans. Harry Cleaver, Michael Ryan and Maurizio Viano (London: Pluto Press, 1991), 189.
77. Negri, *Marx Beyond Marx*, 120–1.
78. Michael Hardt and Antonio Negri, *Multitude* (London: Hamish Hamilton, 2005), 140–1.

79. Badiou, 'Fragments of a Public Journal on the American War Against Iraq,' 44–45.
80. Alain Badiou, *Conditions*, trans. Steve Corcoran (London: Continuum, 2008), 11; Marx and Engels, 'Theses on Feuerbach,' in *The German Ideology*, 574.
81. Slavoj Žižek, *The Ticklish Subject* (London: Verso, 2008), 158.
82. Berardi, *The Soul at Work*, 58.
83. Giddens, *The Third Way*, 122.
84. Karl Marx and Friedrich Engels, *The Communist Manifesto* (London: Penguin, 1985), 105.
85. Friedrich Engels, *Anti-Dühring: Herr Eugen Dühring's Revolution in Science* (New York City: International Publishers, 1972), 306–7.
86. Vladimir Lenin, *The State and Revolution*, trans. Robert Service (London: Penguin, 1992), 38–9.
87. Marx and Engels, *The German Ideology*, 53.
88. Karl Marx, *1844 Economic and Philosophic Manuscripts* (Amherst: Prometheus Books, 1988), 102–3.
89. Marx, *1844 Economic and Philosophic Manuscripts*, 123.
90. Lenin, *The State and Revolution*, 18, 37, 39, 38.
91. Vladimir Lenin, *What is to be Done?*, trans. Joe Fineberg and George Hanna (London: Penguin, 1989), 118–19.
92. Karl Marx, 'Conspectus of Bakunin's *Statism and Anarchy*,' in Karl Marx, *The First International and After*, ed. David Fernbach (London:Verso, 2010), 333.
93. Marx to Joseph Weydemeyer, 5 March 1852, in Karl Marx and Friedrich Engels, *Collected Works*, Volume 39 (London: Lawrence and Wishart, 1983), 62 and 65.
94. Karl Marx, 'Critique of the Gotha Programme,' in Karl Marx, *The First International and After*, ed. David Fernbach (London:Verso, 2010), 355.
95. Hal Draper, 'The Dictatorship of the Proletariat,' in *Marxism: The Inner Dialogues*, ed. Michael Curtis (New Brunswick: Transaction Publishers, 1997), 295–296. This appears to be locus 11, taken from Engels's introduction to Marx's *Civil War in France* in March 1891, with a further locus (12) appearing in June 1891 in his circular to party leaders: 'Critique of the Erfurt Program.' See Draper, *Karl Marx's Theory of Revolution, Volume III: The 'Dictatorship of the Proletariat'* (New York: Monthly Review Press, 1986), 385–6.
96. Karl Marx, 'The Civil War in France: Address of the General Council,' in Karl Marx, *The First International and After*, ed. David Fernbach (London: Verso, 2010), 213.
97. Marx, 'Theses on Feuerbach,' 571.
98. Étienne Balibar, *The Philosophy of Marx*, trans. Chris Turner (London: Verso, 2007), 17.

99. Balibar, *The Philosophy of Marx*, 2–5.
100. François Laruelle, *Philosophies of Difference: A Critical Introduction to Non-philosophy*, trans. Rocco Gangle (London: Continuum, 2010), xiv–xv.
101. François Laruelle, *Anti-Badiou: On the Introduction of Maoism into Philosophy* (London: Bloomsbury Academic, 2013), 5 and xix.
102. François Laruelle, *Introduction to Non-Marxism*, trans. Anthony Paul Smith (Minneapolis: Univocal Publishing, 2015), 1–2 and 10.
103. Laruelle, *Introduction to Non-Marxism*, 139.
104. See Nick Srnicek, 'Capitalism and the Non-Philosophical Subject,' in *The Speculative Turn: Continental Materialism and Realism*, eds. Levi Bryant, Graham Harman & Nick Srnicek (Melbourne: Re:Press, 2011), 164–81.
105. Ray Brassier, Iain Hamilton Grant, Graham Harman, Quentin Meillassoux, 'Speculative Realism,' *Collapse III* (2007), 418.
106. Jacques Rancière, *The Philosopher and His Poor*, trans. John Drury, Corinne Oster and Andrew Parker (Durham: Duke University Press, 2004), 86–7.
107. Moishe Postone, *Time, Labor, and Social Domination: A Reinterpretation of Marx's Critical Theory* (Cambridge: Cambridge University Press, 1993), 357.
108. Endnotes No.2, *Misery and the Value Form* (April 2010), 75. (http://endnotes.org.uk/articles/4)
109. Badiou, 'The Idea of Communism,' in *The Communist Hypothesis*, trans David Macey and Steve Corcoran (London: Verso, 2010), 240.

Chapter 2

1. Alain Badiou, *Théorie de la Contradiction* (1975), 61. http://www.scribd.com/doc/56179831/Alain-Badiou-Theorie-de-la-Contradiction (accessed 15 September 2020). Translation is my own.
2. Newman, 'The Place of Power in Political Discourse,' 150.
3. Newman, *The Politics of Postanarchism*, 2.
4. Newman, *The Politics of Postanarchism*, 1. This term is borrowed from Benjamin Noys, who explored the potential connection between between Badiou and anarchism in 2008. See Benjamin Noys, *Through a Glass Darkly* (2008). Viewed at https://www.academia.edu/216175/Through_a_glass_darkly_Alain_Badiou_s_critique_of_anarchism, accessed 2 August 2015).
5. Saul Newman, *Postanarchism* (Cambridge: Polity Press, 2015), 113.
6. Magda Egoumenides, *Philosophical Anarchism and Political Obligation* (London: Bloomsbury, 2014), 2, 4, 50, 7.
7. Egoumenides, *Philosophical Anarchism*, 166–167.

8. John Horton, *Political Obligation* (Basingstoke: Palgrave Macmillan, 2010), 111, 110, 108–9.
9. A. John Simmons, *Justification and Legitimacy: Essays on Rights and Obligations* (Cambridge: Cambridge University Press, 2001), 103.
10. John P. Clark, *The Impossible Community: Realizing Communitarian Anarchism* (London: Bloomsbury Publishing, 2013), 254.
11. Marx and Engels, *The German Ideology*, 128–476.
12. Alain Badiou, 'The Flux and the Party: In the Margins of Anti-Oedipus,' *Polygraph* 15/16 (2004), 79.
13. Badiou, '*The Cultural Revolution: The Last Revolution?,*' 506–507.
14. Alain Badiou, *Deleuze: The Clamor of Being*, trans. Louise Burchill (Minnesota: The University of Minnesota Press, 2000), 9 and 11.
15. Newman, *Unstable Universalities*, 9 and 11.
16. Alain Badiou, 'Eight Theses on the Universal,' in *Theoretical Writings*, ed. and trans. Ray Brassier and Alberto Toscano (London: Continuum, 2006), 145–54.
17. Benjamin Noys, 'Through a glass darkly: Alain Badiou's critique of anarchism,' Anarchist Studies 16.2 (October 2008), 107–20.
18. Newman, *The Politics of Postanarchism*, 109.
19. Badiou, '*The Cultural Revolution: The Last Revolution?*' 506–7.
20. Alberto Toscano, 'Can Violence Be Thought? Notes on Badiou and the Possibility of (Marxist) Politics,' *Identities: Journal for Politics, Gender, and Culture* 5:1 (2006), 21.
21. Badiou, *Metapolitics*, 58.
22. Stathis Kouvelakis, 'The Crises of Marxism and the Transformation of Capitalism,' in *The Critical Companion to Contemporary Marxism*, eds. Jacques Bidet and Stathis Kouvelakis (Chicago: Haymarket Books, 2009), 24.
23. Toscano, 'Can Violence Be Thought?,' 21, 9, 11.
24. Badiou, *The Cultural Revolution: The Last Revolution?*, 506–7.
25. Newman, *The Politics of Postanarchism*, 11.
26. Alberto Toscano, 'From the State to the World? Badiou and Anti-Capitalism,' *Communication & Cognition*, Vol. 37, Nr. 3 & 4 (2004),199–224; Alberto Toscano, 'Marxism Expatriated: Alain Badiou's Turn,' in *The Critical Companion to Contemporary Marxism* , eds. Jacques Bidet and Stathis Kouvelakis (Chicago: Haymarket Books, 2005), 529–548; Alberto Toscano (2006) 'Can Violence Be Thought?,'; Bruno Bosteels, 'The Speculative Left,' in *The South Atlantic Quarterly* 104:4, Fall (2005), 751–767; Bruno Bosteels, 'Post-Maoism: Badiou and Politics,' *Positions* 13:3 (2005), 575–634.
27. Alain Badiou, *Logics of Worlds,* trans. Alberto Toscano (London: Continuum, 2009), 493–504.
28. See Alain Badiou, *Polemics,* trans. Steve Corcoran (London: Verso, 2006), especially 257–328.

29. Badiou, *The Communist Hypothesis*, 240.
30. Alain Badiou, 'The Idea of Communism,' in *The Idea of Communism*, eds. Costas Douzinas and Slavoj Žižek (London: Verso, 2010), 1–14; Alain Badiou, 'The Communist Idea and the Question of Terror,' in The Idea of Communism 2, ed. Slavoj Žižek (London: Verso, 2013), 1–11.
31. Alain Badiou, *The Rebirth of History* (London: Verso, 2012), 7–9.
32. Newman, *Unstable Universalities*, 100.
33. Alain Badiou, *Ethics*, trans. Peter Hallward (London: Verso, 2001), 77 and 73.
34. Andrew M Koch, 'Post-Structuralism and the Epistemological Basis of Anarchism,' in *Post-anarchism: A Reader*, eds. Duane Rousselle & Süreyyya Evren (London: Pluto Press, 2011), 36.
35. May, *The Political Philosophy of Poststructuralist Anarchism*, 4–7 and 44.
36. Newman, *Unstable Universalities*, 34–5.
37. Call, *Postmodern Anarchism*, 68–9.
38. Alain Badiou, 'Philosophy, Sciences, Mathematics: Interview with Alain Badiou,' *Collapse*, Vol. 1 (2006), 20.
39. Badiou and Tzuchien Tho (2007) 'The Concept of Model, Forty Years Later: An Interview with Alain Badiou,' in Alain Badiou, *The Concept of Model*, ed. and trans. Zachary Luke Fraser and Tzuchien Tho (Melbourne: re.press, 2007), 103.
40. Newman, *From Bakunin to Lacan*, 14–15.
41. Alain Badiou, 'Third Sketch of a Manifesto of Affirmationist Art,' in *Polemics*, trans. Steve Corcoran (London: Verso, 2006), 134.
42. Peter Hallward, *Badiou: A Subject to Truth* (Minneapolis: University of Minnesota Press, 2003), 193.
43. Hallward, *Badiou: A Subject to Truth*, 17.
44. Newman, *Unstable Universalities*, 36.
45. Alain Badiou, 'Eight Theses on the Universal,' 147.
46. Peter Hallward, 'Badiou and the Logic of Interruption,' in *Concept and Form, Volume Two: Interviews and Essays on the Cahiers pour l'Analyse*, eds. Peter Hallward and Knox Peden (London: Verso, 2012), 125.
47. Zachary Luke Fraser, 'Introduction,' in *The Concept of Model*, xv.
48. Hallward, 'Badiou and the Logic of Interruption,' 142.
49. Alain Badiou and François Balmès, *De L'Idéologie* (Paris: François Maspero, 1976), 9.
50. Badiou, *Of Ideology*, 20–1.
51. Bosteels, *Badiou and Politics*, 77.
52. Alain Badiou, *The Adventure of French Philosophy*, ed. and trans. Bruno Bosteels (London: Verso, 2012), 133.
53. Althusser, *For Marx*, 111.
54. Karl Marx, *A Contribution to the Critique of Political Economy* (New York City: International Publishers, 1999), 215.

55. Friedrich Engels, *Socialism: Utopian and Scientific* (Moscow: Progress Publishers, 1978), 10.
56. Althusser, *For Marx*, 174 and 168.
57. Badiou, *The Adventure of French Philosophy*, 140.
58. Badiou, *Theory of the Subject*, 92.
59. Badiou, *Being and Event*, trans. Oliver Feltham (London: Continuum, 2005),176.
60. Badiou, *The Adventure of French Philosophy*, 146-7, 149.
61. Hallward, 'Badiou and the Logic of Interruption,' 137.
62. Alain Badiou, 'Infinitesimal Subversion,' in *Concept and Form, Volume One: Key Texts from the Cahiers pour l'Analyse*, eds. Peter Hallward and Knox Peden (London: Verso, 2012), 192.
63. Badiou, 'Infinitesimal Subversion,'188.
64. Badiou, 'Infinitesimal Subversion,' 192.
65. Badiou, 'Infinitesimal Subversion,' 206.
66. Karl Marx, 'The Civil War in France: Address of the General Council,' in Karl Marx, *The First International and After*, ed. David Fernbach (London: Verso, 2010), 213.
67. Hallward, 'Badiou and the Logic of Interruption,' 141.
68. Alain Badiou, 'Mark and Lack,' in *Concept and Form, Volume One: Key Texts from the Cahiers pour l'Analyse*, eds. Peter Hallward and Knox Peden (London: Verso, 2012), 171-4.
69. Bosteels, *Badiou and Politics*, 132-133.
70. Alain Badiou, 'Metaphysics and the Critique of Metaphysics,' *Pli* 10 (2000), 190.
71. Tzuchien Tho, 'One Divides into Two? Dividing the Conditions,' in *Alain Badiou: The Rational Kernel of the Hegelian Dialectic*, ed. and trans. Tzuchien Tho (Melbourne: re.press, 2011), xi.
72. Slavoj Žižek, *Living in the End Times* (London: Verso, 2011), 185.
73. Immanuel Kant, *Critique of Pure Reason*, ed. Vasilis Politis (London: Everyman: 1993), 243-57.
74. Friedrich Hegel, *Phenomenology of Spirit*, trans. A.V. Miller (Oxford: Oxford University Press, 1977), 14, 19.
75. Friedrich Hegel, *Science of Logic*, trans. A.V. Miller (Amherst: Humanity Books, 1969), 27.
76. Alain Badiou, Jöel Bellassen, Louis Mossot, 'Hegel in France,' in *Alain Badiou: The Rational Kernel of the Hegelian Dialectic*, ed. and trans. Tzuchien Tho (Melbourne: re.press, 2011), 12.
77. Jean-Paul Sartre, *Being and Nothingness*, trans. Hazel E Barnes (London: Routledge, 2003),103.
78. René Descartes, *Discourse on Method and the Meditations*, trans. F E Sutcliffe (London: Penguin Books, 1968), 54-5.
79. Jean-Paul Sartre, *The Transcendence of the Ego*, trans. Andrew Brown (Abingdon: Routledge, 2004), 27, 7.

80. Sartre, *Transcendence of the Ego*, 50–2.
81. Jean-Paul Sartre, *Critique of Dialectical Reason, Volume One*, trans. Alan Sheridan-Smith (London: Verso, 2004), 38–40.
82. Badiou, Bellassen, Mossot, 'Hegel in France,' 12.
83. Zhang Shiying, 'The Rational Kernel of Hegel's Philosophy,' in *Alain Badiou: The Rational Kernel of the Hegelian Dialectic*, ed. and trans. Tzuchien Tho (Melbourne: re.press, 2011), 23–4.
84. Shiying, 'The Rational Kernel of Hegel's Philosophy,' 39.
85. Shiying, 'The Rational Kernel of Hegel's Philosophy,' 43–7.
86. Badiou, *The Rational Kernel of the Hegelian Dialectic*, 7.
87. Alain Badiou and Tzuchien Tho, 'From the 'Red Years' to the Communist Hypothesis: Three Decades of Dividing into Two,' in *Alain Badiou: The Rational Kernel of the Hegelian Dialectic*, ed. and trans. Tzuchien Tho (Melbourne: re.press, 2011), 90.
88. Badiou, *The Rational Kernel of the Hegelian Dialectic*, 58–9.
89. Badiou, *Theory of the Subject*, 35–6.
90. Bruno Bosteels, translator's introduction to *Theory of the Subject* (London: Continuum, 2009), xxxi–xxxii.
91. Badiou, *Theory of the Subject*, 39, 11, 31, 34.
92. Badiou, *Theory of the Subject*, 7.
93. Badiou, *Theory of the Subject*, 11.
94. Alain Badiou, *The Century*, trans. Alberto Toscano, (Cambridge: Polity Press, 2007), 61.
95. Newman, *Unstable Universalities*, 86–7.
96. Badiou, *The Century*, 64–6.
97. Newman, *From Bakunin to Lacan*, 10.

Chapter 3

1. Badiou, *Theory of the Subject*, 7.
2. Newman, *Unstable Universalities*, 70
3. Newman, *Unstable Universalities*, 9 and 11.
4. Badiou, 'The Idea of Communism,' in *The Idea of Communism*, eds. Costas Douzinas and Slavoj Žižek (London: Verso, 2010), 13.
5. Alain Badiou, Peter Hallward and Bruno Bosteels, 'Beyond Formalization: An Interview with Alain Badiou Conducted by Peter Hallward and Bruno Bosteels (Paris, July 2, 2002),' in Bosteels, *Badiou and Politics*, 332–3.
6. Badiou, *The Subject of Change*, 66.
7. Hegel, *Science of Logic*, 137.
8. Badiou, *Theory of the Subject*, 47.
9. Badiou, *Logics of Worlds*, 146–7.
10. Bruno Bosteels, 'Post-Maoism: Badiou and Politics,' *Positions* 13:3 (Winter 2005) 581.

11. Bosteels, 'Post-Maoism,' 580–1, 584.
12. Hakim Bey, *T.A.Z.: The Temporary Autonomous Zone, Ontological Anarchism, Poetic Terrorism*, 2nd edition (New York: Automedia, 2003), 97, 99.
13. Badiou, *Being and Event*, 16–17.
14. Badiou, *Being and Event*, 24–5, 511, 95.
15. Badiou, *Being and Event*, 54–56, 58–9.
16. Badiou, *Being and Event*, 81, 85, 87, 88.
17. Badiou, *Being and Event*, 107.
18. Badiou, *Being and Event*, 99.
19. Alain Badiou, *Second Manifesto for Philosophy*, trans. Louise Burchill (Cambridge: Polity Press, 2011), 61.
20. Mike Davis, *Late Victorian Holocausts: El Niño Famines and the Making of the Third World* (London: Verso, 2001), 4, 28, 31.
21. Davis, *Late Victorian Holocausts*, 8.
22. Badiou, *Being and Event*, 179, 182–3, 190, 201.
23. Badiou, *Being and Event*, 202.
24. Badiou, *Being and Event*, 210–11.
25. Badiou, *Being and Event*, 396–7, 400.
26. Badiou, *Being and Event*, 397, 400–1.
27. Brian A Smith, 'Badiou and Sartre: Freedom, from Imagination to Chance,' in *Badiou and Philosophy*, eds. Sean Bowden and Simon Duffy (Edinburgh, Edinburgh University Press, 2012), 203.
28. Badiou, *Being and Event*, 403, 409, 429.
29. Alain Badiou, *Philosophy for Militants*, trans. Bruno Bosteels (London: Verso, 2012), 19–20.
30. Alejandro de Acosta, 'Anarchist Meditations, or: Three Wild Interstices of Anarchism and Philosophy,' *Anarchist Developments in Cultural Studies: 'Post-Anarchism today,'* 2010 (1), 119–120.
31. Gilles Deleuze, *Difference and Repetition*, trans. Paul Patton (London: Continuum, 2004), 26–7, 30.
32. Badiou, *Deleuze: The Clamor of Being*, 9, 11.
33. Todd May, 'Badiou and Deleuze on the One and the Many,' in *Think Again: Alain Badiou and the Future of Philosophy*, ed. Peter Hallward (London: Continuum, 2004) 67.
34. Roffe, *Badiou's Deleuze*, 9
35. Roffe, *Badiou's Deleuze*, 9–11.
36. Roffe, *Badiou's Deleuze*, 60–1.
37. Deleuze, *Difference and Repetition*, 67.
38. Badiou, *The Rational Kernel of the Hegelian Dialectic*, 60.
39. Badiou, *The Subject of Change*, 66.
40. Simon Critchley, *Infinitely Demanding: Ethics of Commitment, Politics of Resistance* (London: Verso, 2008), 12–13.
41. Alain Badiou and Simon Critchley, *Democracy and*

Disappointment: On the Politics of Resistance, eds. Aaron Levy and Simon Critchley (DVD, 2007). See 1 hour 22 minutes.
42. Newman, *From Bakunin to Lacan*, 98–9.
43. Deleuze, *Difference and Repetition*, 234.
44. Deleuze, *Difference and Repetition*, 234–5.
45. Badiou, *Being and Event*, 110.
46. Badiou, 'The Idea of Communism,' in *The Communist Hypothesis*, trans David Macey and Steve Corcoran (London: Verso, 2010), 240.

Chapter 4

1. Badiou, *The Rebirth of History*, 8.
2. Brian A Smith, 'Badiou and Sartre: Freedom, from Imagination to Chance,' 203.
3. Badiou, 'The Flux and the Party: In the Margins of Anti-Oedipus,' 80.
4. Badiou, 'The Cultural Revolution: The Last Revolution?' 507.
5. Badiou, *Being and Event*, 210.
6. Alain Badiou, *Can Politics Be Thought*, trans. Bruno Bosteels (Durham: Duke University Press, 2918), 80–81.
7. Sartre, *Critique of Dialectical Reason: Volume One*, 266–7.
8. Alain Badiou, *Pocket Pantheon*, trans. David Macey (London: Verso, 2009), 15.
9. Badiou, *The Subject of Change*, 66.
10. Benjamin Franks, 'Post-Anarchism: A Partial Account,' in *Post-anarchism: A Reader*, eds. Duane Rousselle and Süreyyya Evren (London: Pluto Press, 2011), 174.
11. Bey, *T.A.Z.*, 61, 63.
12. Peter Hallward, 'Politics and Philosophy: An Interview with Alain Badiou,' in Alain Badiou, *Ethics: An Essay on the Understanding of Evil*, trans. Peter Hallward (London: Verso, 2001), 114, 107.
13. Newman, *Postanarchism*, 30–1.
14. Bob Black, Anarchy after Leftism (MO: C.A.L. Press Columbia Alternative Library, 1997) chapter 11, accessed 30 November 2013 from http://theanarchistlibrary.org/library/bob-black-anarchy-after-leftism#toc12. The term 'Oriental despotism' is used by Marx in his observations on India, in a passage made 'overly famous' by Edward Said, according to Aijaz Ahmad, in an effort to unconstructively dismiss Marx's relevance to the study of India, without (somewhat hypocritically for someone making the case against orientalism) seeking the views of Indian historians on Marx's thought. See Aijaz Ahmad, *In Theory: Classes, Nations, Literatures* (London: Verso, 2008), 14, 223.
15. Franks, 'Post-Anarchism: A Partial Account,' 175.
16. Balibar, *The Philosophy of Marx*, 17.

17. Karl Marx, 'Theses on Feuerbach,' in The German Ideology, 572–4.
18. Balibar, *The Philosophy of Marx*, 2–5
19. Badiou, *Conditions*, 11.
20. Karl Marx, 'The Civil War in France: Address of the General Council,' 213.
21. Duane Rousselle, 'Georges Bataille's post-anarchism,' *Journal of Political Ideologies* 17(3) (October 2012), 235–6.
22. Lewis Call, 'Buffy the Post-Anarchist Vampire Slayer,' in *Post-anarchism: A Reader*, eds. Duane Rousselle and Süreyyya Evren (London: Pluto Press, 2011), 184.
23. David Graeber, *The Democracy Project*, xx-xxi.
24. Wright, 'Understanding Class: Towards an Integrated Analytical Approach,' 107.
25. Fine and Saad-Filho, *Marx's Capital*, 42–3.
26. Newman, *The Politics of Postanarchism*, 119–20.
27. Wright, *Class Counts*, 10.
28. Newman, *The Politics of Postanarchism*, 120–2.
29. Karl Polanyi, *The Great Transformation: The Political and Economic Origins of Our Time* (Boston: Beacon Press, 2001), 136.
30. Alain Badiou, 'Our Contemporary Impotence,' *Radical Philosophy* 181 (2013), 44.
31. Hallward, *Badiou: A Subject to Truth*, 238–9.
32. Nancy Fraser, 'A Triple Movement? Parsing the Politics of Crisis after Polanyi,' *New Left Review* 81 (2013), 124, 127–8, 130.
33. Hallward, *Badiou: A Subject to Truth*, 36.
34. Alain Badiou, *Second Manifesto for Philosophy*, trans. Louise Burchill (Cambridge: Polity Press, 2011), 61.
35. Hallward, *Badiou: A Subject to Truth*, 39, 239.
36. Slavoj Žižek, 'Who Is Responsible For the US Shutdown?' *The Guardian*, 11 October, 2013, accessed 3 March 2014, http://www.theguardian.com/commentisfree/2013/oct/11/who-responsible-us-shutdown-2008-meltdown-slavoj-zizek.
37. Lukács, *History and class consciousness*, 168, 70, 193.
38. Lukács, *The Ontology of Social Being 2: Marx* (London: The Merlin Press, 1978), 31.
39. Alain Badiou, Joël Bellassen, Louis Mossot, 'Hegel in France,' in Badiou, *The Rational Kernel of the Hegelian Dialectic*, ed. and trans. Tzuchien Tho (Melbourne: re.press, 2011), 12.
40. Badiou, *Being and Event*, 210–211.
41. Badiou, *Theory of the Subject*, 58.
42. Badiou, *Theory of the Subject*, 11, 62, 58–59.
43. Badiou, *Theory of the Subject*, 63.
44. Badiou, *Theory of the Subject*, 63–4.
45. Badiou, *Theory of the Subject*, 64.

46. Badiou, *Theory of the Subject*, 82.
47. Bosteels, 'Post-Maoism: Badiou and Politics,' 581.
48. Badiou, *Being and Event*, 176
49. Badiou, *Being and Event*, 207, 227–228.
50. Badiou, *Theory of the Subject*, 130, 115, 127.
51. Panagiotis Sotiris, 'Beyond Simple Fidelity to the Event: The Limits of Alain Badiou's Ontology,' *Historical Materialism* 19.2 (2011), 42.
52. Badiou, *Theory of the Subject*, 130, 129.
53. Badiou, *Theory of the Subject*, 127, 108, 28, 129.
54. Badiou, *Theory of the Subject*, 129.
55. Badiou, *Theory of the Subject*, 130, 128.
56. Alberto Toscano, 'Marxism Expatriated: Alain Badiou's Turn,' in *Critical Companion to Contemporary Marxism*, eds. Jacques Bidet & Stathis Kouvelakis (Chicago: Haymarket Books, 2009), 530–42.
57. Toscano, 'Marxism Expatriated,' 534–9.
58. Badiou, Hallward and Bosteels, 'Beyond Formalization: An Interview with Alain Badiou Conducted by Peter Hallward and Bruno Bosteels (Paris, July 2, 2002); Bruno Bosteels, *Badiou and Politics* (Durham: Duke University Press, 2011), 332–3.
59. Badiou, Hallward and Bosteels, 'Beyond Formalization,' 332.
60. Badiou, *Being and Event*, 16–17.
61. Toscano, 'Marxism Expatriated,' 534.
62. Toscano, 'Marxism Expatriated,' 542.
63. Costas Douzinas, 'Adikia: On Communism and Rights,' in *The Idea of Communism*, eds. Costas Douzinas and Slavoj Žižek (London: Verso, 2010), 86.
64. Toscano, 'Marxism Expatriated,' 543.
65. Toscano, 'Marxism Expatriated,' 544.
66. David Harvey, *The Enigma of Capitalism and the Crises of Capitalism* (London: Profile Books, 2011), 254.
67. Toscano, 'Marxism Expatriated,' 544–5.
68. Badiou, *The Subject of Change*, 66.
69. Badiou, *Being and Event*, 54–6, 58–9.
70. Sartre, *Being and Nothingness*, 501, 503.
71. Fredric Jameson, foreword to *Critique of Dialectical Reason: Volume Two*, by Jean-Paul Sartre (London: Verso, 2006), xvii.
72. Sartre, *Critique of Dialectical Reason: Volume One*, 46, 266–7.
73. Peter Hallward, 'Order and Event: On Badiou's Logics of Worlds,' *New Left Review* 53 (2008), 121.
74. Henri Lefebvre, *Critique of Everyday Life: Volume 1* (London: Verso, 2008), 75–7.
75. Henri Lefebvre, *Critique of Everyday Life: Volume 2* (London: Verso, 2008), 186.
76. Badiou, *Logics of Worlds*, 208–9.

77. Badiou, *Logics of Worlds*, 374.
78. Sartre, *Critique of Dialectical Reason: Volume One*, 124–5, 266–7, 184.
79. Jean-Paul Sartre, *Search for a Method*, trans. Hazel E. Barnes (New York: Vintage Books, 1968), 89.
80. Sartre, *Critique of Dialectical Reason: Volume One*, 670–1.
81. Jean-Paul Sartre, *Critique of Dialectical Reason: Volume Two*, trans. Quintin Hoare (London: Verso, 2006), 312.
82. Badiou, *Ethics*, 12.
83. Nina Power, 'The Truth of Humanity: The Collective Political Subject in Sartre and Badiou,' *Pli* 20 (2009), 21.
84. Žižek, *Living in the End Times*, 185.
85. Nick Hewlett, 'Politics as Thought? Paradoxes of Alain Badiou's Theory of Politics,' *Contemporary Political Theory* 5 (2006), 388–9.
86. Postone, *Time, Labour and Social Domination: A Reinterpretation of Marx's Critical Theory*, 357.
87. Nina Power, 'The Truth of Humanity,' 2–4.
88. Rancière, *Althusser's Lesson*, 27.
89. Bruno Bosteels, *The Actuality of Communism* (London: Verso, 2011), 24.
90. Badiou, *Theory of the Subject*, 92.
91. Badiou, *Being and Event*, 25.
92. Hallward, *Badiou: A Subject to Truth*, xxiv.
93. Jean-Paul Sartre, 'France: Masses, Spontaneity, Party,' in *Between Existentialism and Marxism*, trans. John Matthews (London:Verso, 2008), 119.
94. Alain Badiou, 'The Idea of Communism,' in *The Idea of Communism*, eds. Costas Douzinas and Slavoj Žižek (London: Verso, 2010), 13.
95. Alain Badiou, 'Roads to Regency: Interview with Eric Hazan,' *New Left Review* 53 (2008), 131.
96. Badiou, Hallward and Bosteels, 'Beyond Formalization,' 335.
97. Antonio Negri, *Insurgencies*, trans. Maurizia Boscagli (Minneapolis: University of Minnesota Press, 1999), 325.
98. Hardt and Negri, *Empire*, 252–3.
99. Badiou, Hallward and Bosteels, 'Beyond Formalization,' 335.
100. Badiou, Hallward and Bosteels, 'Beyond Formalization,' 335.
101. Alain Badiou, *The Communist Hypothesis*, 240, 237.
102. Badiou, *Being and Event*, 391–2, 397.
103. Badiou, *Logics of Worlds*, 146–7.
104. Badiou, *Theory of the Subject*, 128.

Chapter 5

1. Badiou, *Of Ideology*, 20–21.
2. Antonio Negri, 'Some Reflections on the #Accelerate Manifesto,' in #Accelerate: The Accelerationist Reader, eds. Robin Mackay and Armen Avanessian (Falmouth: Urbanomic Media Ltd, 2014), 367–8.
3. Newman, *Power and Politics in Poststructuralist Thought: New Theories of the Political* (London: Routledge, 2005), 63.
4. Alain Badiou, *Théorie de la Contradiction* (1975), 61. Accessed 2 December 2012 from http://www.scribd.com/doc/56179831/Alain-Badiou-Theorie-de-la-Contradiction. Translation is my own.
5. Žižek, *Living in the End Times*, 183.
6. Badiou, *Of Ideology*, 6, 7, 3, 26.
7. Louis Althusser, 'Freud and Lacan,' in *On Ideology* (London: Verso, 2008), 143, 148–9.
8. Althusser, 'Freud and Lacan,' 152.
9. Warren Montag, *Althusser and His Contemporaries: Philosophy's Perpetual War* (Durham and London: Duke University Press, 2013), 118–19.
10. Louis Althusser, On the Reproduction of Capitalism: Ideology and Ideological State Apparatuses (London: Verso, 2014), 190.
11. Althusser, *On the Reproduction of Capitalism,*191.
12. Louis Althusser, *The Humanist Controversy and Other Writings* (London: Verso, 2003), 58.
13. Montag, *Althusser and His Contemporaries*, 112.
14. Alain Badiou and Élisabeth Roudinesco, *Jacques Lacan, Past and Present: A Dialogue*, trans. Jason E. Smith (New York: Columbia University Press, 2014), 8–9.
15. Alain Badiou, *Number and Numbers*, trans. Robin Mackay (Cambridge: Polity, 2008), 1–3, 101.
16. Badiou, *Number and Numbers*, 213.
17. Badiou, *Number and Numbers*, 214.
18. Badiou, *Number and Numbers*, 214.
19. Badiou, *Manifesto for Philosophy*, 55–56.
20. Alberto Toscano, 'From the State to the World? Badiou and Anti-Capitalism,' Communication & Cognition Vol. 37, Nr. 3 & 4 (2004), 206, 207, 213, 211, 209, 220.
21. Alberto Toscano, 'Communism as Separation,' in *Think Again: Alain Badiou and the Future of Philosophy,* ed. Peter Hallward (London: Continuum, 2004), 142.
22. Alberto Toscano, 'Politics in Pre-Political Times,' *Politics and Culture*, September (2004). Accessed 14 September 14 at http://politicsandculture.org/2014/09/01/politics-in-pre-political-times-by-alberto-toscano/
23. Badiou, *Of Ideology*, 26.

24. Badiou, *The Century*, 52–3, 56.
25. Badiou, *Being and Event*, 210.
26. Althusser, *On the Reproduction of Capitalism*, 62.
27. Newman, *From Bakunin to Lacan*, 98–9.
28. Reiner Schürmann, *Heidegger: On Being and Acting—From Principle to Anarchy*, trans. Christine-Marie Gros (Bloomington: Indiana University Press, 1990), 1, 6–7.
29. Newman, The Politics of Postanarchism, 53.
30. Jason Harman, 'Ontological Anarché: Beyond Arché & Anarché,' *Anarchist Developments in Cultural Studies* 2 (2013), 110–11.
31. Newman, *Power and Politics in Poststructuralist Thought*, 63–4.
32. Newman, Power and Politics in Poststructuralist Thought, 67.
33. Slavoj Žižek, The Fragile Absolute, Or Why is the Christian Legacy Worth Fighting For? (London: Verso, 2000), 138.
34. Badiou, *Being and Event*, 429.
35. CB MacPherson, *The Political Theory of Possessive Individualism: Hobbes to Locke* (Oxford: Oxford University Press, 1964), 61.
36. Newman, *Unstable Universalities*, 44.
37. See Saul Newman, 'Anarchism and Law: towards a postanarchist ethics of disobedience,' *Griffith Law Review*, 21 (2012), 308.
38. John Lechte and Saul Newman, 'Agamben, Arendt and human rights: Bearing witness to the human,' *European Journal of Social Theory* 15 (2012), 523.
39. Alain Badiou, *Ethics*, 33.
40. Badiou, *Ethics*, 27–28.
41. Max Stirner, *The Ego and Its Own*, ed David Leopold (Cambridge: Cambridge University Press, 1995), 114–115.
42. Etienne de La Boëtie, *The Politics of Obedience: The Discourse of Voluntary Servitude*, trans. Harry Kurz (Auburn: Ludwig von Mises Institute, 2008), 52–4.
43. Gustav Landauer, 'Weak Statesmen, Weaker People,' in *Revolution and Other Writings: A Political Reader*, ed. and trans. Gabriel Kuhn (Oakland, CA: PM Press, 2010),
44. 213–14.
45. Stirner, *The Ego and Its Own*, 279–80, 198–9.
46. Badiou, *Theory of the Subject*, 219–20.
47. Miguel Abensour, *Democracy Against the State: Marx and the Machiavellian Moment*, trans. Max Blechman and Martin Breaugh (Cambridge: Polity Press, 2011), xxxi–xxxiii, xxiii–xxvi.
48. Badiou, *Logics of Worlds*, 3.
49. Badiou, *Logics of Worlds*, 1–2, 3–4, 99.
50. Badiou, *Theory of the Subject*, 63
51. Gustav Landauer, 'Revolution,' in *Revolution and Other Writings*, 113, 121–2, 115–16.

52. Gustav Landauer, 'The Socialist Way,' in *Revolution and Other Writings*, 192–5.
53. Martin Heidegger, *Being and Time*, trans. John Macquarrie and Edward Robinson (Oxford: Blackwell, 1962), 69.
54. Graham Harman, 'Badiou's Relation to Heidegger in Theory of the Subject,' in *Badiou and Philosophy*, ed. Sean Bowden and Simon Duffy (Edinburgh: Edinburgh University Press, 2012), 241.
55. Harman, 'Badiou's Relation to Heidegger,' 242–3.
56. Badiou, *Being and Event*, 432.
57. Hallward, *Badiou: A Subject to Truth*, 8.
58. Badiou, *Being and Event*, 432–3.
59. Badiou, *Being and Event*, 403.
60. Badiou, *Being and Event*, 396–7, 400.
61. Slavoj Žižek, 'From Purification to Subtraction: Badiou and the Real,' in *Think Again: Alain Badiou and the Future of Philosophy*, ed. Peter Hallward (London: Continuum, 2004), 178–80.
62. Newman, *The Politics of Postanarchism*, 175–6.
63. Herbert Marcuse, *Counterrevolution and Revolt* (London: Allen Lane The Penguin Press, 1972), 4–6.

Chapter 6

1. A shorter alternative to this chapter was published in 2019. Jon Mazzalini, 'The Value of Nothing and the Price of Labour,' *Pli* 30 (2019), 72–97. https://plijournal.com/volume30/jon-mazzalini-the-value-of-nothing-and-the-price-of-labour/
2. Badiou, *The Subject of Change*, 66.
3. Cat Moir, 'In Defence of Speculative Materialism,' *Historical Materialism*, 27.2 (2019), 123–55.
4. Peter Wolfendale, *Object-Oriented Philosophy: The Noumenon's New Clothes* (Falouth: Urbanomic Media Ltd., 2014), 6.
5. Meillassoux, *After Finitude*, 5.
6. William E. Connolly, *The Fragility of Things: Self-Organizing Processes, Neoliberal Fantasies, and Democratic Activism* (Durham: Duke University Press, 2013), 16–17.
7. Quentin Meillassoux, in Ray Brassier, Iain Hamilton Grant, Graham Harman, Quentin Meillassoux, 'Speculative Realism,' *Collapse III* (2007), 449.
8. Meillassoux, *After Finitude*, 1–2, 54.
9. Meillassoux, *After Finitude*, 35, 37, 39.
10. Graham Harman, *Quentin Meillassoux: Philosophy in the Making* (Edinburgh: Edinburgh University Press, 2011), 166.
11. Meillassoux, After Finitude, 103.
12. Harman, *Quentin Meillassoux: Philosophy in the Making*, 167.

13. Elie Ayache, *The Blank Swan: The End of Probability* (Chichester: Wiley & Sons, 2010), 156, 149.
14. Elie Ayache, 'A Formal Deduction of the Market,' *Collapse VIII* (2014), 971.
15. Badiou, *Number and Numbers*, 213.
16. Toscano, 'From the State to the World? Badiou and Anti-Capitalism,' *Communication & Cognition* Vol. 37, Nr. 3 & 4 (2004), 213.
17. Žižek, *Living in the End Times*, 185.
18. Badiou, 'Metaphysics and the Critique of Metaphysics,' 190.
19. Levi R. Bryant, 'Politics and Speculative Realism,' 15, 26, 21.
20. Toscano, 'Marxism Expatriated,' 544.
21. Alain Badiou, *Being and Event*, 210–211.
22. Balibar, 'Communism as Commitment, Imagination, and Politics,' 20.
23. Ben Fine and Alfredo Saad-Filho, *Marx's 'Capital'* (London: Pluto Press, 2016), 19–20. It has also been argued that the labour theory of value does not, on its own, amount to a proof of exploitation. See Diane Elson, *Value: The Representation of Labour in Capitalism* (London: Verso, 2015), 116.
24. Elena Louisa Lange, 'Money versus Value?: Reconsidering the 'Monetary Approach' of the 'post'-Uno School, Benetti/Cartelier, and the Neue Marx-Lektüre,' *Historical Materialism* 28.1 (2020), 78, 51–84.
25. Ayache, *The Blank Swan*, 63.
26. Karl Marx, 'Wage Labour and Capital,' in Karl Marx, *Wage Labour and Capital/Value, Price and Profit* (New York: International Publishers Co., 1976), 35.
27. Michael A. Lebowitz, *Beyond Capital* (Basingstoke: Macmillan, 1992), 12, 16–17. On 'necessary labour,' and the complexity behind the notion of 'necessary means of subsistence,' see Karl Marx, *Capital: Volume 3*, trans. David Fernbach (London: Penguin, 1991), 960–1, 1004–5.
28. Negri, *Marx Beyond Marx*, 128.
29. Marx, *Capital: Volume 1*, 163, 164–165, 165.
30. Marx, *Capital: Volume 1*, 166–7.
31. Marx, *Capital: Volume 3*, 727.
32. Moishe Postone, *Time, Labor, and Social Domination*, 175.
33. Postone, *Time, Labour and Social Domination*, 178.
34. Alfred Sohn-Rethel, *Intellectual and Manual Labour: A Critique of Epistemology* (London: Macmillan, 1978), 35, 37–9, 41, 197.
35. Slavoj Žižek, *The Sublime Object of Ideology* (London: Verso, 2008), 10–11.
36. Žižek, *The Sublime Object of Ideology*, 12–16.
37. Žižek, *The Sublime Object of Ideology*, 16.
38. Žižek, *The Sublime Object of Ideology*, 16–17, 22.
39. Žižek, *The Sublime Object of Ideology*, 28, 30–1, 36.

40. Karatani, *Transcritique*, 9, 10.
41. Karatani, *Transcritique*, 1, 2–3, 10–11.
42. Karatani, *Transcritique*, 22.
43. Karatani, *Transcritique*, 23.
44. Meillassoux, *After Finitude*, 52–53.
45. Meillassoux, *After Finitude*, 79.
46. Meillassoux, *After Finitude*, 10, 17, 27, 60.
47. Quentin Meillassoux, 'Speculative Realism,' 424–6.
48. Suhail Malik, 'The Ontology of Finance: Price, Power, and the Arkhéderivative,' *Collapse VIII* (2014), 640.
49. Elie Ayache, 'A Formal Deduction of the Market,' 975.
50. Ayache, *The Blank Swan*, 167, 18.
51. Nassim Nicholas Taleb, *Fooled by Randomness: The Hidden Role of Chance in Life and in the Markets* (London: Penguin, 2004), 117.
52. Taleb, *Fooled by Randomness*, 72–5.
53. Charles Taylor, *Philosophical Arguments* (Cambridge: Harvard University Press, 1995), 1.
54. Walter Kaufmann, *From Shakespeare to Existentialism: Studies in Poetry, Religion, and Philosophy* (Boston: Beacon Press, 1959), 88–119. Available at https://www.marxists.org/reference/subject/philosophy/works/us/kaufmann.htm (accessed 12 March 2021).
55. Ayache, *The Blank Swan*, 5–6.
56. Ayache, *The Blank Swan*, 62–3.
57. Ayache, *The Blank Swan*, 110–11.
58. Ayache, *The Blank Swan*, 137, 144.
59. Ayache, *The Blank Swan*, 151–5.
60. Ayache, *The Blank Swan*, 189.
61. Ayache, *The Blank Swan*, 380–1.
62. Ayache, *The Blank Swan*, 421.
63. Badiou, *Theory of the Subject*, 92.
64. Ayache, *The Blank Swan*, 126.
65. Joseph E. Stiglitz, *The Price of Inequality* (London: Penguin, 2013), 68.
66. Marx, *Capital: Volume 3*, 132–3.
67. Marx, *Capital: Volume 1*, 683, 339.
68. Negri, *Marx Beyond Marx*, 150.
69. Karl Marx, *The Grundrisse* (London: Penguin, 1973), 708. Quoted in Negri, *Marx Beyond Marx*, 143–4.
70. Negri, *Marx Beyond Marx*, 146, 149–50.
71. Antonio Negri, 'The Constitution of Time,' *Time for Revolution* (London: Continuum, 2003), 25, 39.
72. Alex Williams and Nick Srnicek, '#Accelerate: Manifesto for an Accelerationist Politics,' in *#Accelerate: The Accelerationist Reader*, eds. Robin Mackay and Armen Avanessian (Falmouth: Urbanomic Media Ltd,

2014), 352, 356–60.
73. Antonio Negri, 'Some Reflections on the #Accelerate Manifesto,' in *#Accelerate: The Accelerationist Reader*, 367–8.
74. Berardi, *The Soul at Work*, 74–5.
75. Benjamin Noys, *Malign Velocities: Accelerationism and Capitalism* (Alresford: Zero Books, 2014), 3 and 9.
76. Noys, *Malign Velocities*, 11–12.
77. Marx, *The Grundrisse*, 706.
78. Raya Dunayevskaya, *Philosophy and Revolution: From Hegel to Sartre and from Marx to Mao* (Sussex: Harvester Press, 1982), 70.
79. Dunayevskaya, *Philosophy and Revolution*, 71–3.
80. Newman, *The Politics of Postanarchism*, 130.
81. Alain Badiou, 'The Communist Idea and the Question of Terror,' 9.
82. Badiou, 'The Communist Idea and the Question of Terror,' 9–10.
83. Alain Badiou, 'Interview with Alain Badiou,' in *The Ashville Global Review*, April 20/2005. Accessed 20 April 2015 at http://www.lacan.com/badash.htm.
84. Walter Benjamin, 'Critique of Violence,' in *Walter Benjamin: Selected Writings—Volume 1, 1913–1926*, eds. Marcus Bullock and Michael W. Jennings (Cambridge: Harvard University Press, 2004), 243, 249.
85. Slavoj Žižek, *Violence* (London: Profile Books Ltd., 2009),169.
86. Benjamin, 'Critique of Violence,' 248–250, 246, 252.
87. Judith Butler, 'Critique, Coercion, and Sacred Life in Benjamin's 'Critique of Violence,' in *Political Theologies: Public Religions in a Post-secular World*, eds. Hent de Vries and Lawrence E. Sullivan (New York City: Fordham University Press, 2006), 214.
88. Benjamin, 'Critique of Violence,' 252.
89. Nadine El-Enany, 'Innocence Charged with Guilt: The Criminalisation of Protest from Peterloo to Millbank,' in *Riot, Unrest and Protest on the Global Stage*, eds. David Pritchard and Francis Pakes (Basingstoke: Palgrave Macmillan, 2014), 80–1.
90. Jessica Elgot and Damien Gayle, 'Lawyers Criticise Decision to Prosecute Housing Protester over Sticker,' *The Guardian*, 22 October 2015, http://www.theguardian.com/uk-news/2015/oct/22/lawyers-criticise-decision-to-prosecute-housing-protester.
91. Newman, *Postanarchism*, 69–70.
92. Benjamin, 'Critique of Violence,' 248–50.
93. Badiou, *The Century*, 52–3, 56.
94. Benjamin, 'Critique of Violence,' 249.
95. Badiou, *Theory of the Subject*, 64.

Chapter 7

1. Newman, *The Politics of Postanarchism*, 1–2.
2. Badiou, *Being and Event*, 210–11.
3. Saul Newman, *Postanarchism* (Cambridge: Polity, 2015), 113.
4. Badiou, *Being and Event*, 87, 88.
5. Charles Post, 'Exploring Working-Class Consciousness: A Critique of the Theory of the Labour-Aristocracy,' *Historical Materialism* 18 (2010), 3–38.
6. Wright, 'What is middle about the middle class?,' 115–17.
7. Hallward, *Badiou: A Subject to Truth*, 36.
8. Badiou, *Being and Event*, 207.
9. Badiou, *The Communist Hypothesis*, 246–7, 240.
10. Badiou, *Theory of the Subject*, 128.
11. Karl Marx, 'The Civil War in France: Address of the General Council,' in Karl Marx, *The First International and After*, ed. David Fernbach (London: Verso, 2010), 213.
12. Balibar, *The Philosophy of Marx*, 17, 2–5.
13. Badiou, *The Century*, 52–3, 56.
14. Matt Bernico, 'Anthropodicy: An Anarchism of Things,' *Anarchist Developments in Cultural Studies* (2015:1), 73–85.
15. Lukács, *History and Class Consciousness*, 193.
16. See, for example, Dipesh Chakrabarty, 'Postcoloniality and the Artifice of History: Who Speaks for 'Indian' Pasts?,' in *A Subaltern Studies Reader: 1986–1995*, ed. Ranajit Guha (Minneapolis: University of Minnesota Press, 1999), 267. And Rajnarayan Chandavarkar, 'The Making of the Working Class': E.P. Thompson and Indian History,' in *Mapping Subaltern Studies and the Postcolonial*, ed. Vinayak Chaturvedi (London: Verso, 2000), 52–3.
17. In Neil Lazarus and Rashmi Varma, 'Marxism and Postcolonial Studies,' in *The Critical Companion to Contemporary Marxism*, eds. Jacques Bidet and Stathis Kouvelakis (Chicago: Haymarket Books, 2009), 329.
18. Süreyyya Evren, 'There Ain't No Black in the Anarchist Flag! Race, Ethnicity and Anarchism,' in *The Bloomsbury Companion to Anarchism*, ed. Ruth Kinna (London: Bloomsbury Academic, 2012), 299–314.
19. Cedric J Robinson, *Black Marxism: The Making of the Black Radical Tradition* (North Carolina: University of North Carolina Press, 2000), 218–219, 304–5
20. See David R. Roediger, *The Wages of Whiteness* (London: Verso, 1991).

Appendix

1. Jason Harman, 'Ontological Anarché: Beyond Arché and Anarché,' *Anarchist Developments in Cultural Studies* (2013.2), 110.
2. Michael Schmidt and Lucien van der Walt, *Black Flame: The Revolutionary Class Politics of Anarchism and Syndicalism* (Oakland: AK Press, 2009), 19.
3. Nathan Jun, 'Rethinking the Anarchist Canon: History, Philosophy, and Interpretation,' *Anarchist Developments in Cultural Studies* (2013.1), 89.
4. Alain Badiou, 'The Idea of Communism,' in *The Idea of Communism*, eds. Costas Douzinas and Slavoj Žižek (London: Verso, 2010), 13.
5. Badiou, The Communist Hypothesis, 8.
6. Bosteels, *Badiou and Politics*, xviii
7. Badiou, *Logics of Worlds,* 146–7.
8. Badiou, *Being and Event*, 24–5.
9. Alain Badiou and Tzuchien Tho, 'From the 'Red Years' to the Communist Hypothesis: Three Decades of Dividing into Two,' in *Alain Badiou: The Rational Kernel of the Hegelian Dialectic,* ed. and trans. Tzuchien Tho (Melbourne: re.press, 2011), 90.
10. Badiou, *Being and Event*, 24–5.
11. Badiou, *Being and Event*, 54–6, 58–9.
12. Badiou, *Being and Event*, 81, 85, 87, 88.
13. Badiou, *Being and Event*, 190, 507, 210–211.
14. Badiou, *Being and Event*, 397, 16–17.
15. Alain Badiou, 'Eight Theses on the Universal,' in *Theoretical Writings*, ed. and trans. Ray Brassier and Alberto Toscano (London: Continuum, 2006), 146–7.
16. Badiou, *Being and Event*, 99, 16–17.
17. Badiou, Logics of Worlds, 1–3.

www.ingramcontent.com/pod-product-compliance
Lightning Source LLC
Chambersburg PA
CBHW071730080526
44588CB00013B/1975